Greenwich Village
CATHOLICS

THOMAS J. SHELLEY

Greenwich Village CATHOLICS

St. Joseph's Church and the Evolution of an Urban Faith Community, 1829–2002

The Catholic University of America Press
Washington, D.C.

The paper used in this publication meets the minimum requirements of American National Standards for Information Science—Permanence of Paper for Printed Library materials, ANSI Z39.48–1984.

∞

Library of Congress Cataloging-in-Publication Data

Shelley, Thomas J.

Greenwich Village Catholics : St. Joseph's Church and the evolution of an urban faith community, 1829–2002 / Thomas J. Shelley.

p. cm.

Includes bibliographical references (p.) and index.

ISBN 0-8132-1349-5

1. St. Joseph's Church (Greenwich Village, New York, N.Y.)—History. 2. Greenwich Village (New York, N.Y.)—Church history. 3. New York (N.Y.)—Church history/. I. Title.

BX4603.N6 S387 2003

282'.7471—dc21

2002152749

To the laity, religious, and clergy

—past, present, and future—

of St. Joseph's Church,

Greenwich Village

Contents

Preface

JAY DOLAN TRANSFORMED the writing of American Catholic history a quarter-century ago with his study of New York's Catholics from 1815 to 1865.[1] Abandoning the traditional methodology of telling the story from the top down, he analyzed the Catholic community from the bottom up, exploring their occupations, educational background, ethnic differences, and political allegiances, as well as their sacramental practices and devotional customs. In writing the social history of New York's Catholics in such detail, Dolan drew heavily upon the way that they practiced their religion in their most important local institutions, namely, their parishes. By revealing the unexpected treasure to be found through the study of religious life at that basic level of communal organization, he spurred a new interest in parish history.

Long dismissed as an antiquated form of institutional history, the study of religious belief and practice at the parish level has blossomed into a respected branch of social history. As Dolan has pointed out, at a time when social history became the rage among young academicians, parish history "was seen to provide a unique window to the history of a neighborhood." For Catholic historians in the 1970s, it dovetailed neatly with the ecclesiology of Vatican II and the Council's emphasis on the Church as the People of God.[2]

Monsignor John Tracy Ellis, the foremost representative of the

1. Jay P. Dolan, *The Immigrant Church: New York's Irish and German Catholics, 1815–1865* (Baltimore: The Johns Hopkins University Press, 1975).

2. Jay P. Dolan, "New Dimensions in American Catholic History," in *New Dimensions in American Religious History*, ed. Jay P. Dolan and James P. Winds (Grand Rapids, Mich.: Eerdmans, 1993), 168.

older institutional approach to American Catholic history, was quick to recognize the significance of Dolan's book and called for similar studies of nineteenth-century Catholicism in other American cities. More recently, Canon Roger Aubert, the emeritus professor of ecclesiastical history at the Catholic University of Louvain, compared parishes to "micro-organisms" whose study "enriches general ecclesiastical history and gives it a texture that it often lacks." He added: "Academic historians have therefore been wrong to relegate local history to the status of a pastime for provincial amateurs."[3]

In the United States in recent years a number of parish histories have appeared which reflect and expand the new methodology. Dolan himself edited an extensive study of the regional variations in American Catholic parish life. Both Robert Orsi and Mary Elizabeth Brown have shed light on the distinctive features of Italian American Catholicism by tracing its development in two different New York parishes. Morris MacGregor has performed a similar service for African American Catholicism by focusing on one black parish in Washington, D.C. He had already written a model history of St. Patrick's Church, the oldest Catholic church in the "Federal City." William Warner's history of Holy Trinity parish in Georgetown provides unique insights into the way that the Catholics of colonial Maryland shaped the character of Catholicism in the nation's capital in the early nineteenth century. Robert McNally's study of Catholicism in Florida reveals the unexpected role of one Jesuit parish in Tampa in evangelizing the whole west coast of the state. Charles E. Nolan used St. Mary's Church in Natchez as the focal point to write the first modern history of the Catholic Church in Mississippi.[4]

All of these authors successfully related the life of a local faith community to the larger religious and secular world of which it was

3. Archives of the Catholic University of America (hereafter ACUA), John Tracy Ellis Papers, Ellis to Francis McMenamin, S.J., October 9, 1975. Ellis also recommended Dolan's book to the Apostolic Delegate. Ellis to Archbishop Jean Jadot, October 22, 1975. Roger Aubert, "Les Nouvelles Frontières de l'Historiographie Ecclésiastique," *Revue d'Histoire Ecclésiastique* 95:3 (2000): 762.

4. Jay. P. Dolan, *The American Catholic Parish,* 2 vols. (New York: The Paulist Press, 1987); Robert Orsi, *The Madonna of 115th Street: Faith and Community in Italian Harlem,*

a part, and reciprocally illuminated that bigger world from the perspective of this local community. St. Joseph's Church in Greenwich Village offers a similar opportunity to a historian of New York Catholicism. During the life span of this parish, the Catholic community in New York City grew from a mere thirty or forty thousand to over three million in two dioceses. St. Joseph's Church began as a poor immigrant parish in a hostile Protestant environment, developed into a prosperous working-class parish as the area became predominantly Catholic, survived a series of local economic and social upheavals, and remains today a vibrant spiritual center in the midst of an overwhelmingly secular neighborhood. Its history provides a fascinating glimpse of the evolution of Catholicism in New York City and mirrors in many ways the struggles and achievements of urban American Catholicism during the course of almost two centuries.

St. Joseph's began in 1829 in a rented hall on Sixth Avenue only a few years after the village of Greenwich had been absorbed by the expanding metropolis to the south. During its first dozen years the parish was the scene of bitter struggles between the pastors and lay trustees, which led Bishop John Dubois to place the parish under interdict in 1837. The internal conflict between clergy and laity during this decade illustrates the larger problem of adapting European Catholicism to the American scene. Peace was restored to the parish in the early 1840s during the pastorate of John McCloskey, who later became the second archbishop of New York and the first American cardinal. As pastor in Greenwich Village, McCloskey developed the low-key style of leadership that he would continue as archbishop in

1880–1950 (New Haven, Conn.: Yale University Press, 1985); Mary Elizabeth Brown, *From Italian Villages to Greenwich Village: Our Lady of Pompei, 1892–1992* (New York: Center for Migration Studies, 1992); Morris J. MacGregor, *The Emergence of a Black Catholic Community: St. Augustine's in Washington* (Washington: The Catholic University of America Press, 1999); *A Parish for the Federal City: St. Patrick's in Washington, 1794–1994* (Washington: The Catholic University of America Press, 1994); William W. Warner, *At Peace with All Their Neighbors: Catholics and Catholicism in the Nation's Capital, 1787–1860* (Washington: Georgetown University Press, 1994); Michael J. McNally, *Catholic Parish Life on Florida's West Coast, 1860–1968* (Privately printed); Charles E. Nolan, *St. Mary's of Natchez: The History of a Southern Catholic Congregation, 1716–1988,* 2 vols. (Natchez, Miss.: St. Mary's Church, 1992).

marked contrast to that of his predecessor, the feisty John Hughes.

In the mid- and late nineteenth century St. Joseph's Church achieved fame or notoriety (depending on one's point of view) during the pastorate of Father Thomas Farrell, whose liberal political and theological views aroused the ire of conservative Catholics and led to his temporary removal from office after an unprecedented ecclesiastical trial. However, Father Farrell's legacy lived on long after his death through his sponsorship in Greenwich Village of the first black Catholic church north of the Mason-Dixon line and through the Accademia, a think tank of young "Americanist" New York priests who looked to him for leadership and inspiration.

By the turn of the twentieth century Greenwich Village was fast becoming a predominantly Catholic neighborhood thanks to the influx of Irish and Italian residents. Caroline Ware, in her classic sociological study of Greenwich Village during that era, noted the preeminent position that St. Joseph's Church occupied among the religious institutions in the Village.[5] At that time St. Joseph's Church also became the mother church of a half-dozen other Catholic churches, each of which provided pastoral care for specific ethnic groups in Greenwich Village and the surrounding area.

After World War I Greenwich Village became world-famous as America's bohemia, although both the genuine and would-be bohemians never constituted more than a tiny fraction of the total population. A greater challenge for the local Catholic community was urban renewal and gentrification, which displaced many working-class residents from their homes. The process accelerated after World War II, when the lure of the suburbs siphoned off many younger families at the same time that Greenwich Village became the center of one of the largest gay and lesbian communities in the United States.

In the 1960s and 1970s St. Joseph's Church replicated its early history through a series of wrenching internal conflicts as it attempted

5. Caroline Ware, *Greenwich Village, 1920–1930* (Berkeley: University of California Press, 1994), 309. Reprint; the book was originally published in 1935.

to implement the reforms of Vatican Council II in such areas as liturgy, ecumenism, and social justice. The result was a badly divided parish with the newly constituted parish council playing a role similar to that of the board of trustees a century and a half earlier. The resulting stress and strain took its toll on both the clergy and the laity. Nonetheless, St. Joseph's emerged from this period of turmoil to become one of the most progressive parishes in a conservative archdiocese, offering its parishioners a rare combination of doctrinal integrity, inspiring liturgy, community involvement, and a firm commitment to Catholic principles of social justice.

The history of this parish is worth telling for its own sake as the collective journey of one faith community from immigrant mission to pillar of society and then to spiritual outpost in the Secular City. However, it has significance far beyond the boundaries of Greenwich Village because it documents at the most basic and vital level of Catholic communal organization the interaction between change and continuity that has been one of the most prominent features of urban Catholicism in the United States over the past two centuries.

While attempting to give what I hope is due recognition to the role of the laity in the history of St. Joseph's parish, I have not hesitated to call attention to the vital contribution made by the clergy on both the parish and diocesan levels. Catholics are not Congregationalists. Therefore, social history that ignores the hierarchical structure of the Catholic Church can distort reality as much as the narrowest form of institutional history. To quote Canon Aubert once again: "It is an excellent thing to react against the excessive prominence formerly given to institutional history and to ask historians to take note of the lived experience of ordinary people." Nonetheless, with characteristic balance, Aubert also reminds us that, however wide the gap may appear to be between institutional history and social history, "in the Church as in civil society, institutions create structures that in no small way shape the unfolding of ordinary people's daily lives."[6]

6. Aubert, "Les Nouvelles Frontières," 781.

Acknowledgments

FIRST OF ALL, I wish to thank the Reverend Aldo J. Tos, the pastor of St. Joseph's Church, for inviting me to write the history of his venerable parish. From the perspective of the historian, Father Tos is the ideal pastor to commission a parish history. First, he is a rarity among New York pastors because he has carefully collected and preserved the documentary records of his parish. Secondly, he gave me carte blanche to write the history of St. Joseph's Church as I thought fit without making the slightest effort to influence my judgment in any way. Moreover, he provided constant support, advice, and encouragement at every stage of research and writing. For all of these reasons I am deeply grateful to him.

I also wish to express my thanks to the other members of the pastoral staff at St. Joseph's Church—Sister Anne Tahaney, O.P., the Reverend Michael Holleran, and the Reverend Owen Lafferty—and to Ms. Marie Dunn, sacristan, and Ms. Joanne Willard, the parish secretary, for the assistance that they gave me on my numerous visits to the church. I am grateful also to Mr. Anthony Andreassi, the Reverend John A. Boehning, the Reverend Frank Principe, Msgr. John J. Quinn, and the Reverend Stephen M. Ryan for reading all or part of this book in its early stages and offering me the benefit of their advice. My sister, Ms. Mary A. Shelley, prepared the list of the members of the pastoral staff from 1829 to 2003 that appears in Appendix I.

Every historian depends upon the unseen assistance of generous librarians. I have been fortunate to be able to draw upon the expertise of the staffs of the Archbishop Corrigan Memorial Library at St. Joseph's Seminary, Dunwoodie, the New York Public Library, the

Walsh Family Library of Fordham University, the East Meadow Public Library, and the Library of the New-York Historical Society. I am grateful to Fordham University for affording me a Faculty Fellowship in the fall of 2001, which greatly assisted my research and writing. I wish to express my special thanks to Dr. Susan Ray, former associate vice president for academic affairs, for facilitating this fellowship as well as a research grant.

I am deeply grateful to Dr. David J. McGonagle, the director of the Catholic University of America Press, for many courtesies and for the meticulous care that my book received at the hands of his staff, especially Ms. Susan Needham. Ms. Ellen Coughlin did a superb job as copyeditor and greatly enhanced both the reliability and readability of the text. Finally, I wish to record my deep personal debt to the Reverend John T. Monaghan of Cardinal Spellman High School, Bronx, New York. As in the case of everything that I have ever published, the Reverend Monaghan gave me the invaluable benefit of the personal insights and wise counsel that could come only from a veteran New York diocesan priest.

Thomas J. Shelley
September 1, 2002

Greenwich Village

CATHOLICS

St. Joseph's Church in the Early Nineteenth Century.

1 *In the Beginning*

1834: An Anniversary Year

THE YEAR 1834 was a significant anniversary for the Catholics of New York. Exactly a half-century earlier, at the end of the War of Independence, only a few months after the last British redcoats boarded their transports and sailed out of New York harbor, the State Assembly had repealed the notorious anti-priest law of 1700, which made it illegal for a Catholic priest to set foot in New York. For the first time in almost a century Catholics were free to practice their religion in public. It must have seemed like a quixotic gesture, for the entire Catholic community of New York City consisted of a mere two hundred people, who had neither a church where they could worship nor a priest to minister to them.

Fifty years later, however, the situation was considerably different. Since 1808 New York City had been the seat of a diocese that included all of New York State and the northern half of New Jersey. In the city itself the Catholic population had grown to thirty or forty thousand, only half of whom could squeeze into the five churches for Sunday Mass. No one really knew how many Catholics there were in the rest of the diocese. Bishop John Dubois, New York's third bishop, who was the spiritual leader of the diocese from 1826 until 1842, estimated in 1830 that there were probably another 150,000. On his episcopal visitations of the diocese he had sometimes found ten times as many Catholics in a locality as he had anticipated: "700 where I thought to find 50 or 60," he wrote, "1,000 where I had been told that I would find 200."[1]

Catholic New York: 1784–1834

In New York City in 1834 the origin of the five Catholic churches told the story of the shifting fortunes of Catholicism over the previous half-century. St. Peter's Church on Barclay Street, founded in 1785, was a small frame building that was no longer safe to use. "St. Peter's is the mother church in this city and diocese," said *The Truth Teller,* a local Catholic newspaper, in 1836. "It has literally grown old in the service and is entirely inadequate to accommodate its overflowing congregation." The following year it would be replaced with a new stone church that featured an imposing classical façade. George Templeton Strong, an Episcopalian layman with High Church sympathies and a connoisseur of New York church architecture, called it approvingly "an Ionic temple."[2]

New York's largest Catholic church was St. Patrick's Cathedral at Mott and Prince Streets. It was the second-oldest Catholic church in the city, completed in 1815, a full thirty years after St. Peter's. It was an impressive stone building where fifteen hundred people regularly attended each of the three Sunday Masses. Bishop Dubois wanted to extend the building another forty feet and to decorate the bare interior, but he could initiate neither of these projects until he first found the money to pay off the mortgage of $24,000.[3]

St. Mary's Church on Grand Street, New York City's third-oldest Catholic parish, had been purchased from the Presbyterians in 1826. Although this was the first time that Catholics had bought a former

1. Dubois to the Society for the Propagation of the Faith, March 16, 1830, in *Annales de l'Association de la Propagation de la Foi* 22 (October 1830): 452.

2. *New York Weekly Register and Catholic Diary,* February 1, 1834. *The Truth Teller,* May 21, 1836. *The Diary of George Templeton Strong,* ed. Allan Nevins and Milton Halsey Thomas (New York: Macmillan, 1952), I, 81. On St. Peter's Church, see Leo R. Ryan, *Old St. Peter's: The Mother Church of Catholic New York* (New York: U.S. Catholic Historical Society, 1935).

3. On St. Patrick's Cathedral, see Mary Peter Carthy, *Old St. Patrick's: New York's First Cathedral* (New York: U.S. Catholic Historical Society, 1947).

Protestant church, it soon became common practice for a very practical reason. Quite simply, it was cheaper to renovate old churches than to build new ones, since many Protestant churches in lower Manhattan were put up for sale by their middle-class congregations, who were moving uptown even before the Civil War.[4] St. Mary's Church was the site of one of the first outbursts of anti-Catholic bigotry in New York City when arsonists burned it to the ground in 1831. They even stuffed the steeple bell to prevent the congregation from summoning help. Fortunately, it was insured for $9,000, which paid about half the cost of constructing the new church, which had just been completed in 1834. Before the new church was ready for use, in a rare and much appreciated ecumenical gesture, the nearby First Universalist Church graciously allowed the Catholics to use their church for three Masses every Sunday morning.

Christ Church on Ann Street was New York's fourth Catholic church. It too was a former Protestant church, purchased from the Episcopalians in 1827. A curious Protestant gentleman who poked his head into the church one Thursday afternoon was surprised and edified to discover that it was used during the week as a makeshift schoolhouse for poor children. The pastor of the Church was Father Felix Varela, a Cuban-born priest and patriot who had been exiled from his homeland by the Spanish authorities. In New York he would become enormously popular with his Irish parishioners, first at Christ Church and later at Transfiguration Church.[5]

The fifth and newest Catholic church, St. Nicholas Church on Delancey Street, was one of the few public places in antebellum New York where one was unlikely to hear an Irish accent. Established in 1833 as the first German Catholic parish, it would move in 1835 to

4. In 1857 the New York State Senate complained that the Episcopal Church was abandoning the poorer neighborhoods in lower Manhattan. New York State Senate, *Report of the Select Committee on the Report of Trinity Church Made in 1855* (Albany: C. Van Benthuysen, 1857), 20.

5. *Letters of John Pintard to His Daughter, Elise Noel Davidson, 1816–1833* (New York: New-York Historical Society, 1941), 3, 115. On Felix Varela, see Joseph and Helen McCadden, *Father Varela, Torch Bearer from Cuba* (New York: U.S. Catholic Historical Society, 1969).

more spacious quarters on East 2nd Street in the heart of New York's *Kleindeutschland.* It is indicative of the poverty of the Catholic community that not one of the city's five Catholic churches was heated. It also explains why attendance dropped precipitously at the early morning Masses during the winter, when temperatures in the cathedral sometimes fell to ten degrees below zero.

Alexis de Tocqueville and New York Catholics

In 1831 Alexis de Tocqueville and his friend Gustave de Beaumont began their famous tour of America in New York City. They attended Mass in a large church, probably the cathedral, which they said was full of worshippers. The two French visitors were unable to meet their follow countryman, Bishop Dubois, because he was away on an extended visit to France. However, they had an interview with Father John Power, the Irish-born pastor of St. Peter's Church and the vicar general, who was administering the diocese in the absence of the bishop. Power assured them that the Catholics were already the single largest religious denomination in the city, even though they had only five churches compared to over one hundred Protestant churches. He added that the increase in the number of Catholics was due to conversions as well as immigration. "What struck me most in Mr. Power's conversation," the aristocratic Tocqueville recorded in his diary, "[is] that he appears to have no prejudice against republican institutions [and] that he regards education as favorable to morality and religion."

After a few weeks in New York City, Tocqueville wrote home to a friend that "the religious state of this people is perhaps the most curious thing to examine here." He attended services in several Protestant churches and remarked on the lack of doctrinal content in the sermons. He found the Catholics poor but zealous and praised the local clergy for their devotion to their people. "They are not businessmen of religion like the Protestant ministers," he observed. As for Power's claim about the number of converts, Tocqueville attributed it to the desire for an authoritative religion and the splendor of the Catholic liturgy. He noted too that most of the converts to Catholicism came from the lower classes, while the better-educated Protestants were attracted to Unitarianism.

The young French aristocrat also noticed how Catholicism flourished in the free soil of America, but he observed that Catholics kept aloof from contact with other religious denominations. He wondered how committed they really were to the principle of religious toleration. "I am not sure," he wrote, "that they would not persecute if they found themselves the strongest." It was a latent fear that many American Protestants would continue to harbor until Vatican Council II (1962–1965), when the Catholic Church finally committed itself unambiguously to the principle of freedom of conscience with the Council's "Declaration on Religious Liberty."[6]

On the basis of a few weeks' observation, Tocqueville thought that the Catholics of New York were fairly well provided with churches. Bishop Dubois, who was obviously better informed, thought otherwise and said that at least six more churches were needed. Father Varela believed that the ideal solution would be to have a Catholic church in each of the city's fourteen wards. In 1834 the shortage of churches was somewhat alleviated with the opening of the Church of St. Joseph in Greenwich Village at the corner of Sixth Avenue and Barrow Street (now Washington Place). St. Joseph's was the city's sixth Catholic church, but New Yorkers were still getting used to the fact that the boundaries of the metropolis now extended as far north of the Battery as 14th Street. *The Catholic Almanac* for that year, published in Baltimore, played it safe and gave two entries for St. Joseph's Church. It listed St. Joseph's as both the "new church" in New York City and as the parish church of "upstate" Greenwich Village.[7]

6. George William Pierson, *Tocqueville and Beaumont in America* (New York: Oxford University Press, 1938), 69, 137–38, 153–57.

7. *The United States Catholic Almanac or Laity's Directory for the Year 1834* (Baltimore: John Myers, 1834), 54.

Greenwich Village

Until the 1820s Greenwich Village was a village in fact as well as in name.[8] For thirty years previously it had served as the favorite refuge for better-off New Yorkers during the periodic outbreaks of yellow fever and cholera that devastated the city. A Scottish businessman, Peter Neilson, arrived in the city during the yellow fever epidemic of 1822 and found that many of the city's businessmen and merchants had moved their offices and stores to temporary wooden buildings in Greenwich Village. They spent the whole summer living there with their families in jerry-built wooden houses erected in the middle of open fields while the militia patrolled the streets of the deserted city to prevent looting. Late in October, when the first frost signaled that the danger of contagion was over, the makeshift little city disappeared as quickly as it had arisen. "The consequent numerous removals back to the city," said Neilson, "resembled the breaking up of the camp of some great army."[9]

The year 1822 was just about the last time that Greenwich Village was sufficiently remote from the metropolis to offer New Yorkers a convenient escape from the diseases of their squalid city. The *cordon sanitaire* of the open fields was fast disappearing. (Philip Hone, the future mayor and indefatigable diarist, went to Rockaway during the cholera epidemic ten years later.) An English traveler who witnessed the epidemic of 1822 noted that Greenwich, "though once a separate town, now forms part of the City." Five years earlier, in 1817, the Common Council of the City of New York approved a plan to construct water mains and a sewer through the village of

8. The boundaries of Greenwich Village today are West 14th Street on the north, Fourth Avenue and the Bowery on the east, Houston Street on the south, and the Hudson (or North) River on the west. Jan Seidler Ramirez, "Greenwich Village," in *The Encyclopedia of New York City*, ed. Kenneth J. Jackson (New Haven, Conn., and New York: Yale University Press and the New-York Historical Society, 1995), 506.

9. Peter Neilson, *Recollections of Six Years' Residence in the United States of America* (Glasgow, 1833), in Phelps Stokes, *The Iconography of Manhattan Island* (New York: Robert Dodd, 1926), V, 1624–25. The same quotation is reproduced in Bayrd Still, *Mirror for Gotham* (Westport, Conn.: Greenwood Press, 1980), 103–4.

Greenwich, which it described as "the growing portion of this city."[10]

Another indication that Greenwich Village was no longer a rural retreat came to light in 1822 when residents complained to the Common Council about the "infestation" of pigs. They petitioned for a law "compelling the owners to put rings in their [presumably the pigs'] noses." The complaint may also reflect unhappiness with an influx of unwelcome Irish neighbors, since poor Irish immigrants often settled in the outskirts of the city, where rents were cheaper than in the central wards. The Irish also commonly kept pigs in their yard as a source of cheap food, as they had done in Ireland. References to Paddy's pig in nineteenth-century America had a basis in fact.[11]

Whatever the sociological implications of the growing porcine population, there is no doubt that there was a substantial Irish presence in Greenwich by the 1820s. Many of the Irish weavers who lived in Greenwich Village were Catholics, but there were also many Irish Protestants as well. They lived at peace with one another, at least until July 12, 1824. On that day, the anniversary of the Battle of the Boyne in 1690, the Irish Catholics displayed a green banner from a building at the corner of Sixth Avenue and Amity Street (now West 3rd Street). The Irish Protestants responded by hanging an orange banner from a house across the street. That evening Irish Catholics and Protestants clashed in a riot that involved at least fifty people.

It began when the Catholics attacked a parade of Orangemen proceeding down Sixth Avenue from one tavern to another, accompanied by fifes and drums, calling out provocatively to the Catho-

10. Newnham Blane, *An Excursion through the United States and Canada during the Year 1822–1823* (London, 1824), in Stokes, *Iconography,* V, 1624. *Minutes of the Common Council of the City of New York, 1784–1831* (New York: City of New York, 1917), IX, 33.

11. *Minutes of the Common Council,* XII, 293. In the 1850s, when the northern boundary of the city had moved up to 59th Street, the *New York Times* deplored the fact that the East Fifties were "densely populated with Irish families and pigs." It reported condescendingly that it was an area where "the little ones of Celtic and swinish origin lie around miscellaneously with billy goats here and there interspersed." *New York Times,* June 5, 1858.

lics, "Come forward, you damned croppies." The police arrested thirty-three demonstrators, all of them Catholics. When they came to trial the following September, however, they were all acquitted thanks to the timely intervention of Thomas Addis Emmet, New York's most famous Irishman. He was a Protestant, the older brother of the nationalist martyr Robert Emmet, and himself an exiled hero of the abortive rebellion of 1798.[12]

The riot in July 1824 was the first serious clash between Irish Catholics and Irish Protestants in New York City, the harbinger, unfortunately, of many more to come. It was an indication that, in America as in Ireland, the tenuous alliance that Catholics and Protestants had forged during the rebellion of 1798 was coming apart. At the trial in September 1834 of four Orangemen involved in the July riot, William Sampson, a Protestant champion of the Catholic victims, alluded sardonically to the significance of the violence. "On that day," he said, "the village of Greenwich was alarmed by a new kind of celebration, unknown in this country. In this land of freedom we have not been accustomed heretofore to witness such a celebration."[13]

In 1825 the census returns showed that the population of New York City had reached 166,186. That same year the *Commercial Advertiser* observed in an editorial that "Greenwich is no longer a country village. Such has been the growth of our city that the building of one block more will completely connect the two places; and in three years time, at the rate buildings have been erected the last season, Greenwich will be known only as a part of the city and the suburbs will be beyond it." One person who agreed was John Pintard, a wealthy insurance executive and bank president, who urged a

12. Walter J. Walsh, "Religion, Ethnicity and History," in *The New York Irish,* ed. Ronald H. Bayor and Timothy J. Meagher (Baltimore: The Johns Hopkins University Press, 1996), 61–64; and Paul J. Gilje, *The Road to Mobocracy: Popular Disorder in New York City, 1763–1834* (Chapel Hill: University of North Carolina Press, 1987), 133–38.

13. *The Trial of John Moore and Others for Assault and Battery, New York City, 1824,* in *American State Trials,* ed. John D. Lawson (St. Louis: Thomas Law Book Company, 1921), XIII, 190.

friend not to sell the real estate that he owned in Greenwich Village. "The tide of population and the range of speculation is setting that way," he predicted. "You will be reimbursed handsomely for your purchase."[14]

The real estate boom hardly seemed to be affected by the presence in the middle of Greenwich Village of an undesirable neighbor, Newgate State Prison, which occupied four acres bounded by Christopher Street, Washington Street, Charles Lane, and the Hudson River. By 1825 private homes had been built to the very edge of the twenty-three-foot-high prison walls on the three landward sides. Then, the opening of the new state prison in upstate Sing Sing in 1828 paved the way for the sale of the old facility to the city. The following year the Common Council sold off most of the property (but not the buildings) together with additional municipal land on Barrow, Christopher, and West Streets. It also ordered the extension of 14th Street to the Hudson River, and the improvement of Sixth and Tenth Avenues north of 14th Street. Part of the former prison property was also earmarked for a public market to be known as Greenwich Market. Unfortunately, it did not prosper, but the construction of the more centrally located Jefferson Market at Greenwich Avenue and Sixth Avenue helped to promote the development of Sixth Avenue as the main shopping street in the neighborhood.[15]

The Old Ninth Ward

Until 1832 Greenwich Village was located entirely within the confines of the Ninth Ward, which was bounded by 14th Street on the north, West Houston Street on the south, the Bowery on the east, and the Hudson River on the west. Between 1825 and 1830 the population of the Ninth Ward more than doubled, from 10,956 to 22,752, a higher rate of growth (108 percent) than that of any other ward.

14. *New York Commercial Advertiser,* January 18, 1825. John Pintard to Samuel Bayard, January 20, 1825, *Letters of John Pintard,* I, 161. On Pintard, see *Dictionary of American Biography,* XIV, 629–30.

15. *New York Evening Post,* April 23, 30, 1829. *Minutes of the Common Council,* XVIII, 131–33, 235–36.

During that same five-year period, the assessed value of property more than doubled as well, from $4,498,550 to $9,073,450, an increase of 102 percent, almost double the growth rate of any other ward. By 1830 the Ninth Ward accounted for almost ten percent of all the assessed property in New York City.[16]

In May 1831 the *New York Evening Post* reported that "the growth of that part of the city that lies above Canal Street, on both sides of Broadway, is astonishingly rapid, and the new edifices for the most part are handsome permanent structures." The writer called attention especially to the area around Washington Square. Only six years earlier, it had been the city's potter's field, a public cemetery for the poor and destitute where some 22,000 bodies had been interred. Aware that the "subterranean occupancy" made it unattractive for residential use, a committee of the Common Council recommended in 1831 that interments should cease "in a part of our city so rapidly improving." Now, said a reporter for the *New York Evening Post*, "preparations are immediately to be commenced for a line of superb edifices, to front on the north side of Washington Square and to extend nearly the whole length of that beautiful enclosure."[17]

The following year the Ninth Ward was divided into two, with Sixth Avenue as the boundary line. The Ninth Ward was now reduced to the West Village between Sixth Avenue and the Hudson River, while a new Fifteenth Ward was created for the area between Sixth Avenue and the Bowery. The new ward quickly became one of the city's prime residential neighborhoods. By 1833 the "superb edifices" on the north side of Washington Square were ready for occupancy, and their owners successfully petitioned the city to change the name of the street from 6th Street to Waverly Place in honor of Sir Walter Scott and his Waverly novels. Lower Fifth Avenue was soon dotted with fashionable mansions and churches. The area re-

16. Elizabeth Blackmar, *Manhattan For Rent, 1785–1850* (Ithaca, N.Y.: Cornell University Press, 1989), 274, 308 n.64.

17. Bayrd Still, "The Washington Square Neighborhood, 1830–1855," in *Greenwich Village: Culture and Counterculture,* ed. Rick Beard and Leslie Cohen Berlowitz (New Brunswick, N.J.: Rutgers University Press, 1993), 112. *New York Evening Post,* May 7, 1831.

ceived another boost when the trustees of New York University selected a site on the east side of Washington Square as the location for their new institution. By the 1840s the property values in the Fifteenth Ward were the second highest in the city. It included among its residents many lawyers and doctors as well as businessmen who were seeking relief from the crowded living conditions of lower Manhattan. A solitary distillery was the only factory in the whole ward. It had the second-smallest foreign-born population and the second-smallest tenement-house population in the city. In 1865 the Council of Hygiene declared that it was the healthiest ward in the entire city.

In contrast to the posh Fifteenth Ward, the Ninth Ward in the West Village contained a much greater variety of industrial and residential buildings and greater social diversity among its residents. There were iron works, cotton factories, breweries, distilleries, sawmills, and even a gristmill. Many of the residential buildings were small wooden houses occupied by artisans, laborers, and cartmen who worked in the neighborhood and in businesses along the Hudson River. The Ninth Ward was sometimes called the American Ward because in the mid-nineteenth century it had the smallest foreign-born population in the city. It also had the largest number of churches (twenty-one), relatively few grog shops and taverns (only 237!), and not a single brothel. The contrast in wealth between the Ninth and Fifteenth Wards should not be pressed too far, however, for every ward had a mixed population of rich and poor. As Juliana Gilheany points out in her study of British immigrants in antebellum New York City, "The wards did not constitute ghettos [because] merchants, attorneys, and manufacturers lived in wards with grocers, tailors and shoemakers, and with riggers, cartmen and laborers."[18]

By the mid-1830s improvements in transportation were transforming the face of the city. There was stagecoach service on Broad-

18. Juliana Gilheany, "Subjects of History: English, Scottish and Welsh Immigrants in New York City, 1820–1860," Ph.D. dissertation, New York University, 1989, 170–71, 188.

way between Wall Street and Greenwich Village every fifteen minutes. Commuters could purchase six-trip tickets for the bargain price of fifty cents. Broadway itself was crowded with traffic during much of the day. "[It] is such a thoroughfare," John Pintard told his daughter in 1833, "as to render it hazardous crossing the street, to avoid which I usually take a side street where I feel safe." Even the old state prison became an asset for Greenwich Village. Jacob Lorillard purchased the building and turned it into a fashionable sanitarium complete with vapor baths. He boasted that the front portico "commands a splendid prospect of the city, part of Staten Island, the Jersey shore, North River, and all the variety of life and being that animates that interesting scene."[19]

A Catholic Church for Greenwich Village

The building boom in Greenwich Village created a need for new churches. Among the first to respond were the Episcopalians. As early as October 1820 a group of them met for a religious service in Obadiah Parker's schoolhouse on Amos Street (now West 10th Street). That same month they petitioned the Common Council for the use of the Watch House at the corner of Hudson and Christopher Streets, a request that the Council granted for a fee of thirty dollars per annum. The Episcopalians did not have to pay the fee very long. On June 4, 1821, they blessed the cornerstone for their new Church of St. Luke. Apparently Protestant New Yorkers did not share Thomas Jefferson's strict views about a wall of separation between church and state. In 1822 the Quakers followed the example of the Episcopalians and asked the Common Council for the use of the upper room in the Engine House at Hudson and Christopher Streets.[20]

The Catholics of Greenwich Village did not have their own

19. John Pintard, February 14, 1832; March 1, 1833, in *Letters of John Pintard,* IV, 14, 130. *New York Evening Post,* May 20, 1831.

20. *Minutes of the Common Council,* XI, 356; XII, 293. H. P. Croswell Tuttle, *History of St. Luke's Church in the City of New York* (New York: Appeal Printing Company, 1927), 5–9.

church building until 1834, but the parish of St. Joseph dates back to 1829. At least that date seems like a reasonable supposition for the founding of the parish. Bishop Dubois told the French-based Society for the Propagation of the Faith in March 1830: "Finding myself unable to obtain the means to build a church in a certain suburb [Greenwich Village] where the Catholic population is quite large and too distant from other churches to be able to attend them, I was obliged to rent at $200 a year a large hall capable of holding some seven hundred or eight hundred people. It is an additional burden, falling entirely on myself, poor as I am; but what would I not do to serve the souls entrusted to my care!" Since Dubois sailed from New York on September 20, 1829, for a two-year visit to Europe, he must have established the parish before his departure. (He wrote the letter to the Society for the Propagation of the Faith from Rome.)[21]

Prior to 1829 the closest Catholic church to Greenwich Village was St. Patrick's Cathedral, eighteen city blocks from the future site of St. Joseph's Church. Although Greenwich Village was already provided with stagecoach service to the downtown business district, New York City, like most American cities of that era, was essentially a "walking city" where most people, especially the working class, lived within a short distance of their place of employment. They walked to work, school, shops, taverns, and places of amusement, and on Sundays they were accustomed to walking to their parish churches. St. Joseph's Church was conveniently located for Catholics who lived in the heart of Greenwich Village, but the boundaries of the parish extended from Canal Street to West 32nd Street, necessitating a considerable trek to Mass for those who lived in the southern and northern areas of the parish.

The ubiquitous omnibuses, which so impressed visitors to the city, were less appreciated by native New Yorkers and were already the object of their jokes and complaints. "The omnibuses of this city should hereafter be styled Nuisances or perhaps more appropriately "packing boxes," said the editor of *The Truth Teller* in 1836. "The

21. Dubois, *Annales* 22 (October 1836): 453.

drivers of them are generally reckless and impudent, as ready in uttering abusive language to passengers as they are careless in endangering lives." George Templeton Strong made the mistake of taking the Greenwich Street omnibus home from church one Christmas Day. "The driver was drunk," he said, "and the progress of the vehicle was like that of a hippopotamus through one of the quagmires of Africa."[22]

The first two years of the parish's history, from 1829 to 1831, are a total blank. There is no indication how often Mass was celebrated, or where or by whom, perhaps by priests who came occasionally from other parishes. The first resident pastor of St. Joseph's Church, Father Patrick Duffy, is a shadowy figure about whom nothing is known except that he is said to have ministered to the Catholics of Greenwich Village from 1831 until his death there on February 5, 1833. He was replaced by Father James Cummiskey, who came to New York from Philadelphia, where his brother Eugene was a well-known Catholic bookseller.[23] The parishioners were then worshipping in a temporary "chapel" on Sixth Avenue across from the site of the present church. The chapel in question may very well have been the same hall that Dubois had rented in 1829, for the minutes of a meeting of the parish trustees in 1833 refer to "the large room now occupied as a place of publick worship by the Roman Catholics of Greenwich Village."[24]

22. *The Truth Teller,* August 27, 1836; Strong, *Diary,* December 26, 1848, cit. in Gilheany, "Subjects of History," 192.

23. For Duffy, see Michael Augustine Corrigan, "Register of the Clergy Laboring in the Archdiocese of New York from Early Missionary Times to 1885," *Historical Records and Studies* 2 (1900): 58. For Cummiskey, see ibid., 64–65. After leaving St. Joseph's Church, Cummiskey ministered at Yonkers and at Sing Sing (Ossining) to the Irish laborers who were constructing the first Croton Aqueduct. He suffered a stroke around 1841, which left him paralyzed until his death on April 24, 1850, at St. Columba's Church, New York City.

24. Archives of St. Joseph's Church (hereafter ASJC), Minutes of the Meetings of the Board of Trustees, March 17. A former parishioner, writing fifty years later, recalled attending Mass as a child "in the second story of an old building at the junction of Grove and Christopher Streets, where now is a public or city park." ASJC, G. J. Phelan to William Quinn, April 19, 1882.

In the summer of 1832 a cholera epidemic devastated the city, claiming 3,527 lives between July and September. As always, the poor suffered the most, and that meant that a high percentage of the victims were Irish Catholic immigrants. John Pintard watched the digging of the special cholera graves, deep enough to hold four coffins, in the cathedral graveyard. The interments there became so frequent that the neighbors complained of the danger of contagion. "More than half the victims this dreadful month have been Irish Roman Catholics whose last request was to be buried in Holy Ground," Pintard wrote in June. It was hardly the right moment for Father Cummiskey to solicit funds for the building of a new Catholic church.[25]

However, a year later, on June 10, 1833, under Father Cummiskey's guidance, the construction of a church for the Catholics of Greenwich Village finally got under way with the laying of the cornerstone. According to contemporary newspaper accounts, Cummiskey started the project with only $50 on hand, but he was able to complete it thanks to "the liberality of the contributions from a few Catholics of New York." Cummiskey must have had a reliable source of financing, for construction continued without interruption throughout the summer of 1833. A visitor marveled at the progress four months later, when the exterior of the stone structure began to take shape, 102 feet long, 66 feet wide, and 38 feet high. "If such a church were built by a rich congregation, in so short a time," the same visitor observed, "the wonder would not be so great."[26]

The church was designed by John Doran in the Greek Revival style that was popular in New York in the 1830s. The "superb edifices" on Waverly Place to which the *Evening Post* alluded had been built in that style in 1832 and 1833. However, Greek Revival no longer reigned unchallenged as the preferred style for churches and public

25. Pintard, June 27, 1832, *Letters of John Pintard,* IV, 78. Pintard complained that the Catholics already had so much political influence that no city official would dare to curtail the burials in the cathedral graveyard. "Were it a Protestant burial place," he said, "it would be interdicted, but so many of our Corporation depend on Irish votes at elections that the nuisance passes unheeded by."

26. *New York Weekly Register and Catholic Diary,* October 5, 1833; March 22, 1834.

buildings; the Gothic Revival had already begun to make its presence felt in New York City. St. Thomas Episcopal Church, at the corner of Broadway and Houston Street, completed in 1826, set new standards for Gothic architecture in New York City. John Pintard, one of the founding members of the congregation, noted proudly that it was "the only one approaching the Gothic order" among the 101 churches in the city. A few months after the dedication of St. Joseph's Church in 1834, New York University moved into its new home on the east side of Washington Square Park. It was a handsome, four-story, brick and marble Gothic building, the first American college built in the Gothic style. It received generally favorable reviews from the critics, though Doran may have taken malicious satisfaction in the remark of one acerbic Englishman who referred to the ornate structure scathingly as "Carpenter's Gothic." The same critic added, "No wonder that the Greek, 'the classic and simple Greek,' is preferred by the people who will not be gulled into admiration of anything so *outré* as this university."[27]

One reason for the choice of Greek Revival over Gothic at St. Joseph's may have been lower construction costs. Cummiskey had originally wanted a Gothic church and even obtained plans for such a church from a Philadelphia architect. However, he had to abandon the idea because Bishop Dubois would not allow a Gothic church to be erected in his diocese.[28] Even a decade later, in 1847, when Father Sylvester Malone proposed to build New York's first Catholic Gothic church, the Church of Saints Peter and Paul in Williamsburg, he had to overcome the strenuous objections of Bishop John Hughes that it would be too expensive. Money may not have been the only consideration in choosing the Greek Revival style for St. Joseph's. Another

27. Pintard, February 23, 1826, *Letters of John Pintard,* II, 232–33. The disparaging remarks about the New York University building appeared in *The Architectural Magazine* (London, 1835), 493, cit. in Stokes, *Iconography,* V, 1730.

28. Cummiskey to Miss Aline Rodrigue, May 15, 1833, in "Plan of St. Joseph's Church, New York," *Records of the American Catholic Historical Society of Philadelphia* 21 (1910): 107–8. Aline Rodrigue was the sister of William Rodrigue, the architect whom Cummiskey consulted. William Rodrigue married John Hughes' sister and came to New York with him.

factor may have been Doran's limitations as an architect. Like many church designers of that period, he may not have been a trained architect at all but an ordinary builder, who lacked the expertise to construct a church in the more complicated Gothic style.[29]

Whatever Doran's limitations, the church he designed was larger than any other Catholic church in New York City except the cathedral. Doran showed considerable imagination also in combining the Greek Revival exterior with a warmer and softer Georgian interior. He also made remarkably efficient use of the available interior space, providing enough pews to give the church an estimated seating capacity of over a thousand. One highly admired feature was the arrangement of the pews in the balcony, where each row was raised nine inches above the other to afford everyone an unobstructed view of the altar. The altar itself, imported from Italy and valued at $3,000, was the showpiece of the church. "On entering the door," said one visitor, "the first thing which the eye beholds with delight is a superb and magnificent altar piece."[30]

In February 1834 no fewer than thirty-four carpenters were busy at work installing the pews for the dedication that was scheduled for Sunday, March 9th. At the last minute, the ceremony had to be postponed until the following Sunday because of the illness of one of the indispensable participants, the man in charge of the music, Maestro Carlo Salvioni, a director of the recently opened Italian Opera House at the corner of Church and Leonard Streets. Attendance was by ticket only, available for the price of one dollar at the Catholic churches and bookstores throughout the city. The tickets, however,

29. The point is made by Sarah Bradford Landau, "Greek and Gothic Side by Side: Architecture in the Village," in *Greenwich Village: Culture and Counterculture*, 69. The New York University building was razed in 1894 to make room for the new main building. Ibid., 79. The author does not mention St. Joseph's Church in her article.

Malone's Church of Saints Peter and Paul was begun on May 30, 1847. It was the first of more than five hundred churches designed by Patrick Keely, an Irish-born architect, who was known for the quantity rather than the quality of his work. Richard Purcell, "Patrick Keely, Builder of Churches," *Records of the American Catholic Historical Society of Philadelphia* 54 (1943): 208–27.

30. *New York Weekly Register and Catholic Diary*, March 22, 1834; *The Truth Teller*, June 28, 1834.

did not provide the worshippers with immunity from another collection taken up during the Mass, which raised the total amount collected from them to $1,500.[31]

The Dedication of St. Joseph's Church

St. Joseph's Church was filled but not crowded when Bishop Dubois began the Pontifical High Mass on March 16, 1834, at 10:30 A.M. He was assisted by Father William Quarter of St. Mary's Church, the future bishop of Chicago, as deacon, and by the young Father John McCloskey, the future cardinal archbishop of New York, as sub-deacon. Three other local priests were also present, an exceptionally large turnout of the clergy on a Sunday morning in a city that had a total of only nine Catholic priests. Another guest was a young Philadelphia pastor whose name would soon become familiar to all New Yorkers, John Hughes. About one-third of the congregation were thought to be Protestants, which was not all that unusual, for the high quality of the music in the city's Catholic churches reguıarly attracted Protestant worshippers.

The preacher was Father Charles Constantine Pise, who had been a student at Mount St. Mary's Seminary in Emmitsburg, Maryland, when Bishop Dubois was the rector. Pise had just completed a term as chaplain to the U.S. Senate, the only Catholic priest ever to hold the post. He spoke for a full hour, not unreasonably long by the standards of the day. In typical classical style, Pise ranged widely in his sermon, beginning with Noah and the Flood, traveling with Moses to Mt. Sinai, visiting Solomon's temple in Jerusalem, moving on through the Old Testament with Daniel, Susanna, Mordecai, and Esther, and tarrying for a moment on the banks of the Tigris and Euphrates, before reaching the central moment of revelation with Jesus and the Twelve. From them he traced the descent of the evangelists, the Fathers of the Church, the patriarchs, and the bishops "down to the prelate who this day presides with so much zeal and respectability in the diocese of New York."

31. *New York Weekly Register and Catholic Diary,* March 22, 1834.

Even Pise's patient audience may have grown alarmed when he exclaimed: "How can I find time to rehearse the sees of more than three thousand bishops whose succession has been unbroken from the earliest times?" Fortunately, it was only a rhetorical flourish, and he made no attempt to do so. Conscious perhaps of the many Protestants in the congregation that morning, Pise emphasized that "we preach no other faith than that of the primitive Christians" and invited his listeners to reflect on the historical continuity of the Catholic faith and liturgy. It was a theme to which he returned in a series of lectures that he gave in the church on Sunday afternoons in the spring and fall of 1834.[32]

The account of the dedication of St. Joseph's Church that appeared in the *New York Weekly Register and Catholic Diary* was reprinted in the Catholic press in cities as far distant as Boston and Charleston, South Carolina.[33] Such national attention for a local event was not unusual among American Catholics, for they were still a minuscule group of outsiders in America who drew strength from one another by sharing their triumphs and perils. Later that same year, when a Nativist mob destroyed the Ursuline convent in Charlestown, Massachusetts, New York's Catholic press gave it as much coverage as if it had happened in the heart of Manhattan.

In contrast to the Catholic press, New York's secular newspapers ignored the opening of the new Catholic church in Greenwich Village. (The fire that destroyed Christ Church in August got more attention.) Far more significant to most New Yorkers than the affairs of the local Catholics was the fact that their city entered the railway age in May 1834 with the opening of the New York and Harlem Rail Road from Prince Street to Yorkville. In April of that year Brooklyn was incorporated as a city and the Long Island Rail Road received a state charter; in July New York University held its first commencement, graduating nine students; and in December President Andrew

32. Ibid., March 29, October 11, 1834.

33. *The Jesuit*, March 29, 1834; *U.S. Catholic Miscellany*, March 29, 1834. *The Jesuit* was the forerunner of the Boston *Pilot*.

Jackson fulfilled a promise often made and as often forgotten by other American presidents when he announced to Congress that he had extinguished the national debt. Two aspects of New York life that impressed a visitor from South Carolina the year that St. Joseph's Church was dedicated were the large number of omnibuses "roll[ing] incessantly over the paved streets," and the high price of real estate. Ominously that year also witnessed three days of rioting by anti-abolitionists who attacked two African American churches and the homes of abolitionist leaders Arthur and Lewis Tappan.[34]

Another portent, at least for the history of New York City, was the three days of rioting that accompanied the municipal elections in April 1834. In the heavily Irish Sixth Ward there were pitched battles between Irish-born Democrats and native-born Whigs. Like the riot of 1824 between Catholic Irishmen and Orangemen in Greenwich Village, the violence in 1834 signaled the end of the uneasy *modus vivendi* between Catholic and Protestant Irish immigrants in New York City that had been one of the happy side effects of the rebellion of the United Irishmen in 1798 on the other side of the Atlantic. In the future, Irish Catholics in New York City would remain firmly in the Democratic camp, while Irish Protestants would find their political home with the Whigs. Irish Catholics would now find few allies like Thomas Addis Emmet and William Sampson among their Protestant countrymen as they faced a rising tide of Nativist and Know Nothing attacks upon them and their religion.[35]

Getting Started

No parish in the diocese of New York was rich in the early nineteenth century, but some were less poor than others. Despite serious and persistent financial problems in the early days, St. Joseph's was incomparably better off than a parish like St. Mary of the Snow in

34. Stokes, *Iconography,* V, 1727–30. The *New York Weekly Register and Catholic Diary* blamed the victims for the riots and castigated the abolitionists for promoting "wicked and abominable doctrines" such as the equality of whites and blacks. June 29, 1834.

35. Walsh, "Religion, Ethnicity and History," 64–69; Gilje, *Road to Mobocracy,* 138–42.

the Hudson River town of Saugerties. In Saugerties they erected the walls of their church in 1833, but then had to wait two years before they could afford the price of a roof. Even then the church building was only an empty shell without furnishings or doors or windows or even a floor.[36]

Another indication that St. Joseph's Church was relatively well off was that the parish never felt the need to publish a list of donors to the new church in the local Catholic newspapers. That was a common way of spurring contributions that was employed by both St. Peter's Church and St. James Church in the 1830s. One of the few objective yardsticks for comparing the relative affluence or poverty of Catholic parishes in New York City at that time was the annual Christmas collection, the proceeds of which went to St. Patrick's Orphan Asylum on Prince Street. Judged by this standard, St. Joseph's cut a sorry figure in Christmas 1834, raising only $110.00 and finishing well behind St. Peter's ($368.31), the Cathedral ($273.00), and St. Mary's ($201.00).[37]

However, St. Joseph's poor showing that year was misleading, for the parish had just been instrumental in providing New York's Catholics with a second orphan asylum. The key figure in founding this institution was Thomas Glover, a parishioner and trustee of St. Joseph's Church. Glover wanted a Catholic charitable institution in New York City to care specifically for children who had lost one parent. "In many instances," he said, "their lot is more deplorable than those who have lost both father and mother because bad example and want are too often united in the surviving parent." Since these children were ineligible for admission to St. Patrick's Orphan Asylum, Glover's wife helped organize an Association of Ladies and Patrons to establish a "half-orphan" asylum. They managed to purchase a building for this purpose, but their major problem was to find an adequate staff for the institution. Glover found a solution in the spring of 1833 when he persuaded the Sisters of

36. *The Truth Teller,* July 26, 1834; October 10, 1835.
37. *The Truth Teller,* December 27, 1834.

Charity in Emmitsburg, Maryland, to take charge of the institution.[38]

St. Joseph's Half-Orphan Asylum was located at 68 Sixth Avenue, across the street from the site of the new parish church. Although it was not a parish institution, it received generous support from the priests and people of St. Joseph's. The parish's poor showing in the diocesan Christmas collection of 1834 may be due to the fact that only two months earlier the parishioners had sponsored a fund-raising event for St. Joseph's Half-Orphan Asylum that included a performance of a Mozart Mass and a charity sermon by Father Pise. The parish continued to be a source of financial aid even after the asylum moved in 1838 to more spacious accommodations on Fifth Avenue between 15th and 16th Streets. It continued as a separate institution until 1855, when the last children were transferred to St. Patrick's Orphan Asylum.[39]

By the end of 1834 the Catholics of Greenwich Village possessed the beginnings of what a later age would call a parish plant, that is, a church, rectory, orphan asylum, and eventually a parochial school as well. At the orphan asylum the Sisters of Charity held undisputed sway, but, across the street, at St. Joseph's Church, the lines of authority were less clearly drawn. The first decade of the parish's history would be marked by a long and sometimes bitter dispute as to how leadership was to be shared by clergy and laity, providing a graphic example of a common phenomenon in the American Catholic Church of that era—lay trusteeism.

38. Archives of St. Joseph's Provincial House, Emmitsburg, Maryland (hereafter ASJPH), Thomas Glover to Sister Mary Augustine, January 11, 1833.

39. For the history of St. Joseph's Half-Orphan Asylum, see Sister Marie de Lourdes Walsh, S.C., *The Sisters of Charity of New York, 1809–1959* (New York: Fordham University Press, 1960), I, 82–89.

2 *Clergy and Laity*

Lay Trusteeism

VIRTUALLY EVERY Catholic parish founded in the United States prior to 1830 (except those under the care of religious orders) included a board of lay trustees, who wielded considerable authority over many aspects of parish life. They were usually the legal owners of the church property and managed the finances. The system worked well in places like southern Maryland where there was an ethnically homogeneous population and a long tradition of lay involvement in church affairs.[1] Elsewhere, however, most notably in Philadelphia, Norfolk, Charleston, and New York, it led to major difficulties when the lay trustees tried to control the appointment of pastors. Several highly publicized confrontations between lay trustees and bishops led to suspensions, interdicts, and even schisms. As early as 1786, Father John Carroll, a native of Maryland who was then the Superior of the Mission—that is, the priest appointed by Rome to administer the Church in the new republic—discovered that the situation in New York was different from that in his home state. In that year Carroll categorically rejected the claim put forward by the trustees of St. Peter's Church that

1. With regard to Maryland in the post-Revolutionary period, the historian of the Archdiocese of Baltimore wrote: "It never occurred to these early Catholic communities that there was any other way of doing business. The first task of a new congregation was to raise a church, and for this trustees were deemed indispensable." Thomas W. Spalding, *The Premier See: A History of the Archdiocese of Baltimore* (Baltimore: Johns Hopkins University Press, 1989), 28.

they had the sole authority to appoint and dismiss the pastor. "If ever the principles laid down there should become predominant," he said, "the unity and catholicity of our church would be at an end." In fact the assertiveness of the trustees in New York was one of the principal reasons that Carroll decided that it was necessary to have a bishop in the United States. However, New York's first resident bishop, John Connolly, quickly discovered that his episcopal authority made little difference to the trustees at St. Peter's Church, who were also the trustees of his own cathedral. He spent much of his ten years in New York (1815–1825) doing battle with them and their clerical allies. In February 1817 the embattled bishop told Carroll, now the Archbishop of Baltimore, that the trustees had not even paid his salary for the previous three months.[2]

In 1829, at the First Provincial Council of Baltimore, the U.S. bishops effectively outlawed lay trusteeism by decreeing that henceforth all church property should be vested in the local bishop.[3] In New York, however, where lay trusteeism was well entrenched, the laity continued to play an important and even a dominant role in the day-to-day operation of the parishes throughout the 1830s, especially since they were in firm control of the finances. Announcements of parish social events, the annual auction of pews, and other fund-raising activities were invariably issued in the name of the trustees as well as that of the pastor, and frequently in the name of the trustees alone. Thanks to trusteeism, the laity in New York had far more authority over parish affairs than they did later in the century, when pastors sometimes became the ecclesiastical equivalents of feudal barons, accountable only to the bishop and his chancery office.

However, this so-called republican model of church polity was

2. John Carroll to Dominick Lynch and Thomas Stoughton, January 24, 1786, in *The John Carroll Papers*, ed. Thomas O'Brien Hanley, S.J. (Notre Dame, Ind.: University of Notre Dame Press, 1976), I, 203–6. Archives of the Archdiocese of Baltimore (hereafter AAB), Connolly to Carroll, February 13, 1817. For an account of lay trusteeism in New York during the episcopate of John Connolly, see Peter Guilday, "Lay Trusteeism in New York," *Historical Records and Studies* 18 (1928): 7–73.

3. Patrick Carey, *People, Priests and Prelates: Ecclesiastical Democracy and the Tensions of Trusteeism* (Notre Dame, Ind.: University of Notre Dame Press, 1987), 264–65. Rome actually softened the decrees to make them less offensive to the laity.

far from democratic. The lay trustees were elected each year, not by the whole congregation, but only by those parishioners who had purchased or rented pews. The franchise was thus limited to the better-off members of the congregation. Those who were too poor to purchase or rent a pew were ineligible to take part in the election of the trustees—rather like the disappointed sans-culottes during the French Revolution, who found themselves unexpectedly relegated to the role of "passive citizens" by the Constitution of 1791.

Despite the legislation of the First Provincial Council of Baltimore in 1829, trusteeism was accepted by both the clergy and laity in New York in the 1830s as the normal state of affairs. When the new parish of St. Paul was established in suburban Harlem in 1835, the pew holders matter-of-factly elected nine trustees to solicit funds for the construction of a church. They issued the appeal in their name, not in the name of the pastor, whom they did not even mention. The same thing happened in 1836 when the congregation of Christ Church moved from their original building on Ann Street to a former Dutch Reformed Church on Chambers Street. It was announced that "two weeks after opening the pew holders will meet and appoint a treasurer and three individuals to receive the income and make the payments."[4]

When the clergy and laity worked well together, the trustees could relieve the pastor of much unwelcome administrative work. At St. Mary's Church, after the fire of 1831, it was the trustees who undertook the task of building a new church. At St. Peter's Church, where Father John Power was highly esteemed by his parishioners, he was happy to leave the burden of fund-raising for his new church in the hands of the trustees. They excused him from the onerous task because, they said, "his services are in such frequent requisition in the performance of religious duties . . . and his health [is] so delicate." It is worth noting, however, that neither obstacle prevented him from speaking all over the diocese at the drop of a hat.[5]

Finances were also one area of parish and charitable activity

4. *The Truth Teller,* May 30, 1835; February 6, May 28, 1836; January 21, 1837.

5. *The Truth Teller,* September 12, 1829; April 28, 1832; November 26, 1836.

where women sometimes played a significant role. In December 1834 at St. Mary's Church, a group of lay women formed a Ladies Charitable Society to assist the Sisters of Charity in the operation of the girls' parish school. The women not only raised money for the school, but they also solicited donations of clothing for children whose parents were too poor to buy them dresses to wear to school. As mentioned earlier, a few years before women also played a key role in establishing St. Joseph's Half-Orphan Asylum.[6]

The Bylaws of St. Joseph's Church

The Catholics of Greenwich Village were only following the established custom in New York, therefore, when they set up a board of lay trustees for St. Joseph's Church. The legal basis for the board was the "Act to Provide for the Incorporation of Religious Societies" enacted by the New York state legislature on April 5, 1813. At the first meeting of the board of St. Joseph's Church, on January 21, 1833, the trustees drew up the bylaws of the parish corporation. They were clearly trying to anticipate and prevent the difficulties that had made lay trusteeism a problem elsewhere. They acknowledged a clear line of demarcation between temporal and spiritual affairs, with the latter belonging exclusively to the pastor and the bishop.

Article Two of the bylaws stated: "The Board shall confine its deliberations to matters merely temporal, and may not in any way directly or indirectly interfere with spiritual concerns, which exclusively belong to the Bishop and the Pastor." Moreover, the bylaws explicitly authorized the pastor to determine where the line was to be drawn between spiritual and temporal affairs. "Should any resolution or measure be adopted against which the President [the pastor] shall protest, and shall under his hand and seal testify that it is contrary to the doctrine and discipline of the Roman Catholic Church, it shall be considered as rescinded and annulled, and such protest and certificate shall be registered on the books of the corporation."[7]

6. *The Truth Teller*, December 16, 1837.

7. Archives of St. Joseph's Church, Minutes of the Meetings of the Board of Trustees

Doctrine and discipline, therefore, were to be the exclusive prerogative of the pastor, but the parish finances were to be the domain of the lay trustees. The treasurer of the board of trustees was to "receive and keep in trust all monies, deeds, securities, and other evidences of deeds belonging to the board." Apparently the first election of the trustees took place on January 21, 1833, in the hall that served as a temporary chapel. The pastor, Father James Cummiskey, was unanimously elected the president of the board of trustees, and Mr. Andrew O'Leary was elected the vice president.

Three other lay trustees were also elected: John Devlin (treasurer), Joseph Lamb (secretary), and Patrick Kinsella. Later the number of trustees was increased to nine. It is not clear who was eligible to vote in this first election, but at a meeting of the trustees on April 8, 1833, they carefully defined the qualifications required to vote in future elections. They determined that "*he only* being a Roman Catholic of full age and in whose name a full pew shall have been registered at least six months previous to any subsequent election shall be entitled to a vote and besides that he shall have paid the advance rent of six months to May following."[8]

In accordance with the bylaws of the parish, the board of trustees, not the pastor, authorized the purchase of the property for the church at the corner of Sixth Avenue and Barrow Street. On February 6, 1833, the board appointed Father Cummiskey and Mr. Devlin to negotiate with the city about the terms of the sale, and on March 3, 1833, they approved the purchase of the property. Lay sensitivity about this transaction surfaced a few months later in an open letter to Bishop Dubois in *The Truth Teller*. "In whose name have the lots

(hereafter ASJC, MMBT), January 21, 1833. The minutes of the meetings of the Board of Trustees from January 21, 1833, to February 6, 1845, have been preserved in a much-thumbed register in the archives of St. Joseph's Church. It is the main source of information for this chapter.

8. ASJC, MMBT, April 8, 1833. May 1st was the traditional moving day in New York City, when leases expired in the tenement houses and the streets were filled with poor people pushing their few possessions on wheelbarrows from one location to another. See Dolan, *The Immigrant Church*, 41–42. Pews in the Catholic churches were offered for rent at the end of April, with the leases beginning on the first Sunday in May. See the advertisement in *The Truth Teller*, April 28, 1832.

been bought?" asked the author of the letter, who identified himself only as "One of the People." "If the church be in Mr. C[ummiskey's] name alone," this anonymous writer added, "have the goodness to state the advantages that accrue to the people." The trustees assured the readers of *The Truth Teller* that church property had been incorporated in their name, not in the pastor's name. In the meantime, they urged the parishioners to solicit funds from all the Catholics of the city to pay for the construction of the new church.[9]

Another function of the board of trustees, one that they guarded jealously, was the supervision of the annual rental of pews, which provided the parish with the bulk of its income. The pews were divided into three classes (depending on their proximity to the altar) and were rented for annual fees of fifteen, twelve, and ten dollars respectively. Competition for the best pews must have been keen, for applicants for each category were obliged to cast lots and were then exhorted to "take and occupy the pew which fortune may put in [your] way." The rental price must have been adjusted periodically. In 1841 the cost of a pew on the center aisle was $13 while a pew in the balcony could be rented for $8.50. In order to raise more money, a certain number of pews were offered for sale at the price of three hundred dollars, but it does not appear that there were many takers.[10]

Pew rental, like lay trustees, was a common practice in the city's Protestant churches. At St. Thomas Episcopal Church, John Pintard was willing to bid as much as five hundred dollars to buy a choice pew when that church was opened in 1826. He was delighted to get

9. ASJC, MMBT, February 6, March 3, 1833. *The Truth Teller,* September 21, 28, 1833.

10. ASJC, MMBT, March 17, 1833; March 14, 1831. Archives of the Archdiocese of New York (hereafter AANY), Financial Report of St. Joseph's Church, June 29, 1841. Even after purchasing a pew for three hundred dollars, the owner was expected to pay an annual "ground rent" of thirteen dollars. In 1882 a former parishioner threatened to sue the parish because the pastor, Father John Salter, disputed his ownership of Pew 110, which his mother had purchased in 1834. It was settled out of court when Salter bought back the pew for five hundred dollars. ASJC, G. J. Phelan to William Quinn, April 19, 1882; G. J. Phelan to John Salter, May 5, 1882.

the pew he wanted for the bargain price of four hundred dollars. He was shrewd as well as pious and made a neat profit by selling his old pew at Grace Church for one hundred dollars more than he had paid for it. A few days later his wife met other pew holders from St. Thomas Church at a fancy upholstery shop, where they were busy selecting materials for their pew cushions. It is not likely that they met many women from St. Joseph's Church there.[11]

Father Cummiskey and Father Pise

Father Cummiskey and the lay trustees seem to have gotten on well together during the parish's first few years. At their meeting on April 3, 1833, the trustees voted to give him an annual salary of $800. The first hint of trouble did not come until three years later. At the regular monthly meeting of the trustees on February 24, 1836, Cummiskey was not present. In his absence, the trustees replaced him as president of the board with a layman, Thomas Glover. Glover was an exemplary layman who had demonstrated his commitment to the Church by helping to establish St. Joseph's Half-Orphan Asylum, but the bylaws of the parish envisioned that the office of president would be filled by the pastor. At that same meeting, the trustees also appointed one of their innumerable ad hoc committees, this one with the mandate to obtain from Father Cummiskey "all the books and accounts relative to the Church affairs."[12]

It was not Cummiskey's first unpleasant experience with lay trusteeism. A decade earlier, Cummiskey had been a curate in St. Mary's Church in Philadelphia during the notorious "Hogan Schism." At that time he had sided with his bishop, Henry Conwell, against the lay trustees who tried to make Father William Hogan the pastor in defiance of the bishop's wishes. At St. Joseph's in 1836, Cummiskey refused to hand over the financial records of the parish to the trustees, leading to a four-month standoff. All the while the

11. The pious John Pintard donated his $100 windfall to charity, sharing it equally between St. Thomas Church and Grace Church. Pintard, February 28, 1826, *Letters of John Pintard*, II, 238–39.

12. ASJC, MMBT, February 24, 1836.

trustees methodically increased the pressure on Cummiskey. In March they asked Bishop Dubois to force Cummiskey to comply with their wishes. When they got no satisfaction from the bishop, they decided to publish a pamphlet detailing the financial condition of the parish and the reasons for their dissatisfaction with Cummiskey. They then voted to discontinue Cummiskey's salary and to demand that he pay $1,800 in back rent for the use of the rectory, where he had been living for the previous two and a half years. Not surprisingly, in June Cummiskey resigned as pastor, but his difficulties with the trustees were not yet finished. For the next several months they hounded him to move out of the rectory, threatening him with legal action if he failed to do so. They even laid claim to his furniture, saying that it was parish property.[13]

As Cummiskey's replacement, Bishop Dubois appointed Father Charles Constantine Pise, the guest speaker at the parish's dedication. A Baltimore priest whom the bishop had invited into the diocese a few years earlier, Pise was a quiet scholarly gentleman, the author of several books and a former seminary professor. He remained in the parish as assistant pastor from 1834 to 1836 and must have been well known to the trustees. Years later Archbishop Michael Corrigan described Pise as "one of the gentlest and meekest of men, never resorting to a harsh word." Unfortunately those virtues were not the ones that he needed to survive as the pastor of St. Joseph's Church in the 1830s.[14]

13. Francis E. Tourscher, O.S.A., *The Hogan Schism and Trustee Troubles in St. Mary's Church, Philadelphia, 1820–1829* (Philadelphia: The Peter Reilly Company, 1930), 30–31. ASJC, MMBT, February 28, March 13, March 20, March 27, June 6, July 7, July 10, September 7, November 1, 1836. It is not known whether or not the pamphlet criticizing Cummiskey was ever published.

14. Pise was born in Annapolis, Maryland, on November 22, 1801, attended Georgetown College, and was briefly a member of the Society of Jesus. After theological studies in Rome and at Mount St. Mary's Seminary in Emmitsburg, Maryland, Pise was ordained a priest of the Archdiocese of Baltimore on March 19, 1825. In the 1820s he published several apologetical and historical books, which constituted, according to Richard Purcell, "the most extended literary work achieved by an American Catholic up to that time." On a brief visit to Rome in 1832 he acquired a doctorate in divinity. Upon his return to America, he served as chaplain to the U.S. Senate in 1833–1834. After his unhappy

Initially the trustees accepted the appointment of Pise as pastor without demur, voted to continue his existing salary of six hundred dollars per year, and even borrowed four hundred dollars in order to pay it. They also offered him free accommodation in the rectory from which they were trying to dislodge Cummiskey. However, when they described it as "the house of the trustees attached to the church," they made it plain that he would live there at their sufferance. It is significant too that Pise was never elected president of the board of trustees. The board was now exclusively in lay hands and became considerably more assertive after several new trustees were voted into office in the elections of May 1837.[15]

Jay Dolan, the church historian, has observed that, in the parishes that he studied in antebellum New York, the trustees came from a higher social class than most of the parishioners. That was true also at St. Joseph's Church. The trustees whose occupations can be identified were skilled workers, merchants, or professional people. Joseph Lamb and Patrick Kinsella, two of the original trustees, were a dyer and a blacksmith respectively. John Hoey was a tailor, Patrick Duffy was a milkman, and Patrick Quinn described himself as a contractor. Thomas Glover, the secretary of the Eagle Insurance Company at 59 Wall Street, was easily the most affluent of the early trustees.[16]

Two of the new trustees elected in 1837, Patrick Casserly and Francis Cooper, were well-known figures in the Catholic community in New York City. Both of them were to give Father Pise considerable grief. Casserly was an Irish-born schoolmaster who emigrated to America in 1824 and founded his own school, the Chrestomathic

---

experience at St. Joseph's Church between 1834 and 1837, he lived with John Power at St. Peter's Church until 1849, when he founded St. Charles Borromeo Church in Brooklyn, New York, where he remained as pastor until his death on May 26, 1866. Pise continued to publish apologetical and historical works throughout the 1830s and 1840s. Richard Purcell, "Charles Constantine Pise," *Dictionary of American Biography*, XIV, 634–35. Corrigan, "Register of Priests," *Historical Records and Studies* 2 (1900): 68–69.

15. ASJC, MMBT, June 6, 1836; May 19, 1837.

16. *Longworth's American Almanac, New-York Register and City Directory* (New York: Thomas Longworth, 1833–1837), passim.

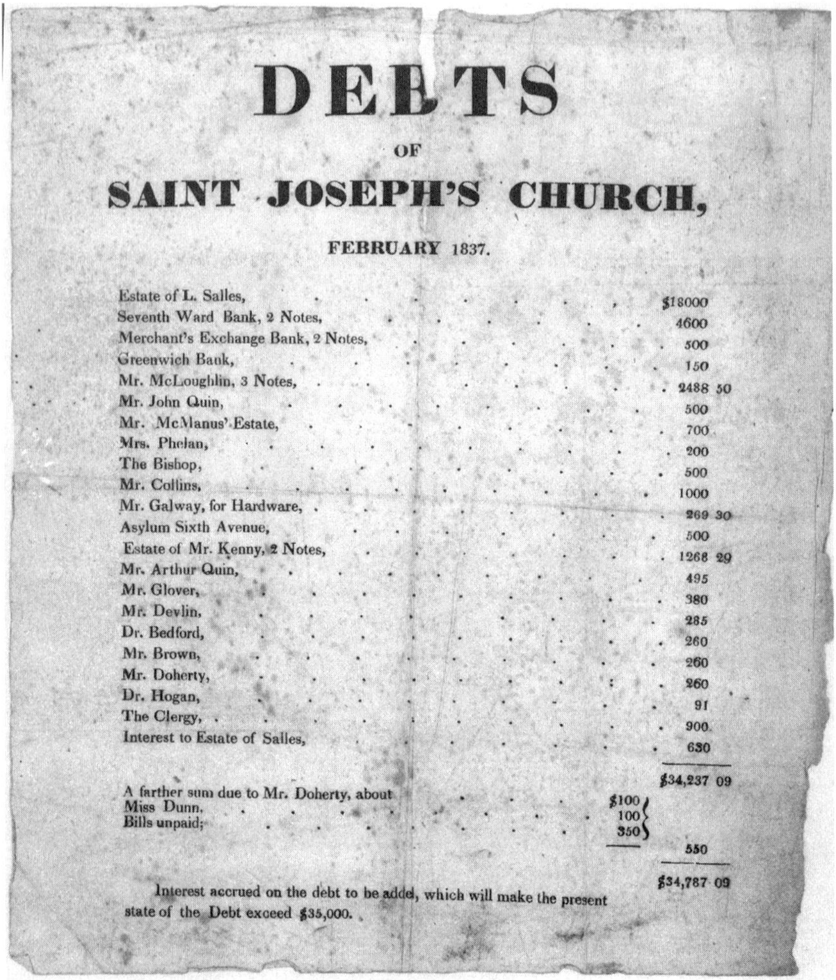

DEBTS
OF
SAINT JOSEPH'S CHURCH,
FEBRUARY 1837.

Estate of L. Salles,	$18000
Seventh Ward Bank, 2 Notes,	4600
Merchant's Exchange Bank, 2 Notes,	500
Greenwich Bank,	150
Mr. McLoughlin, 3 Notes,	2488 50
Mr. John Quin,	500
Mr. McManus' Estate,	700
Mrs. Phelan,	200
The Bishop,	500
Mr. Collins,	1000
Mr. Galway, for Hardware,	269 30
Asylum Sixth Avenue,	500
Estate of Mr. Kenny, 2 Notes,	1268 29
Mr. Arthur Quin,	495
Mr. Glover,	380
Mr. Devlin,	285
Dr. Bedford,	260
Mr. Brown,	260
Mr. Doherty,	260
Dr. Hogan,	91
The Clergy,	900
Interest to Estate of Salles,	630
	$34,237 09

A farther sum due to Mr. Doherty, about	$100	
Miss Dunn,	100	
Bills unpaid;	350	
		550
		$34,787 09

Interest accrued on the debt to be added, which will make the present state of the Debt exceed $35,000.

Source: Archive of St. Joseph's Church. The equivalent of the debt in 2002 dollars is $660,377.36.

Institution, which was located at 43 Henry Street. He was also a classical scholar who published translations of several Greek and Latin authors as well as a Greek reader and *A Complete System of Latin Prosody*. His son Eugene became a prominent lawyer in New York in the 1840s before moving to San Francisco, where he was elected a U.S. senator in 1869. Francis Cooper was an even more significant figure. A coppersmith by trade, he became a hero to local Catholics in 1806 when he was elected to the New York State Assembly and refused to take the offensive anti-Catholic oath requiring abjuration of allegiance to all foreign potentates "in matters ecclesiastical as well as civil." At his insistence the phrase was dropped from the state constitution.[17]

In 1837 Cooper was elected president of the board of trustees and Casserly was elected vice president. Within two months they were at loggerheads with Pise over the financial condition of the parish and also over the organist and the management of the choir. The main source of conflict, however, was the curate, Father James Quinn, a popular young priest who had been transferred from Greenwich Village to the upstate city of Troy shortly after Pise became the pastor. The trustees accused Pise of initiating the transfer of Quinn and claimed that Bishop Dubois had broken his word to them by failing to consult them about the transfer.[18] The trustees sent a peremptory note to Dubois "requiring" him to attend the next meeting of the board of trustees. They also called a public meeting of all pew holders for Sunday, August 24, 1837. The ostensible reason for the meeting was to decide on a farewell present for Quinn, but it was obvious that the trustees had a wider purpose in mind. They announced that the meeting would also "take into consideration the present state of affairs of St. Joseph's Church." To rub salt into the wounds, they asked Father Pise to announce the meeting from the pulpit on Sunday morning at Mass.[19]

17. Thomas F. Meehan, "Some Schools in Old New York," *Historical Records and Studies* 2 (1901): 441–43. William H. Bennett, "Francis Cooper: New York's First Catholic Legislator," *Historical Records and Studies* 12 (1918): 29–38.

18. ASJC, MMBT, May 19, July 3, July 25, August 3, August 17, August 24, 1837.

19. ASJC, MMBT, August 24, 1837.

At the meeting on August 24, the crowd was overwhelmingly on the side of the trustees, although one person made a brave but fruitless effort to defend Father Pise. The pew holders who were present passed nine resolutions, each introduced and seconded by one of the trustees, deploring the transfer of Father Quinn, praising his services at St. Joseph's, and criticizing Pise for dereliction of duty and for treating his parishioners in a condescending manner. One resolution, introduced by the trustee Patrick Quinn and seconded by Patrick Casserly, stated: "From the contemptuous terms in which the Rev. Dr. Pise has been heard repeatedly to express himself in regard to the humble positions in the social scale which Providence has assigned to a majority of the congregation, his ministry can no longer be serviceable in St. Joseph's Church." The final resolution, introduced by John Hoey and seconded by Francis Mann, defined the purpose of the whole meeting: "Resolved that the bishop be respectfully requested to accept the resignation of the Rev. Dr. Pise as pastor of St. Joseph's Church." Pise, of course, had not offered his resignation, but he did so that very day. The trustees accepted it without any consultation with the bishop.[20]

Bishop Dubois and the Trustees

Bishop Dubois received varying accounts of the meeting from both the trustees and from friends of Father Pise. He declared the meeting illegal and told the trustees that their actions belied their protestations of respect for him and his office. He claimed that the trustees had packed the meeting with their own partisans so that anyone who dared to defend the pastor was "hooted and insulted." Furthermore, he accused the trustees of insulting him under the guise of praising Father Quinn and criticizing Father Pise. He denounced their whole proceeding as a usurpation of power on the part of ignorant people.[21]

20. ASJC, MMBT, August 28, 1837. AANY, List of Resolutions of Pewholders of St. Joseph's Church, August 24, 1837, typed copy.

21. AANY, Letter of the Trustees of St. Joseph's Church to Bishop Dubois, September 6, 1837.

Stung by Dubois' strong response to them, the trustees heatedly insisted that the meeting of the pew holders was legal because it had been called for the specific purpose of selecting a present for Quinn. They expressed shock at the bishop's "unprovoked tone of irascibility." They protested that they had never challenged his authority to transfer Quinn, but were only asking him to reconsider his decision. "We never for a moment questioned your right to remove a clergyman," they told him. "But, Rt. Rev. Sir, permit us to claim the privilege as free agents to express our sense of the manner in which that inherent right has been exercised." They professed surprise that any "dispassionate mind" would see in their praise of Quinn "the most remote intention of insulting you." They also rejected Dubois' assertion that the meeting had been wild and disorderly. On the contrary, they claimed that it was "as orderly an assembly as had ever been convened." When the trustees got down to brass tacks, however, they did not retreat an inch from their criticism of Pise, claiming that he was a snob who said he would not preach on Sundays if the pews in the center aisle were "ever to be occupied by hod-carriers and milkmen." They even claimed to have an affidavit from a parishioner asserting that Pise had refused to come to the bedside of a dying woman unless a coach was provided for him.

There was also an unmistakable ethnic dimension to the conflict between Dubois and Pise on the one side, and Quinn, the trustees, and the pew holders on the other side. The French-born bishop was never popular with the Irish in New York. Some of that same resentment was directed at Pise, a native of Annapolis, Maryland, who was the son of an American-born mother and an Italian father. Dubois said that much of the opposition to Pise stemmed from the fact that he was American-born, not Irish. "We disclaim the petty ungenerous insinuation," the trustees retorted. They were also sensitive to accusations that the Catholic Church in America was becoming too Irish. "[We] reject the wretched driveling insinuation that the Irish want to form here a nation distinct from the American," they told Dubois. They also took a gratuitous swipe at "those *soi-disant* Catholic countries" like France and Italy where the Catholic clergy were not nearly as well respected as they were in Ireland."[22]

Since Dubois did not capitulate to their demands, the trustees adopted a twofold plan of action. First they decided to appeal to legitimate ecclesiastical authority by sending a list of their grievances to the Sacred Congregation for the Propagation of the Faith, the Roman curial congregation directly responsible for the American Church. At the same time they decided on a demagogic appeal to popular opinion by threatening to publish a pamphlet with a full account of their difficulties with Bishop Dubois. Interestingly, they themselves identified the source of "the recent difficulties" as "the unpleasant removal of Rev. Mr. Quinn from the assistant pastorate of St. Joseph's Church." Once again they descended to the same mean-spirited tactics that they had employed against Father Cummiskey, demanding that Pise leave the rectory immediately. They revealed their own notion of their authority vis-à-vis the pastor when they informed Pise: "From your resignation from your pastoral duties on Sunday, the 24th of August last, and from the acceptance of that resignation by the congregation, you ceased from that day to be the pastor of St. Joseph's Church."[23]

Dubois fought back by using the same two tactics that the trustees were employing against him, church authority and public opinion. First he imposed an interdict on the parish, forbidding the celebration of Mass or any other religious service. At the same time he made his own appeal to the parishioners of St. Joseph's by summoning a meeting of the pew holders for Sunday, September 17, in the basement of the church. Now it was the turn of the trustees to protest and to complain that this meeting was "irregularly and in-

22. AANY, ibid., and List of Resolutions Passed by Pewholders of St. Joseph's Church, August 24, 1837, typed copy.

23. ASJC, MMBT, September 11, 15, 20, 1837. Letter of Trustees to Pise, September 15, 1837, in Minutes of Meeting of September 15, 1837. There is no mention of an appeal to Rome in the Catholic press, nor is there any reference to such an appeal in Finbar Kenealy, O.F.M., et al., ed., *United States Documents in the Propaganda Fide Archives: A Calendar,* 11 vols. (Washington: Academy of American Franciscan History, 1966–1987).

formally convened." They accused Dubois of packing the meeting with nonparishioners and even Protestants in an effort to produce a majority favorable to Pise. The result, said the trustees, was "a desecration of the sabbath day by as disorderly an assembly as the trustees ever witnessed."[24]

In this tug of war between the bishop and the trustees, the trustees blinked first. Dubois said that he would not lift the interdict until the trustees either restored Father Pise's salary or resigned. On October 11, 1837, they chose the easier course of action and restored Pise's salary, although insisting that Pise could no longer remain as pastor. They made this concession, they told Dubois, "in order that they may be guiltless of the sins inevitably attendant on the lamentable state of destitution in which a whole congregation, the innocent as well as the guilty, has been so wantonly thrown."[25] Having successfully asserted his authority, Dubois was also willing to make a concession and agreed to let Father Pise step down as pastor, something that Pise was more than willing to do to restore peace to the troubled parish.

Parish Finances

By 1837 the trustees of St. Joseph's Church had driven from the parish two pastors in as many years and had provoked the bishop to place the parish under interdict. However, despite these explosive developments, it would be a great mistake to conclude that the main preoccupation of the trustees was feuding with the pastor or bishop. Nor did they devote their monthly meetings to formulating a "republican ecclesiology" to match the Jacksonian politics of most of their parishioners. On the contrary, during those first dozen years of the parish, from 1833 to 1845, the trustees spent 90 percent of their time coping with the more mundane problem of the precarious state of the parish finances. It was hard and unglamorous work.

24. AANY, Letter of Trustees of St. Joseph's Church to Bishop Dubois, September 20, 1837, typed copy.

25. ASJC, MMBT, October 11, 1837.

They worked diligently if not always effectively at the task, even during the most bitter moments of conflict with the pastor and the bishop. Their basic problem was the one that confronted the trustees of all the Catholic churches in New York City, the heavy indebtedness which was itself a reflection of the poverty of the Catholic community. Bishop John Hughes said that in 1838 the total debt of the churches was greater than the value of the property on the open market. He claimed that the annual interest alone would have sufficed to build several new churches every year.[26]

St. Joseph's Church was built largely with borrowed money. The single biggest loan was one of $18,000 from the Salles estate, but there were many other loans both from banks and from private individuals. The trustees frequently made personal loans of several hundred dollars to the church. Thus they had more than a spiritual interest in the solvency of the parish. In March 1841 one creditor demanded the immediate payment of the interest on his four-year loan. Since there was no money in the treasury, the trustees dug into their own pockets and each contributed $32 to raise the necessary funds.[27]

Loans both large and small were constantly recycled because there was no money to repay them in full. When loans came due, the trustees frequently made a minimum payment to the creditor and then renewed the loan for almost the original amount. In March 1839, when a loan of $1,800 from the Seventh Ward Bank came due, the trustees paid the bank $200 and then took out another loan for $1,600. On two separate occasions, in December 1837 and October 1840, the trustees appealed for help to the trustees of St. Patrick's Cathedral. On the first occasion they were successful and got a loan of $2,000. The second time they got nothing, despite their plea "to help us in our present embarrassment."[28]

26. John Hughes to Abbot Bernard Smith, March 23, 1853, published as "A Memoir of Archbishop Hughes, 1838–1858," ed. Henry J. Browne, *Historical Records and Studies* 29–40 (1952): 134.

27. ASJC, MMBT, March 26, 1841.

28. ASJC, MMBT, March 19, 1839; December 17, 1837; January 11, 1838; October 5, 1840.

The first detailed account of the parish's financial condition was drawn up by Thomas Glover while he was the parish treasurer in 1841. He revealed that, from February 1840 to February 1841, the total income was $6,288.03 and the total expenses were $6,496.50, leaving a deficit of $208.47. Glover's breakdown of both income and expenses reveals why it was so difficult to keep the parish solvent. Almost half of the income ($3,134.41) came from pew rents. The Sunday collections brought in another $1,299.24, but most of the rest of the income came from loans from the Greenwich Bank and from two of the parish trustees, James Mooney and James Ryan. On the other side of the balance sheet, almost three-quarters of the expenses ($4,456.36) went either to liquidating loans ($2,309.19) or paying the interest on them ($2,147.17). The total parish debt amounted to $36,092.96. Glover reported sadly: "The reduction of the principal of the debt during the present year is merely nominal., not exceeding $300."[29]

Pew Rents and Class Differences

There was no way to get out from under the crushing burden of debt without increasing income. That meant increasing the revenue from pew rents, many of which were paid late or were not paid at all. In March 1841 Glover estimated that the unpaid pew rents amounted to $1,051.54. Since the rent for a pew on the center aisle was a modest $13 per year, and a pew in the balcony cost only $8.50 per year, there must have been a rather long list of defaulters. In June 1841 Glover, John Hoey, and John Phelan made an extensive analysis of the arrears in pew rentals. They concluded that, for the years 1838, 1839, and 1840, the total unpaid pew rents amounted to $3,818.68. "The congregation cannot expect a better state of things," they warned, "while matters go on as they have for the past three

29. ASJC, MMBT, March 14, 1841. The financial situation was worse at St. Peter's Church, where the debt rose from $116,500 to $135,000 between 1838 and 1844, when the trustees declared bankruptcy. Five years later Bishop Hughes bought the property through a third party at a sheriff's auction. John Hassard, *Life of the Most Reverend John Hughes* (New York: D. Appleton and Company, 1866), 353–55.

years." If all of the pew rentals had been paid on time, they pointed out, "we might now have the pleasure of stating that four thousand dollars of the debt have been liquidated in three years."[30]

The recalcitrant pew holders were periodically threatened with punishments usually reserved for unruly schoolchildren, such as having their names read from the pulpit or posted on the front door of the church. It was especially infuriating when parishioners signed up for pews and then failed to make the payments. As a result of this experience, the trustees required payment of the first quarter's rental by the end of May. Those who failed to comply found their pew locked and a "To Let" sign posted on the door.

One unfortunate side effect of pew rents was to accentuate the class differences in the congregation. On Sundays at St. Joseph's Church the aisles were clogged with poor people standing throughout the Mass because they could not or would not rent one of the many vacant pews. The trustees urged them to attend the early morning Masses so that they did not block the aisles at the high Mass. A note of desperation is evident in the plea of the trustees to the pastor in April 1841 "to urge upon those persons who wish to attend at the High Mass the necessity that exists that every individual should hire a pew or part of a pew or at least a seat—the pecuniary affairs of the Church requiring that everyone should do their part to help in extracting it from present embarrassment."[31]

Parish Concerts

One of the few ways of raising money from sources outside the parish was through concerts. They were usually a success because the Catholic churches in New York City had a reputation for good music. When George Templeton Strong attended the dedication of the new St. Peter's Church in 1838, he had nothing but praise for the music, and he was equally complimentary when he attended Christ-

30. ASJC, MMBT, March 14, 1841. AANY, Financial Report of St. Joseph's Church, June 29, 1841.

31. ASJC, MMBT, May 9, 1841; November 7, 1837; March 1, 1839; August 30, 1838; April 4, 1839; April 4, 1841.

mas Mass there three years later. Snob that he was, however, he could not refrain from adding: "It's a shame that The Church [St. Paul's Episcopal Church] can't or don't [sic] have such music as is thrown away on those rowdies at St. Peter's." John Pintard shared Strong's favorable impression of the music in the Catholic churches. He regretted missing the benefit concert for the orphan asylum in St. Patrick's Cathedral in February 1830. "I should have been gratified to hear the superb music usual on those occasions which attracts great numbers of other denominations," he said.[32]

St. Patrick's Cathedral, St. Peter's Church, and St. Mary's Church regularly scheduled concerts to raise funds either for the Catholic orphan asylum or for their own churches. An oratorio presented in the cathedral in November 1836 drew a capacity crowd of 1,500 people and raised $1,800 for the orphans. Mention has already been made of the concert held in St. Joseph's brand new church in November 1834 for the benefit of St. Joseph's Half-Orphan Asylum. Four years later, on September 16, 1838, the parish put on an even more ambitious presentation, which was styled a Grand Oratorio and consisted largely of selections from Handel and Haydn. Tickets were fifty cents each and the forthcoming concert received extensive coverage in *The Truth Teller.* However, the financial returns may have been disappointing, judging from the total silence about the concert afterwards in the minutes of the trustees' meetings.[33]

Even one or two successful concerts every year would not have eliminated the need for a regular source of income from the pew rents. At St. Joseph's Church the collection of this indispensable revenue was not left to chance. The pew rents were collected by a parish employee who was hired specifically for this purpose and was paid on a commission basis. Unfortunately the first two individuals hired

32. Strong, February 25, 1838, *Diary,* I, 81; December 25, 1841, *Diary,* I, 171. Pintard, June 11, 1830, *Letters of John Pintard,* III, 152–53. After attending a service at St. Peter's Church on April 26, 1839, Strong recorded in his diary: "I never heard anything equal for richness and softness and grandeur the magnificent body of sound that the full band with kettle drums or the sub-bass of the organ produced." *Diary,* I, 102.

33. *The Truth Teller,* September 15, 1838.

by the trustees proved to be unsatisfactory. The first collector of pew rents was James Dornan, who combined the job with that of sexton at a salary of $250 per year. The trustees hired him on April 3, 1833. He held the job until February 1838 when the trustees fired him from both jobs for what they euphemistically called "his intemperate habits," after he lost the account books, or "allegedly" lost them, according to the skeptical trustees.[34]

Dornan's successor was James Doherty, who was also hired by the trustees. He held the job until Glover, Hoey, and Phelan began to sift through the financial records in June 1841. They discovered that, between March 1, 1838, and May 1, 1841, Doherty had collected $10,406.36 in pew rents but had deposited in the parish treasury only $9,695.54, leaving a shortfall of $710.82. Part of the problem was Doherty's sloppy bookkeeping, especially his bad habit of paying his own salary in advance. Even after taking these factors into consideration, however, Glover, Hoey, and Phelan declared that "Mr. Doherty is a defaulter to the amount of about $400." They fired him on the spot, whereupon he sued the parish. The third collector of pew rents, Nicholas Walsh, proved to be a better choice than either of his predecessors. Nonetheless, the trustees took no chances and ordered him to give a weekly report of the pew rents that he collected.[35]

The first real improvement in the financial picture at St. Joseph's Church came from an unexpected quarter. This was the Church Debt Association, established by Bishop John Hughes to help the parishes to reduce their crippling debt. Between October 1841 and April 1842, St. Joseph's Church received $2,343.38 from the fund and paid into it only $100. Thanks to John Hughes, in 1842 St. Joseph's Church was able to pay $2,994.22 on the principal of the debt. By 1844 the annual parish income had increased to $8,228.96, but expenses had also increased, leaving a grand surplus that year of thirty-nine cents. As usual the main reason for the bleak financial pic-

34. ASJC, MMBT, April 8, 1833; February 9, 13, 1838.

35. AANY, Financial Report of St. Joseph's Church, June 29, 1841; ASJC, MMBT, July 16, June 29, September 12, 1841.

ture was the size of the debt. That year the parish paid $1,890 in interest just on the money borrowed from the Salles estate. However, by 1845, the last year that the trustees were in charge of the finances, the debt had finally begun to shrink, to $29,148.34. Servicing the debt became much more manageable after 1847, when annual parish income topped $10,000 for the first time.[36]

Father John McCloskey

By the time that the financial situation of the parish began to improve in the mid-1840s, a major transformation had taken place in the relationship between the pastor and the trustees of St. Joseph's Church. The change may be traced to the pastor whom Bishop Dubois selected in 1837 as a replacement for Father Pise. The new appointee, who could hardly have regarded his assignment as a reward, was Father John McCloskey, the future archbishop of New York and the first American cardinal. McCloskey was then ordained only three years and had just returned from several years of theological studies in Rome. The parishioners of St. Joseph's Church hardly greeted him with open arms. For the next several months McCloskey celebrated Mass every Sunday in an almost empty church. Not only was the church empty, but so was the parish treasury. One of the first requests that the trustees made of their new pastor (though they could not bring themselves to address him by name) was to issue an appeal from the pulpit begging the pew holders to pay their long overdue rental fees. In lieu of salary, they offered to provide McCloskey with food packages from a local baker, butcher, and grocer. At the same time, however, the empty parish treasury did not prevent them from voting to pay Father Quinn his back salary as soon as possible.[37]

In early December the trustees carried their dispute with Dubois to the point of open rupture with the Catholic Church. At the meet-

36. ASJC, MMBT, July 6, 1842; AANY, Financial Report of St. Joseph's Church 1844, 1845.

37. ASJC, MMBT, November 6, 19, 24, 1837.

ing of the board on December 3, 1837, they appointed Patrick Quinn and Francis Cooper to a committee for the purpose of petitioning the state legislature at its next session to grant them a new charter for the parish, thus raising the possibility of open schism. They also decided to place a notice in *The Truth Teller* announcing their intentions. Fortunately, however, cooler heads prevailed and they drew back from the brink. At their next meeting, on a motion of Patrick Casserly seconded by John Hoey, the trustees changed their minds and rescinded the resolution.[38]

Often when severe conflicts erupted between a parish's lay trustees and the bishop, there was a third party acting as an instigator, usually a priest who encouraged or manipulated the trustees. At St. Joseph's Church, Father James Quinn filled that role, although it would appear that in his case it was the trustees who were manipulating him. Despite the near bankruptcy of the parish, the trustees presented Quinn with a gold watch as a farewell present and used the occasion to take a swipe at both the bishop and the former pastor. While heaping praise upon Quinn, they made clear their dislike of Pise by voicing regret that Bishop Dubois' "credulity in the . . . insinuations of a certain individual who can never enjoy . . . the affections of his flock should unhappily predominate over the united voices of a devoted congregation."[39]

38. ASJC, MMBT, December 3, 17, 1837.

39. ASJC, MMBT, Letter of Trustees to Rev. James Quinn, n.d., in Minutes of Meeting of December 17, 1837. James Quinn was ordained on October 4, 1835, at Mount St. Mary's Seminary, Emmitsburg, Maryland. After serving in Greenwich Village, he was assigned to Troy, New York, and later to Paterson, New Jersey, where he died on June 13, 1851. Corrigan, "Register of Clergy," *Historical Records and Studies* 2 (1900): 76. From the slender evidence available, Quinn appears to have been much flattered by the attention paid to him as a young priest in his first assignment. In thanking the trustees for their gold watch, he told them that what impressed him the most was that it had come from so many "disinterested, discerning and worthy persons." He expressed satisfaction that his "first humble efforts as a laborer in the vineyard of Christ were not entirely in vain." He made no mention of the controversy swirling around him, nor did he urge the trustees to effect a reconciliation with the pastor or to restore peace to the parish that had been so good to him. ASJC, MMBT, Letter of Quinn to the Trustees, February 5, 1837, in Minutes of the Meeting of February 13, 1837.

Like skittish cats on a backyard fence, McCloskey and the trustees eyed each other warily during their first few months together. "Difficulties soon passed away," was McCloskey's bland recollection of the events twenty-nine years later when he came back to visit his old parish as the new Archbishop of New York. Nonetheless, his first few months in the parish were very unpleasant. Not until May 1838 did the trustees agree to pay him a salary of $500 per year. Even then they were still pestering Dubois to replace him with their own candidate, Father John Urquhart, an Irish-born Dominican friar who was a curate at St. Patrick's Cathedral.[40] The resignation of Cooper and Casserly from the board of trustees removed two of the most contentious figures from the scene. Other firebrands like John Hoey and Francis Mann also withdrew from the board over the next few years. Last but not least, Father McCloskey played a crucial role in restoring peace to the troubled parish. A gentle, self-effacing man, he had to endure humiliations like being called out of the rectory in the middle of the night on bogus sick calls. However, his tenacity and dedication to duty eventually wore down the opposition and won for him the respect and the affection of his parishioners.[41]

The End of an Era

In 1839 a decided change took place in the character of New York Catholicism, when the young and determined coadjutor bishop, John Hughes, became the administrator of the diocese for the aging and ailing John Dubois. Hughes had already demonstrated his opposition to lay trusteeism the year before, when he routed the trustees of the cathedral parish at a dramatic meeting of the pew

40. Urquhart was the pastor of St. Mary's Church in Albany from 1836 to 1837 before coming to the cathedral in 1838. He returned to Ireland in 1841. Archbishop Corrigan described him as "a fine commanding figure," but also mentioned cryptically that "his lot was cast in evil days on account of the evils of the trustee system, which was yet in active existence." Corrigan, "Register of the Clergy," *Historical Records and Studies* 2:1 (1900): 78.

41. ASJC, MMBT, February 9, 1838; May 3, 1838. See also John Cardinal Farley, *The Life of John Cardinal McCloskey* (New York: Longmans, Green and Company, 1918), 129. AANY, John McCloskey, Notes for a Sermon in St. Joseph's Church. n.d. [1866].

holders. Two years later he gave the final coup de grâce to trusteeism in New York during the first diocesan synod, which met in the cathedral on August 29, 1842. At Hughes' direction, the synod enacted statutes that severely limited the authority of the trustees over church property and parish finances, and required them to obtain the pastor's approval for virtually all of their decisions.[42]

The minutes of the trustees' meetings in St. Joseph's Church give no indication that they were aware of Hughes' radical reconstruction of the whole trustee system in the diocese. However, like the justices of the United States Supreme Court, who are alleged to follow the election returns, the trustees of St. Joseph's Church showed a marked change in attitude toward their pastor in the course of the year 1842. In February of that year McCloskey returned to the parish after a temporary absence during which he had served as the first president of St. John's College at Fordham. The trustees expressed "great satisfaction" at his return and voted to increase his salary by $100. They now referred to the rectory as "the house of the pastor" rather than "the house of the trustees." They even agreed to paint the rectory for McCloskey and to pay the cost of the insurance (the annual premium was $2.18). On February 17, 1843, an event took place that would have been unthinkable a few years earlier. The trustees elected McCloskey president of the board, called upon him in the rectory, escorted him to the meeting room, and installed him in the president's chair.[43]

What was hardly less surprising was the fact that, of the seven active trustees, only two, John Gibbons and John McCarthy, were newcomers to the board. The other five, Dr. Robert Hogan, Peter McLaughlin, Thomas Glover, John Phelan, and John Boulger, were

42. Hassard, *Life of the Most Reverend John Hughes,* 259–60. Hughes made no effort to eliminate lay trustees in the parishes where they already existed. In fact, he said that his critics "may still be further surprised to learn that many trustees of churches have tendered their trust into my hands, and that I have declined to receive it." "Bishop Hughes' Apology for his Pastoral Letter," November 1842, in *Complete Works of the Most Reverend John Hughes* (New York: Lawrence Kehoe, 1866), I, 334.

43. ASJC, MMBT, February 14, April 24, June 21, 1842; February 17, 1843.

all veterans of the parish wars of the previous seven years. In fact, some of them had been vociferous critics of the former pastors. John Boulger had been the chairman of the famous meeting of the pew holders on August 24, 1837, that led to the resignation of Father Pise. Dr. Robert Hogan had been the co-author of the blistering report of that meeting to Bishop Dubois on September 6, 1837. Thomas Glover had served as the first lay president of the board, replacing Father Cummiskey in February 1836. The rapprochement between the pastor and the trustees, therefore, was not due to any radical change in the composition of the board, but to a change in the attitude of the trustees themselves. That remarkable turnaround may be traced in considerable measure to the combination of the stick and the carrot wielded respectively by Bishop John Hughes and Father John McCloskey.

The trustees reelected McCloskey president of the board in February 1844. Shortly thereafter he was appointed the coadjutor bishop of New York. The trustees voted to purchase an episcopal throne for the church, and a miter and vestments for McCloskey, whom they described as "their beloved pastor." McCloskey remained as pastor for only a few more months, but the problem of lay trusteeism had been effectively resolved at St. Joseph's Church before his departure. The board itself disappeared shortly after McCloskey left to take up his episcopal duties at St. Patrick's Cathedral. For reasons that are not clear, at the regular monthly meeting of the board of trustees on February 6, 1845, five of the nine trustees resigned. Deprived of a quorum, the board simply expired, bringing to a close twelve tumultuous years in the parish's history.[44]

44. ASJC, MMBT, February 14, 28, 1844; February 6, 1845. In April 1844 the trustees of Transfiguration Church gave the deed to the church to their pastor, Father Varela. Jay Dolan notes that the trustees in several parishes in New York were not notably successful in the very area where they claimed special competence, financial management. Dolan, *Immigrant Church*, 49–50.

3 *Antebellum Greenwich Village*

FOUR MONTHS AFTER the dissolution of the board of trustees of St. Joseph's Church, Bishop John Hughes issued a statement in which he noted that lay trusteeism had practically disappeared throughout his diocese. He disclaimed any credit for it, but he obviously regarded it as a happy development. At the synod of 1842 he said that he had never intended to destroy the trustee system itself, only "to limit the exercise of its powers by holding the trustees to a strict and direct ecclesiastical responsibility." Nevertheless, Hughes observed with considerable satisfaction in 1845 that "the effect . . . has been that both the trustees themselves, and for the most part the congregations generally, have practically set the system aside. . . ." Lay trustees, he said, "have been, as by general consent, dispensed with in nearly all the congregations of this diocese." The bishop was happy to see the old system disappear. "The consequence has been," he claimed, "an improvement in the financial condition of the churches, a great diminution of strife and contention, and, we have reason to hope, a very considerable increase of piety and attention to religious observance."[1]

New York's First Archbishop

John Hughes was the outstanding figure in the history of nineteenth-century Catholicism in New York. During the quarter-century (1839–1864) that he presided over the

1. Statement of Bishop John Hughes, June 4, 1845, in *Freeman's Journal and Catholic Register*, July 5, 1845.

Church in New York, the poverty-stricken, struggling diocese that he inherited developed into the largest and most important archdiocese in the country. A poor administrator and worse financial manager, Hughes nevertheless became the best known, if not the best loved, Catholic prelate in the whole country because of his courageous defense of the rights of his immigrant flock in the face of widespread Nativist bigotry. In a famous incident in 1844, when Nativist mobs threatened the safety of Catholic churches, Hughes placed armed guards around his churches and vowed to "turn the city into a second Moscow" if any harm came to them.[2]

John Hughes headed a diocese that was constantly shrinking in size but growing in Catholic population. After the creation of two new dioceses in Buffalo and Albany in 1847, and two more in Brooklyn and Newark in 1853, the original Diocese of New York was reduced to one-tenth its former size. Nonetheless, in that remaining portion, the Catholic population soared from about fifteen thousand in 1815 to almost four hundred thousand by the time of Hughes' death in 1864. In the meantime, on July 19,1850, New York was made an archdiocese, with John Hughes as the first archbishop.

Nowhere was the growth of the Catholic population more astonishing than in New York City, where by 1864 half of the total population may have been Catholic. The city itself experienced a massive population explosion that led to a major geographical expansion. When John Hughes arrived in New York as coadjutor to Bishop Dubois in 1838, the northern boundary of the city was 14th Street. According to the census of 1840, only 46,907 people lived north of that street, and 2,773 residents of New York City still listed their occupation as agricultural. Twenty years later no fewer than 423,107 people (including seven Native Americans) lived north of 14th Street and a whole "second city" had grown up between 14th Street and 59th Street.[3]

2. Hassard, *Life of the Most Reverend John Hughes*, 276.

3. Ira Rosenwaike, *Population History of New York City* (Syracuse, N.Y.: Syracuse University Press, 1972), 16, 48.

East Village and West Village

As the city expanded northward, it followed the rigid grid pattern of streets and avenues that had been laid out in 1811, which all but obliterated the natural features of Manhattan's landscape. An exception to the rule was Greenwich Village, whose winding streets and meandering alleys set it apart from the rest of Manhattan. Greenwich Village also differed from the rest of the city in that it was less affected than most Manhattan neighborhoods by the huge influx of immigrants to antebellum New York. The Irish tended to settle in the Fourth, Fifth, and Sixth Wards, the area south of Canal Street, which included the notorious Five Points slum. They were among the poorest of the immigrants. In 1855, 20 percent of them were laborers while another 26.4 percent were domestic servants, a far higher percentage than among other immigrant groups. The Germans were concentrated in the Tenth, Eleventh, Thirteenth, and Seventeenth Wards, the area east of the Bowery between Grand Street and 14th Street, which became known as *Kleindeutschland*, or "Little Germany."[4] So great was the tide of immigration that, by the end of the Civil War, one out of every four New Yorkers was born in Ireland, and one out of every seven New Yorkers was born in Germany.[5]

4. Dolan, *The Immigrant Church*, 27–29.

5. Rosenwaike, *Population History*, 41, 43. It was common for native-born American Protestants to express their preference for German Protestant immigrants instead of Irish Catholics. The New York Association for Improving the Condition of the Poor drew this contrast in 1860:

"Unfortunately [the Irish] are mostly rude, uninstructed laborers of the lowest grade, who have but little knowledge of work beyond what has been derived from farming their impoverishing potato patch, to which they were pertinaciously attached in their own country. . . . It is not surprising, therefore, that so many soon find themselves at the foot of the social ladder,—or that their wives are often deserted, their children neglected, and themselves and families beyond any other class of our population in the way of becoming subjects of the Almshouse or Penitentiary."

"The Germans supply the next most considerable part of our immigrant population and ratio of pauperism. Of them it may be said that they are the opposite of the Irish, being generally a self-reliant, sober, frugal, thrifty people. . . . They often move in families, sometimes by villages, accompanied by their minister and doctor, bringing with

The state census of 1855 revealed that 52 percent of the city's population was foreign-born. However, in the Ninth and Fifteenth Wards, which covered the West Village and East Village, the proportion of foreign-born residents was only 34 percent and 41 percent respectively. Even the immigrant population in Greenwich Village was different from the immigrant population of the rest of the city. The English and Scots were overrepresented, and the Irish and Germans were underrepresented, in proportion to their total numbers in the city's population. Parts of the Village, especially the area around Washington Square, lower Fifth Avenue, Union Square, and Gramercy Park, formed one of the most exclusive residential sections of the city. Broadway between Houston Street and 14th Street was dotted with fine hotels, shops, and theaters. It was said that in the 1840s the two sights that tourists were most eager to see were the elegant mansions around Washington Square and the notorious slums of the Five Points.[6]

The West Village, the area between Sixth Avenue and the Hudson River, lacked the social cachet of the East Village, but it became a solid middle-class neighborhood that was home to many native-born American artisans who had moved up from lower Manhattan. In the early and mid-nineteenth century, said one historian, the West Village "was one of the few neighborhoods where middle-class families could live at a reasonable cost in their own homes on quiet, sunny, largely residential streets." Another historian noted that in

---

them ample means to establish themselves in the country of their adoption. . . . They can work for less wages than Americans and live where an Irishman would starve. As they limit their wants to their necessities, and rarely spend all they earn, they generally become prosperous, money-making citizens." New York Association for Improving the Condition of the Poor, *Seventeenth Annual Report*, 1860, 50–51.

Four of the six founders of the New York Association for Improving the Condition of the Poor, in July 1863, were Presbyterians and leaders of the New York Tract Society. Dorothy Ganfield Fowler, *A City Church: The First Presbyterian Church in the City of New York, 1716–1976* (New York: The First Presbyterian Church in the City of New York, 1981), 105.

6. Robert Ernst, *Immigrant Life in New York City, 1825–1863* (Syracuse, N.Y.: Syracuse University Press, 1994), 44. This classic work was first published in 1949. Charles Lockwood, *Manhattan Moves Uptown* (Boston: Houghton Mifflin Company, 1976), 108.

that era "Greenwich Village became known as an area where the residents were well mannered and largely native born, and was often approvingly called the 'American ward.'"[7] Together with the East Village, the West Village was ranked by a private relief agency in the 1850s as one of the two healthiest neighborhoods in the city. Its "salubrity" was attributed to the "better condition and circumstances of the population." There were few tenement houses and few people on public relief (only 318 families in 1854). Nonetheless, even in this relatively affluent neighborhood, there were pockets of poverty, which were inhabited by many of the poor Irish immigrants who made up the bulk of St. Joseph's congregation. The same private relief agency that praised the "salubrity" of the West Village also noted that "most of the houses occupied by the poor in this ward are very deficient in the requisites for health, decency and comfort. Sewerage is but partially introduced and the consequent accumulations of fluid, filth and putrid mud, poisoning the atmosphere, squalor and debasement are visible in all locations."[8]

Dr. Ambrose Manahan

Shortly after John McCloskey was made the coadjutor bishop of New York, he relinquished his role as pastor of St. Joseph's Church and moved into Bishop Hughes' residence on Mulberry Street. He served as a member of the cathedral staff and relieved Bishop Hughes of the upstate confirmation tours, until he was made the first bishop of Albany in 1847. To replace McCloskey as pastor of St. Joseph's Church, Hughes made the risky decision to appoint Ambrose Manahan. Like McCloskey, Manahan was a native New Yorker, born in either 1813 or 1814. Like McCloskey, he was also one of the first New York priests sent by the diocese to study in Rome, where he

7. Blackmar, *Manhattan for Rent,* 101; Lockwood, *Manhattan Moves Uptown,* 71. James F. Richardson, "Wards," *Encyclopedia of the City of New York,* 1237; Jan Seidler Ramirez, "Greenwich Village," ibid., 508.

8. New York Association for Improving the Condition of the Poor, *First Report of a Committee on the Sanitary Condition of the Laboring Classes in the City of New York with Remedial Suggestions* (New York: John F. Trow, 1853), 12. Ibid., *Eleventh Annual Report,* 1854, 24; *Sixteenth Annual Report,* 1859, 40.

spent seven years and received a Doctor of Divinity degree from the College of the Propaganda Fide. A charming conversationalist and popular lecturer, Manahan in later life was the author of *Triumph of the Church in the Early Ages,* a book which won the favorable attention of both Orestes Brownson and Archbishop Corrigan. John Talbot Smith, an early-twentieth-century priest-historian of the archdiocese, described him as "clever and accomplished, born to great things, but never arriving."[9]

In 1844 Manahan was under a cloud. Ordained only four years, he had already had three assignments. One of the assignments was the rectorship of St. John's College at Fordham, where he succeeded John McCloskey. However, his authoritarian style of leadership alienated the faculty and drove the students to the brink of rebellion. One faculty member, Father John Harley, told Hughes: "What was before the home of harmony and happiness is now the abode of discord and unhappiness. . . . Mr. [sic] Manahan has come among us, full to overflowing of wild and useless schemes." As for the students, Harley warned Hughes that "nothing but the paucity of their number restrains them from open eruption." Harley was so unhappy with Manahan's leadership that he offered Hughes his resignation from the faculty. Instead, Hughes fired Manahan and replaced him with Harley, who proved to be a huge success.[10]

John Hughes was taking a calculated risk, therefore, when he appointed Manahan to St. Joseph's Church. Unfortunately, Manahan proved to be no more successful as a pastor than he had been as a college rector. As a result, in September 1845, he was unceremoniously dismissed from St. Joseph's Church by Hughes. The reasons for his dismissal are not known, but Hughes' letter was short, brutally blunt, and tantalizingly cryptic. "Not wishing to have the pain of

9. John Talbot Smith, *The Catholic Church in New York* (New York and Boston: Hall & Locke Company, 1905), I, 171. Brownson's favorable review of Manahan's book appeared in *Brownson's Quarterly Review,* 3rd series, 1 (January 1860): 51–74.

10. AANY, A-14, John Harley to Hughes, February 28, 1842. On Manahan and the situation at St. John's College, see Thomas J. Shelley, "Fordham Before the Jesuits: Bishop John Hughes and St. John's College, 1838–1846," in *Fordham: The Early Years,* ed. Thomas C. Hennessy, S.J. (n.p.: Something More Publications, 1998), 53–76.

inflicting any public censure on your character," Hughes told him, "I advise you to resign, to ask [for] your *exeat,* in the almost extinguished hope that on a new scene where your future character will be determined by your future conduct, you may disappoint the melancholy anticipations which the past is too well calculated to inspire."[11]

For all of Hughes' bluster, there was also a softer side to him that he occasionally chose to exhibit. Indeed, Manahan once characterized him as "a tyrant, but with feeling." He gave Manahan a second chance a decade after his fiasco in St. Joseph's Church. He allowed him to return to the diocese from his exile in Boston and appointed him the chaplain in the charity hospital on Ward's Island, hardly a coveted assignment. Manahan served there from 1853 to 1864. While acting as the temporary administrator of St. Stephen's Church in 1857, however, Manahan had a further run-in with Hughes when he walked off with the financial records and receipt books of the parish after refurbishing the rectory. He died outside the diocese, in Troy, New York, on December 7, 1867.[12]

One of Manahan's friends was James McMaster, the irascible and ultra-conservative editor of the *New York Freeman's Journal and Catholic Register.* "Dr. Manahan was a rare genius," said McMaster enigmatically. "He was fitted for great things, but could not adapt himself to little things." During their younger days McMaster and Manahan were part of a circle of friends who met every Thursday afternoon to discuss theology. At one of these sessions Manahan delivered himself of what McMaster called "the most eloquent and fascinating discourse we ever listened to," when he proceeded to demonstrate that the human intellect could prove that "God is One

11. AANY, A-5, Hughes to Manahan, September 4, 1845.

12. Manahan's comment about Hughes is quoted by Richard Burtsell, AANY, Burtsell, Diary, July 24, 1865. AANY, A-7, Hughes to Manahan, November 4, December 9, 1857. There is a brief sketch of Manahan in Archbishop Corrigan's "Register of the Clergy Laboring in the Archdiocese of New York from Early Missionary Times to 1885," *Historical Records and Studies* 2 (1901): 260. Corrigan merely mentions that Manahan "did not remain long" as pastor of St. Joseph's Church.

in Nature and Three in Persons." "We never heard eloquence like that before or since," said McMaster, tongue in cheek. He also admitted that the whisky flowed fairly freely at these Thursday gatherings, although he added, perhaps also tongue in cheek, that, at least in the summer, Dr. Manahan's favorite beverage was current jelly and ice water.[13]

The Archdeacon: Michael McCarron

Bishop Hughes replaced Manahan at St. Joseph's Church with two rough-hewn, flinty Ulstermen much like himself. The first was Michael McCarron, who was appointed the pastor in 1846, and the other was William Quinn, almost twenty years younger, who arrived six months later to take up the duties of curate. Despite the difference in age, they were birds of a feather who took an immediate liking to one another and remained close friends for the rest of their lives. "He was my first friend in the priesthood," said Quinn of McCarron, and "that friendship [was] uninterrupted for a day."

McCarron was born in 1803 in County Monaghan, not far from the town in County Tyrone where John Hughes had been born six years earlier. As a young man in Ireland, McCarron witnessed the excitement among the Catholic peasantry aroused by Daniel O'Connell and the Catholic Association in their struggle for civil rights for Irish Catholics. He was twenty-six years old when the Catholic Emancipation Act became law in 1829. Even in post-Emancipation Ireland, however, Catholics still suffered from various forms of discrimination. John Hughes once said: "They told me when I was a boy that for five days I was on social and civil equality with the most favored subjects of the British Empire. These five days," he explained, "would be the interval between my birth and my baptism."[14] Forty years later, in 1837, McCarron, then a young layman,

13. James McMaster, *New York Freeman's Journal and Catholic Register,* December 21, 1867.

14. Richard Shaw, *Dagger John: The Unquiet Life and Times of Archbishop John Hughes of New York* (New York: Paulist Press, 1977), 14.

wrote to a friend in the United States, indicating that conditions were not notably better. "I have always had a great affection for the land of freedom," McCarron told his American friend, "and when I contemplate how liberty is enjoyed in Republican America, and contrast it with the oppression practiced in this ill-fated land by a tyrannical oligarchy . . . I feel an insatiable desire of leaving this degraded country, and I envy your felicity in having escaped out if it altogether."[15]

McCarron entered St. Patrick's College, Maynooth, and was ordained a priest around 1840 at the relatively late age of thirty-seven or thirty-eight. Almost immediately he volunteered for service in America, motivated not only by dissatisfaction with conditions in Ireland but also by the constant appeals for help from American bishops. According to his friend William Quinn, McCarron selected New York as his adopted diocese because of his admiration for John Hughes. Hughes accepted McCarron into the diocese, assigning him first to St. James Church and to the cathedral as a curate before entrusting him with St. Joseph's Church, where he was to remain as pastor for twelve years.[16]

During his first six months at St. Joseph's, Father McCarron was the only priest in the parish. He celebrated two Masses every Sunday as well as Vespers in the afternoon, and took care of all the sick calls in a parish that still extended from Canal Street to 20th Street and from Broadway to the Hudson River. He heard confessions every morning, and on Saturdays he frequently remained in the confessional in the dank basement of St. Joseph's Church from 3:00 until 10:00 or 11:00 at night. Years later Quinn recalled seeing McCarron on Saturday evenings "surrounded most of the time with crowds of penitents so great that the very sight of them was appalling to the confessor."

McCarron's training at Maynooth left him with a lifelong love of

15. McCarron to Michael Curran, 1837, cit. in *New York Freeman's Journal and Catholic Register,* March 9, 1867.

16. Corrigan, "Register of the Clergy," 254–55.

learning and a respect for education, which he tried unsuccessfully to pass on to his younger colleague. McCarron's interests were not limited to theology, but included the Greek and Latin classics as well. An avid reader, as a pastime he liked to collate the text of the Latin Vulgate with the Greek text of the Septuagint. Like Hughes, he realized that education was essential for the Catholic immigrants and their children if they were to escape from the debilitating cycle of poverty. For that reason McCarron gave strong support to St. John's College at Fordham, sending students there and raising funds for it. "He rejoiced at its success," said Quinn, "almost as much as its illustrious founder and first distinguished president."[17]

Closer to home, McCarron made his own contribution to Catholic education when in 1855 he established the first permanent parochial school in his own parish. Several earlier attempts going back as far as 1835 had ended in failure.[18] McCarron not only erected a large school building on Leroy Street, but also assured the success of the school when he secured the services of both the Sisters of Charity for the girls' department and the Christian Brothers for the boys' department. The initial enrollment was eight hundred students, evenly divided between girls and boys. Quinn gave McCarron full credit for the achievement, noting that he bought the property, raised the funds for the construction of the building, and persuaded both the Sisters and Brothers to serve on the staff.[19]

In 1857, after launching the parochial school, McCarron asked Archbishop Hughes for a change of assignment and was appointed pastor of St. Mary's Church on Grand Street. There he showed the same interest in Catholic education as he had at St. Joseph's Church.

17. William Quinn, *New York Freeman's Journal and Catholic Register,* March 9, 1867.

18. In 1835, one year after the completion of St. Joseph's Church, Father Cummiskey advertised for a teacher for the "School of St. Joseph's Church." The requirements were that "he must be a good English Scholar, a good Arithmatician, a good Penman, and be well acquainted with Geography, as it is usually taught in the schools of this City." *The Truth Teller,* October 2, 1835. A month later it was announced that Mr. Bartholomew McGowans had opened a school "under St. Joseph's Church." It is not known how long the basement school lasted. *The Truth Teller,* November 7, 1835.

19. Walsh, *Sisters of Charity,* II, 8.

Since the parochial school in St. Mary's was too small for the needs of the parish, McCarron purchased the Rutgers Institute, one of the most fashionable Protestant academies in the city, and turned it into a free Catholic school. It was suggested that he might want to preserve the name of the prestigious Rutgers Institute. "I will not call it Rutgers Institute," McCarron said emphatically. "What do I care for Rutgers? I will call it St. Mary's Institute."

McCarron's health had already begun to fail when he went to St. Mary's. He died on February 23, 1867, after a long illness. Like Manahan, McCarron too was a friend of James McMaster, but for different reasons. The dour, former Presbyterian newspaper editor and the stern Ulster-born priest had much in common. McMaster admired McCarron as a person "who never feared the face of any man" and who was "inaccessible to flattery." Archbishop Hughes gave McCarron the title of "Archdeacon," one that was rarely if ever used in the United States, perhaps because of his habit of correcting the clergy for what he regarded as their lapses and shortcomings. "He was instant and unsparing," said McMaster, "in his rebuke of anything that seemed an infraction of the strict old-fashioned rule of faith or morals. In a company, we have known him openly and crushingly rebuke an indiscreet utterance of an ecclesiastic," although McMaster was quick to add that he "would take the pains to see everyone present and speak in the kindest and most honorable way of the man he had corrected."[20]

Monsignor William Quinn

Father McCarron's friend and protégé William Quinn was born in Donoughmore, County Donegal, in 1821. He emigrated to America twenty years later, enrolled in the newly established St. Joseph's Seminary at Fordham, and was ordained a priest by Bishop John McCloskey in Old St. Patrick's Cathedral on December 17, 1845. His first assignment was to St. Joseph's Church in Greenwich Village, where he remained as the curate for four years. Except for John Mc-

20. James McMaster, *New York Freeman's Journal and Catholic Register,* March 2, 1867.

Closkey, no other priest connected with St. Joseph's Church has risen to comparable influence in the archdiocese. After a brief stint as pastor in upstate Rondout, New York, in 1849, Quinn was made pastor of St. Peter's Church in Barclay Street. There he paid off a debt of $140,000 and restored the shattered finances of the parish, a feat that even his predecessor, the legendary John Power, had been unable to accomplish. Archbishop McCloskey called him higher, making him rector of the new cathedral in 1873 and one of the two vicars general of the archdiocese. He was offered the coadjutorship of Cincinnati after Archbishop John Purcell nearly bankrupted that archdiocese, but he turned down the offer and in 1881 settled for the title of Monsignor, which was then a rare honor among the New York clergy.[21]

The diocesan clergy of Quinn's day were still largely foreign-born, either Irish or German, and they retained the clerical characteristics of their native land. Quinn was a born autocrat, who treated clergy and laity alike with the lofty disdain of an Irish country pastor for his peasant flock. He had a genuine gift for administration and finance, but his social graces were those of a drill sergeant. By sheer ability and force of personality, he overshadowed the senior vicar general, Father William Starrs, and became, in Monsignor Florence Cohalan's telling phrase, "the strong man of the McCloskey administration." The shy and self-effacing McCloskey was happy to float above the clouds and allow Quinn to be the enforcer in the archdiocese.[22]

John Talbot Smith admitted that Quinn "ruled with energy," but complained that "he was an absolutist in church government." "For the conventions he had not the slightest regard," added Talbot Smith, "and walked his own path through custom and etiquette with perfect unconsciousness of their demands." Quinn's friend, Bishop Michael O'Farrell of Trenton, New Jersey, described him in

21. New York *Catholic American,* April 23, 1887; New York *Catholic Review,* May 28, 1887.

22. Florence D. Cohalan, *A Popular History of the Archdiocese of New York* (New York: U.S. Catholic Historical Society, 1983), 99.

his funeral eulogy before a congregation of some five thousand people in St. Patrick's Cathedral as "a strong unbending character of the Roman type, rough and possibly rude." Many in the congregation at one time or another would have been the object of Quinn's barbs. With unusual candor in a eulogy, O'Farrell made the best case that he could for his deceased friend. "He was neither a great orator, a clever writer, nor a profound scholar," admitted O'Farrell, "yet he was a great man and a great ecclesiastic. His bluntness often gave offence, but he had a loving heart and a tender soul beneath his rough exterior."[23]

The Sisters of Charity

In the nineteenth century, the Sisters of Charity were to become the preeminent congregation of women religious in the Archdiocese of New York, staffing the bulk of the parochial schools and many of the charitable institutions. Founded by St. Elizabeth Ann Seton, a native New Yorker and convert to Catholicism, the first Sisters came from their mother house in Emmitsburg, Maryland, to New York City in 1817 to operate St. Patrick's Orphan Asylum. In 1822 they began their long and indispensable contribution to Catholic education in New York when they took charge of the girls' department of St. Patrick's parochial school. In 1831 they assumed the same responsibilities at St. Peter's parochial school.

The connection between the Sisters of Charity and St. Joseph's Church dates from 1833. Over the following sixteen years they opened no fewer than seven Catholic institutions in the parish, not all of which proved to be permanent and not all of which originated or remained within the confines of the parish. The Sisters of Charity first came to Greenwich Village when two of them arrived from Emmitsburg to take charge of St. Joseph's Half-Orphan Asylum, originally located on Sixth Avenue across the street from the site of the present church. The need for larger facilities twice necessitated the

23. Smith, *Catholic Church in New York*, II, 302–3. Michael O'Farrell, New York *Catholic News*, May 22, 1887.

relocation of the asylum to more spacious quarters, first to Fifth Avenue between 15th and 16th Streets, and then to West 11th Street, both of which locations were then in St. Joseph's parish. By 1846 eight Sisters were caring for more than one hundred children in the orphanage. However, it was closed in 1855 and the children were transferred to the larger St. Patrick's Orphan Asylum on Prince Street.[24]

In 1833, the same year that they took charge of St. Joseph's Half-Orphan Asylum, the Sisters established an institution of their own in Greenwich Village, St. Joseph's Select School. "Select schools" were tuition-charging schools that catered to a better-off clientele than the free parochial schools and offered their students a more advanced curriculum. It was a common practice at the time for religious communities to conduct both kinds of school and to use the tuition collected from the select schools to subsidize the operation of the free schools. The Sisters of Charity were already doing this in New York with their one "pay" school, St. Patrick's Academy on Mulberry Street. Their calculation that New York's growing Catholic population could support two such schools proved correct. St. Joseph's Select School prospered in its original location, a small house on Washington Square, to such an extent that the building could no longer accommodate the number of students. In 1836 or 1837, the school was moved to a larger building on Oliver Street in St. James parish. It lasted until 1847, when it was absorbed into the Academy of Mt. St. Vincent.[25]

The "third coming" of the Sisters of Charity to Greenwich Village proved to be even more ephemeral than their first two. In 1834 a fire destroyed St. Patrick's parochial school. For the next two years the Sisters from St. Patrick's traveled across town every day to Greenwich Village to operate a makeshift school for their students in the basement of St. Joseph's Church. (Apparently they shared the basement with a short-lived parish school run by laymen.) Once again,

24. Walsh, *Sisters of Charity,* II, 80–89.
25. Ibid., I, 106–10, 142.

in 1850, the Sisters of Charity returned to the parish, this time to conduct a Female Sunday School, but this venture also failed to endure and was discontinued in 1856.[26]

Finally, after this series of erratic and complicated beginnings, in 1855 the Sisters put down permanent roots in St. Joseph's parish when they took charge of the girls' department of the spacious new parochial school erected by Father McCarron on Leroy Street. The following year Catholic education in Greenwich Village got a further boost when the Sisters reestablished a "select school" in the parish. This time they called it St. Joseph's Academy. It was originally located on Sixth Avenue near Barrow Street, a few doors away from St. Joseph's Church and across the street from the original site of St. Joseph's Half-Orphan Asylum. As the enrollment increased, the academy was moved several times, but always within the parish boundaries, first to 194 West 4th Street, then to 33 Grove Street, and finally in 1894 to 152 and 154 Waverly Place.[27]

The most important of the seven institutions established by the Sisters of Charity in St. Joseph's parish was St. Vincent's Hospital, which admitted its first patients on November 1, 1849. It should be mentioned that three years earlier, under pressure from Bishop Hughes, the Sisters had severed their ties with the mother house in Emmitsburg and formed their own diocesan community, the Sisters of Charity of St. Vincent de Paul. The foundation of St. Vincent's hospital was the first major undertaking of the new community.

A Catholic hospital had long been needed in New York City, where priests frequently found it difficult to gain access to Catholic patients in public and private institutions. In his pastoral letter for Lent in 1847, Bishop Hughes lamented that "our poor people in their sickness are obliged, at great expense to themselves or their friends, to go into public infirmaries in which the prevailing sympathies of religion are adverse to their faith. Should there not then be established among ourselves," he asked, "an [sic] hospital under the care

26. Ibid., II, 7–9.
27. Ibid., II, 19–23.

of the Sisters of Charity?" An outbreak of cholera in 1849 brought the matter to a head and led to the decision to establish New York's first Catholic hospital.[28]

The original St. Vincent's Hospital was a thirty-bed institution located just outside the boundaries of St. Joseph's parish in a three-story rented building at 102 East 13th Street between Third and Fourth Avenues. It had no running water. The only light came from oil lamps and the only heat from a small stove in the basement. The founder of the hospital and the superior of the community of three Sisters was Sister Angela Hughes, John Hughes' sister, who had spent four years on the staff of the Mullanphy Hospital in St. Louis, the first Catholic hospital in the United States. In 1856 St. Vincent's Hospital moved to its permanent home in St. Joseph's parish. On April 17 of that year, amid torrents of rain, a cavalcade of horse-drawn carriages transported the seventy-four patients in the old hospital to a four-story building at 195 West 11th Street that had previously housed the now-closed St. Joseph's Half-Orphan Asylum.[29]

In 1871 St. Vincent's Hospital was described as "the principal establishment" of the Sisters of Charity in New York City. By that date the number of Sisters had grown from the original thirty-one who formed the New York community in 1846 to no fewer than 420. In addition to St. Vincent's Hospital, they also operated forty-nine other educational and charitable institutions in New York City. At the hospital, the weekly fee was $6 for men and $5 for women.[30]

28. John Hughes, Lenten Pastoral, February 10, 1847, in *New York Freeman's Journal and Catholic Register,* February 20, 1847. In 1848 Father George McCloskey asked the House of Industry, a private charitable institution at East 2nd Street and First Avenue, to admit a Catholic patient; the patient was refused. When McCloskey appealed to the mayor for help, the mayor declined to intervene on the grounds that his authority was limited to public institutions. *New York Freeman's Journal and Catholic Register,* February 5, 1848.

29. Walsh, *Sisters of Charity,* III, 133–39.

30. *New York Freeman's Journal and Catholic Register,* February 18, 1871. In addition to St. Vincent's Hospital, the Sisters of Charity operated thirty free parochial schools, fourteen select academies, three orphan asylums, and two shelters.

Catholic Revivalism in Greenwich Village

The nineteenth-century Catholic equivalent of a Protestant revival meeting was the parish mission, an occasion when a team of outside priests descended upon a parish for several weeks. Typically they conducted a round-the-clock series of religious services that were designed to rekindle the fervor of the regular churchgoers and to bring the fallen-away Catholics back to the practice of their faith. Gerard Manley Hopkins once described a parish mission to a skeptical Protestant inquirer in England as "a revival without heresy or hysteria."

While the first part of Hopkins' description is undoubtedly true, the second part is open to some question. The highlight of the parish mission was the sermon preached each evening in the church before a packed congregation. The object of most of these sermons was to stress the heinousness of sin and the need for repentance. In the Tridentine Catholic tradition, this repentance was to take the form of an integral confession of all of one's mortal sins since the last "good" confession. In order to induce sinners to take this often difficult step, the mission preachers put great stress on the threat of eternal damnation, which was typically described in vivid fire-and-brimstone terms. One veteran Redemptorist mission preacher, Father Henri Giesen, was so adept at this kind of pyrotechnic pulpit oratory that on one occasion the firemen in a nearby firehouse thought that the church was on fire and rushed over to put out the blaze.[31]

Parish missions were usually conducted by religious order priests, Jesuits, Franciscans, Dominicans, and others. One religious congregation that specialized in this apostolate was the Congregation of the Most Holy Redeemer, better known as the Redemptorists. It was one of the traditions handed down to them by their founder, St. Alphonsus Ligouri, and the Redemptorists brought this apostolate with them when they came to America in 1832. However,

31. Dolan, *Immigrant Church*, 155.

the early Redemptorists in America were almost exclusively German, and they conducted virtually all of their parish missions in the German language in German national parishes. After two decades in the United States, however, they were ready to expand their apostolate beyond those confines. By 1851 they had formed and trained a group of priests who were to devote themselves exclusively to giving missions in English-speaking parishes.

A half-century later, when the Redemptorists had become famous for their parish missions, John Talbot Smith gave a highly laudatory description of how they conducted them. "The Redemptorists take possession of a parish for a period of a week, or of two, three and four weeks, according to the need," he said. "Their preaching is of the simple and vivid order on the chief doctrines and duties of a Catholic; it would be thought coarse by the more cultured people, and even extravagant; the pictures of hell and purgatory are medieval in color; the consequences of sin, the judgment deserved by faithless parents and ungrateful children, the woe of drunkards and fornicators and thieves, are described with vigor; but the result justifies the method, for the people flock to the confessional, their good resolutions are strengthened by the vivid impressions made upon them, and the revival of faith and religious life is sincere and enduring."[32]

The first parish in the United States selected by the Redemptorists for these new English-language missions was St. Joseph's Church in Greenwich Village, where they conducted a parish mission from April 6 to April 20 in 1851. The leader of the team was their American provincial, Father Bernard Hafkenscheid. He was assisted by four other Redemptorists, Fathers John B. Duffy, Clarence Walworth, Augustine Hewitt, and Isaac Hecker. All four were native English speakers, and the last three were converts to Catholicism. Isaac Hecker would later part company with the Redemptorists and found the first male religious congregation in the United States, the Missionary Society of St. Paul, or the Paulists. Hecker would be

32. Smith, *Catholic Church in New York,* I, 202.

joined by both Walworth and Hewitt, who was to succeed him as the second superior general of the Paulists.

The Redemptorist mission preachers estimated that there were about ten thousand Catholics in St. Joseph's parish. They described the people who attended the mission as mostly Irish, "servants, laborers and other persons of the poorer class," although some Catholics "of a higher class" also attended out of curiosity. The four American Redemptorists were apprehensive about their first attempt to conduct a European-style mission in an English-speaking parish, but they were delighted with the results. St. Joseph's Church was so crowded that the priests could hardly make their way to the sanctuary. People knelt to kiss their habits as they walked down the aisle. News of the mission spread throughout Greenwich Village, attracting Catholics who had not been to confession in thirty or forty years. Some were so poor that they had to borrow clothes to come to church. Before the mission was over, the Redemptorists heard six thousand confessions and prepared sixty adults to receive their first Communion. On the last evening, as Father Walworth conducted the concluding ceremony, emotions ran so high that he could hardly be heard above the weeping of the congregation.[33]

New Parishes

Until the late 1840s, St. Joseph's parish still stretched from Canal Street to 14th Street, and from Broadway to the Hudson River. However, as the Catholic population continued to increase and more priests became available, Bishop Hughes created three additional parishes in the area: St. Alphonsus in 1847, St. Francis Xavier in 1850, and St. Ann's in 1852. Each had its own unique character.

St. Alphonsus Church was located on Thompson Street between Canal and Grand Streets about a mile south of St. Joseph's Church. It was established as a German national parish and entrusted to the

33. Archives of the Paulist Fathers, Chronicle of Missions of the English Missions Given by the Redemptorist Fathers in the United States of North America, 1851, Mission at St. Joseph's Church, New York City. See also John F. Byrne, C.Ss.R., *The Redemptorist Centenaries* (Philadelphia: The Dolphin Press, 1932), 261–63.

Redemptorist Fathers with the mandate to care for all the German-speaking Catholics between the Battery and West 14th Street. However, from its inception, St. Alphonsus Church attracted many English-speaking Catholics, mainly Irish, who found it more convenient to attend Mass there than at St. Peter's, St. Joseph's, or St. Patrick's. When confirmation was first administered in the new parish in 1854, of the 160 candidates, thirty-five were German, forty-eight were Irish, and seventy-six were listed as "other."[34] In 1866 Archbishop McCloskey recognized the polyglot nature of the congregation and authorized the Redemptorists "to preach and to hear confessions in all those languages which they believe to be beneficial to the faithful."[35]

A few years later, when the Redemptorists made known their plans to build a new and bigger St. Alphonsus Church one block farther east on South Fifth Avenue (present-day West Broadway), the newspaper editor James Alphonsus McMaster, who had once been a Redemptorist seminarian, was delighted. "We are to have a strictly *Mission* Church in this city," he announced. He proceeded to explain the purpose of such a church in terms that the Redemptorists may not have appreciated because of the additional work that it was likely to create for them. "There are to be priests there," he said, "at all hours of the day, to hear confessions. There are to be priests there who can hear confessions not only in English, French and German, but in Spanish, in Italian, in Hollandish or Dutch, in Flemish, etc. etc."[36]

The Irish continued to flock to St. Alphonsus Church in such numbers that they soon outnumbered the Germans. The German parishioners resented the numerical predominance of the Irish in what was supposed to be a German national parish and resisted the

34. Francis X. Murphy, C.Ss.R., *The Centennial History of St. Alphonsus Parish* (New York: St. Alphonsus Church, 1947), 14. Writing under the alias of Xavier Rynne during Vatican Council II, Father Murphy later became famous for his "Letters from Vatican City" in *The New Yorker.*

35. McCloskey to Rev. Frederick Brandstetter, C.Ss.R., September 14, 1866, ibid., 18.

36. *New York Freeman's Journal and Weekly Register,* September 3, 1870.

introduction of English-language services. When the plans were drawn up for the new church in 1870, the Redemptorists wished to have both an upstairs church and a downstairs church. The proposal was vetoed by the vehement protests of the German parishioners who suspected that they would be relegated to the basement. "We will not go downstairs and have the Irish over our heads," they said."[37] However, by the turn of the century, ethnic friction had faded, and the harmony among the German, Irish, and American-born parishioners in St. Alphonsus parish was cited by John Talbot Smith as a model for all American Catholic parishes.[38]

No pastor likes to preside over the dissolution of his parochial empire, but Father McCarron may have been happy to see St. Alphonsus Church erected as a mission church in the southern part of St. Joseph's parish. The Redemptorist Church was located close to some of the poorest and least desirable parts of the Ninth Ward. A church with round-the-clock confessions was a definite asset in a neighborhood with a red light district that contained over one hundred brothels. These establishments were said to be "of the most respectable class," since they catered to customers in the fashionable Broadway hotels. By way of contrast, south of Houston Street, between Varick and Greenwich Streets, there was a densely populated area of run-down tenements. Unlike the brothels, there was nothing upscale about these buildings. An inspector described them as "universally unclean and offensive, with the emanations of the decomposing refuse which surround and permeate the apartments of the poor." The social pathology of the neighborhood could not have been improved by the presence of 198 liquor stores and groceries that sold liquor.[39]

Unlike the neighborhood in the vicinity of St. Alphonsus Church, the area north of 14th Street was developing into a prime residential

37. Dolan, *Immigrant Church*, 96.

38. Smith, *Church in New York*, I, 201. Smith's favorable assessment of the situation at St. Alphonsus Church may reflect the fact that the Irish had won the tug of war with the Germans.

39. *Report of the Council of Hygiene of the Citizens' Association of New York upon the Sanitary Condition of the City* (New York: D. Appleton and Company, 1865), 67–68.

area that no pastor would care to lose. When the Society of Jesus established the Church of St. Francis Xavier on West 16th Street between Fifth and Sixth Avenues in 1850, it immediately created competition for St. Joseph's Church. The Jesuits had been present in New York City briefly during colonial times and again between 1808 and 1815 under Father Anthony Kohlmann, when they had played a major role in the establishment of the diocese. However, their permanent presence in New York dates from 1846. In that year a group of exiled French Jesuits who were conducting a languishing college in Kentucky accepted Bishop Hughes' invitation to take charge of St. John's College at Fordham. The next year they opened their first church in New York, Holy Name of Jesus Church, on Elizabeth Street, but it burned to the ground six months later. Finally in 1850 they bought property on West 16th Street where they established St. Francis Xavier College and a parish church of the same name. The church was blessed by Archbishop Hughes on July 6, 1851.[40]

Hughes quarreled with the Jesuits over a number of issues, among them the title to St. Francis Xavier Church. Before the construction of the church even began, Hughes insisted that the Jesuits surrender the title of the church to him. Despite repeated requests from the Jesuits, who feared that a future Archbishop of New York might hand the parish over to the diocesan clergy, Hughes never returned the title to them. They only got it back in 1872 from Archbishop McCloskey.[41]

Father McCarron may have been one of the diocesan priests who, according to Hughes, were jealous of the large number of people going to confession at St. Francis Xavier. Hughes' bizarre solution was to forbid the Jesuits from hearing men's confessions except in the confessionals of the church, which, the local Jesuit superior said, "are always besieged by women." On the other hand, McCarron

40. John Gilmary Shea, *The Catholic Churches of New York* (New York: Lawrence G. Goulding and Company, 1878), 296–310.

41. Francis X. Curran, S.J., "Archbishop Hughes and the Jesuits: An Anatomy of Their Quarrels," in Hennessy, *Fordham: The Early Years*, 177–221. This article originally was published as "Archbishop Hughes and the Jesuits," *Woodstock Letters* (winter 1968): 5–56.

must have been grateful to the Jesuits for taking over the ministry to the patients at St. Vincent's Hospital. The Jesuits at St. Francis Xavier also did yeomen's work as chaplains at the Tombs prison and at the hospitals on Blackwell's Island, Randall's Island, and Ward's Island in the East River.[42]

In March 1877, St. Francis Xavier Church was the scene of a terrible incident. On an evening when the church was filled to capacity for the women's mission, some prankster opened the front door and yelled "Fire." In the ensuing panic seven people were killed and seven others were seriously injured. The tragedy led the Jesuits to act on their long-standing plans to replace the church with a much bigger structure. They commissioned Patrick Keely, the famous Irish American architect, to design a large Baroque church in the European Jesuit style. The cornerstone was blessed on May 5, 1878.[43]

To the east of St. Joseph's parish, the new parish of St. Ann was established in 1852. St. Ann's was originally located in a former Presbyterian church at Astor Place, a few hundred feet west of Fourth Avenue on 8th Street. In 1870 it moved to a new and larger church at its present location on East 12th Street between Third and Fourth Avenues. The first pastor was John Murray Forbes, a former Episcopalian clergyman who—much to the dismay of Archbishop Hughes—returned to the Episcopal Church in 1859. As a hurried replacement, Father Hugh Brady, the curate at St. Joseph's Church, was dispatched across town to take Forbes' place. Brady in turn was replaced for a year by another young priest who, two decades later, would become the most controversial cleric in the archdiocese, Edward McGlynn. Finally, late in 1862, Archbishop Hughes found a suitable replacement for Forbes in the person of Father Thomas Preston, another former Episcopalian clergyman who had actually been Forbes' assistant at St. Luke's Episcopal Church and had been received into the Catholic Church with him.[44]

42. Curran, ibid., 189, 207. Shea, *Catholic Churches of New York*, 310.
43. Ibid., 301–2.
44. For the origins of St. Ann's Church, see the model parish history written by Hen-

Preston remained as pastor of St. Ann's from 1862 until his death in 1891. He also served as chancellor and then vicar general under three archbishops of New York: John Hughes, John McCloskey, and Michael Corrigan. Preston's reputation as a preacher and the high quality of the choir helped to make St. Ann's for several decades the most fashionable Catholic church in New York City. On special occasions, when Preston was the featured preacher, carriages lined East 12th Street from Second Avenue to Fifth Avenue. One may wonder, however, how many Catholics in the plush Fifteenth Ward could claim the same social status as the wealthy congregations of Grace Episcopal Church on Broadway, or the Church of the Ascension and the First Presbyterian Church on lower Fifth Avenue. In fact, despite St. Ann's reputation as a bon ton parish, when Preston died in 1891, he left a staggering debt of over $93,000. It was little solace to his successors that Preston was fondly remembered by the parishioners for never talking about money.[45]

The Diocese in Miniature

Just as the Diocese of New York was shrinking in size but growing in population throughout the antebellum years, so was St. Joseph's parish. Between 1847 and 1853, new dioceses were created in Buffalo, Albany, Brooklyn, and Newark, reducing the New York diocese (archdiocese after 1850) to 10 percent of its original size. Thereafter the geographical boundaries of the archdiocese were limited to Manhattan, Staten Island, and seven counties north of the city line. However, even within these greatly diminished boundaries, the

ry J. Browne, *St. Ann's on East Twelfth Street, New York City, 1851–1952* (New York: Church of St. Ann, 1952), 2–16.

45. Ibid., 29. Preston's successor was his faithful first assistant, Father Andrew J. Clancy, who paid off $8,000 of the debt before dying three years later at the age of thirty-four. Clancy's successor, Father William O'Neill, told Archbishop Corrigan that the number of parishioners had been declining for years and that the parish was "practically bankrupt." In 1901 O'Neill asked for another parish. Archbishop Corrigan was unsympathetic and turned down his request. He told O'Neill to thank God for what he had accomplished at St. Ann's, adding pointedly "of which not a little has been done by your assistants." AANY, O'Neill to Corrigan, December 30, 1895; Corrigan to O'Neill, April 23, 1901.

Catholic population continued to grow from about four hundred thousand at the end of the Civil War to well over a million by the end of the century, maintaining New York's position as the most populous archdiocese in the United States.

St. Joseph's parish experienced similar changes on a smaller scale. With the establishment of three new parishes on the north, south, and east, the parish boundaries by 1852 were reduced to perhaps one-quarter of their original extent. They were now practically the same as those of the Ninth Ward, namely West 14th Street on the north, Houston Street on the south, University Place and South Fifth Avenue on the east, and, of course, the Hudson River on the west. As a result St. Joseph's became increasingly identified with its core territory, Greenwich Village. The Catholic population, estimated at ten thousand in 1851, continued to increase until, by the end of the century, the Catholics, mainly Irish and Italians, transformed the old American Ward into a predominantly Catholic neighborhood, where the most important local religious institution was St. Joseph's Church.

4 *Liberal Catholicism in a Conservative Diocese*

Father Thomas Farrell

OF ALL THE PASTORS of St. Joseph's Church, none was more controversial than Father Thomas Farrell. Born in Ireland on August 23, 1823, he came to the United States as a young man, around 1840, studied for the priesthood at Mount St. Mary's Seminary in Emmitsburg, Maryland, and was ordained to the priesthood by Bishop John Hughes in 1848. He served as a curate at St. Patrick's Cathedral and at St. Bridget's Church, and then as pastor of St. Paul's Church in Harlem and St. Mary's Church on Grand Street, before coming to St. Joseph's Church in 1857 as pastor, a post which he held until his death on July 20,1880.

Farrell was the first, but not the last, pastor of St. Joseph's Church to reach beyond the confines of his own parish to address important public issues in both church and state. As one of the few Catholic abolitionists in a city where Irish Catholics were notorious for their hostility to African Americans, he was a maverick among the New York diocesan clergy of his day. During the Civil War he flew the Stars and Stripes from his church as a demonstration of his loyalty to the Union. After the war he became a radical Republican at a time when virtually every New York priest was a staunch supporter of Tammany Hall, the local Democratic organization. On a tour of the postwar South with his friend Father Sylvester Malone, Farrell and Malone expressed such open sympathy for the emancipated black population that the Bishop of Richmond, John McGill, accused the two of them of "negrophily," as if it were a crime or a sin. "But, apart from their extravagance about the negro," McGill warned Archbishop John McCloskey of New York, "their views and feelings about the Holy Father and his spiritual and temporal authority make me fear that they will not prove reliable pastors and spiritual fathers."[1]

Farrell and Church Authorities

Back in New York, on June 6, 1869, Farrell gave a lecture in his church entitled "The South: Catholics and Their Difficulties." He said that it would be the first of several talks on subjects of the day. Farrell criticized his fellow Catholics for their opposition to the abolitionists and regretted that the American bishops had done so little for the emancipated slaves. Egged on perhaps by a favorable response from the friendly audience, Farrell interjected provocative polemical remarks that would have been more appropriate on a political platform than in a pulpit. "The clergy sat in solemn session," he said, referring to the Second Plenary Council of Baltimore in 1866, "very solemn indeed, especially [since] there [were] many old fogies among them, but they accomplish[ed] nothing."

Turning to the condition of the Catholic Church in Europe, he deplored the union of church and state, which he traced back to Constantine, and he dismissed the doctrine of the divine right of kings as "divine humbug." By way of contrast, Farrell pointed proudly to the example set by the United States, where, he said, the Catholics of colonial Maryland "first established the principle of liberty of conscience, and the sword of Washington and the pluck and tenacity of the American people confirmed the true Catholic doctrine of the freedom of conscience." He could not resist adding the comment that it was a pity that "the sword of Washington did not find its way to Spain."

If Farrell's remarks were reported accurately, he made some claims that defy logical analysis, such as the assertion that "it was the first principle of Catholic teaching that the people can never be

1. AANY, A-52, McGill to McCloskey, June 14, 1869.

wrong, for they do not wish their own injury." He was on firmer ground, but still tiptoeing through a minefield, when he said that "the Church is a constitutional government with an executive which cannot change the fundamental law, and neither take from it nor add to it." Unfortunately, he then coupled this careful formulation with the questionable claim that "everything outside is left to reason and to the judgment of mankind." Once more playing to the gallery, he added that "religion is unchangeable," but that he was "not compelled to swallow what every pious fool might say." For good measure, he also denounced the Inquisition and ecclesiastical courts, deplored Catholic prejudice against Protestants, and closed his lecture with a plea for the unity of all Christians.

The lecture was reported in James Gordon Bennett's *New York Herald*[2] and came to the attention of Archbishop Martin Spalding of Baltimore, who thought that some of Farrell's comments "smacked of heresy." "Did you see that scandalous lecture of Rev. Farrell in New York?" he asked Archbishop John Purcell of Cincinnati. "We are coming to a pretty pass." Spalding took particular offense at Farrell's reference to the American bishops as "old foggies." "If a priest delivered such a speech in one of my churches," he complained to Archbishop McCloskey, "he would never preach or say that again at least without doing public penance."[3]

When McCloskey questioned Farrell about his lecture, Farrell offered to publish the full text. "I will follow the advice of my Bishop," he assured McCloskey, "but I will not submit to cowardly sneaking inquisition, for I do despise all jesuitical cunning." In the meantime, Spalding supplied McCloskey with further accusations

2. *New York Herald*, June 7, 1869.

3. Archives of the University of Notre Dame (hereafter AUND), Spalding to Purcell, June 18, 1869; AANY, A-32, Spalding to McCloskey, June 16, 1869. Spalding himself was a victim of the "old foggies" at the Second Plenary Council of Baltimore. Recognizing the need to evangelize four million emancipated slaves, Spalding wanted to establish a special diocese for them similar to the military archdiocese today. His fellow bishops flatly rejected the proposal. "It is a golden opportunity for reaping a harvest of souls," he said prophetically, "which neglected may not return." Cyprian Davis, O.S.B., *The History of Black Catholics in the United States* (New York: Crossroad, 1990), 118–20.

against Farrell, alleging that in his lecture he had referred to the Church as a "rotten ship." The story in the *New York Herald* reminded Spalding that he had come across Farrell's name before in connection with the bête noire of the Papacy, Giuseppe Garibaldi, a leader of the *Risorgimento,* the movement for the unification of Italy. He claimed that Farrell had been present at a dinner in New York City in which a toast had been proposed to Garibaldi. Farrell supposedly responded to the toast with an offer to give Garibaldi absolution (in the extremely unlikely event that he asked for it).

Neither McCloskey nor Spalding wanted Farrell to publish his lecture for fear of giving it a wider audience. Farrell was quite deferential about the whole matter. He told his archbishop: "I have always tried to please you, but somehow or another I don't succeed." McCloskey may also have been stung by Farrell's lament "that everything that passes between us becomes known so very soon." McCloskey assured Spalding (somewhat prematurely, it turned out) that "an end has been put to [Farrell's] political preaching." McCloskey did not pursue the matter further, and Father Farrell escaped relatively unscathed from his first major brush with the ecclesiastical authorities.[4]

As far as McCloskey was concerned, Farrell's theological views were more alarming than his political views. He accused Farrell of belonging to a school of clerics "who do not accept of anything except what is defined *de fide.*" It was an accusation that Farrell indignantly denied, but the fact of the matter is that Farrell did not share the emotional ultramontanism that was becoming common among most of the Catholic clergy in both Europe and America. In contrast to the ultramontanes, who emphasized papal power almost to the

4. AANY, A-32, Spalding to McCloskey, June 25, 1869; I-35, Farrell to McCloskey, June 21, 1869. AAB, 36A-N14, McCloskey to Spalding, June 21, 1869. Sympathy for Garibaldi was one of the most damaging accusations that one could make against any priest at that time. John Henry Newman was the victim of such slanders on more than one occasion. See Newman to Robert Ornsby, July 23, 1862; Newman to James Hope-Scott, July 6, 1864, *The Letters and Diaries of John Henry Newman,* ed. C. S. Dessain and Edward E. Kelly, S.J. (London: Nelson, 1970–1971), XX, 241; XXI, 144–45.

exclusion of that of the bishops, Farrell's ecclesiology reflected an older model of church with a more balanced division of authority. Farrell had difficulty expressing himself in exact theological terminology, but his more restrained view of papal authority was similar to that of European liberal Catholics like Bishop Félix Dupanloup and Père Henri Lacordaire.

Such liberal Catholics were few and far between in America, however, which is why Father Farrell acquired the dubious distinction of being the favorite priest of the secular press in New York City. "A certain Catholic priest in this city, Rev. Father Farrell, pastor of St. Joseph's Church," said the *New York Times* in a flattering editorial in 1871,"has long been known to our citizens as an extraordinary exception in many respects to the Roman Catholic priesthood. Though a devout, and, we believe, extreme Romanist in his religious views, he has been a Republican in American politics and a Liberal in European [politics]." Charles Dana's *New York Sun* hailed Farrell for "his liberal Americanized views on all questions pertaining to the connection of the Church with the state." Unfortunately for Farrell, however, when the secular press compared him to European liberal Catholics, the Old World counterpart they usually mentioned was neither Dupanloup nor Lacordaire, but Père Hyacinthe Loyson, the Carmelite friar who left the Church.[5]

Farrell aroused the suspicions of the New York Chancery Office not only because of his avant-garde opinions, but also because of his influence over some of the brightest of the younger clergy. He was the unofficial leader of a group of priests known as the Accademia, who met regularly in St. Joseph's rectory to discuss such controversial theological topics as papal infallibility, biblical inspiration, the temporal power of the pope, a vernacular liturgy, and the relevance of religious orders in the modern world. At the time of Farrell's lecture in June 1869, McCloskey told Spalding: "I wish to avail myself of the opportunity now afforded of dealing not alone with Rev. Mr. Farrell, but with the whole school of which he seems to be the ac-

5. *New York Times*, February 19, 1871; *New York Sun*, February 14, 1871.

knowledged leader."[6] Among the members of this school were Edward McGlynn, Richard Burtsell, James Nilan, and Patrick McSweeny, young priests who were to become the leading Americanists or liberals in the New York presbyterate in the late nineteenth century.[7]

By 1870, therefore, Father Farrell was a well-known, if rather unconventional, figure in Catholic circles in New York City. "A good man, but crazy on some points," is how he was described by another New York priest, William McCloskey, the Bishop of Louisville.[8] That year he began to express his views on a topic even more delicate than abolition, namely the temporal power of the papacy.

The Roman Question

On September 20, 1870, the Italian army breached the walls of Rome and raised the red-white-green tricolor over the Eternal City, ending a thousand years of papal rule. It was the culmination of a struggle that had been going on for decades. Throughout the nineteenth century Italian nationalists and the popes had been on a collision course over what was called the Roman Question. Italian nationalists insisted that the Papal States must become part of a united

6. AAB, 36A-N14, McCloskey to Spalding, June 21, 1869.

7. On the Accademia, see Robert Emmett Curran, "Prelude to 'Americanism': The New York Accademia and Clerical Radicalism in the Late Nineteenth Century," *Church History* 47 (1978): 48–65. For a more critical view of the Accademia, see Cohalan, *Popular History of the Archdiocese of New York,* 119–24. The basic source for the history of the Accademia is the diary of Richard Burtsell, a manuscript of almost five thousand pages recorded between 1865 and 1912, which is preserved in the archives of the Archdiocese of New York. On Burtsell, see Anthony D. Andreassi, "'The Cunning Leader of a Dangerous Clique'?: The Burtsell Affair and Archbishop Michael Augustine Corrigan," *Catholic Historical Review* 86 (1999): 620–39. The members of the Accademia followed closely the latest developments in European theology such as the writings of John William Colenso, the controversial Anglican Bishop of Natal. AANY, Burtsell, Diary, March 2, 1865. Burtsell defended Colenso from the accusation of being an "out-and-out rationalist." Ibid., March 10, 1865.

8. AUND, William McCloskey to Purcell, July 7, 1869. When John Lancaster Spalding was seeking funds to start a black church in Louisville, McCloskey told him to appeal to Farrell "in the hope that his love for the Negro would prove itself by substantial assistance from his parish." Ibid. Farrell took up a special collection and sent Spalding $300.13. AANY, Financial Report of St. Joseph's Church, January 1, 1869, to January 1, 1870.

Italy with Rome as its capital; the popes were equally insistent that they must remain the temporal sovereigns of central Italy to safeguard their independence as the spiritual leaders of a multinational Church.

In 1929 both sides were to reach an amicable settlement. With the signing of the Lateran Treaties of that year, the Holy See renounced its claims to the former Papal States and the Italian government recognized the temporal sovereignty of the popes over the 103 acres that constituted Vatican City State. Mussolini was surprised that the Holy See was willing to settle for so little real estate in 1929. The papal secretary of state, Pietro Cardinal Gasparri, is reputed to have explained: "We do not want to have to deal with a trolley car strike."

In 1870, however, the settlement of 1929 was far in the future. Relations between Italy and the Holy See were bitterly hostile. In 1861 the papacy had already lost most of the Papal States to the Italians, and it retained control of Rome only because of the presence of a French garrison. The withdrawal of the French troops during the Franco-Prussian War of 1870–1871 paved the way for the Italian seizure of Rome a few months later. Pope Pius IX protested vehemently and refused to compromise with a government that rejected all claims of papal sovereignty and adopted numerous anticlerical laws.

Catholic public opinion overwhelmingly supported the pope, who was viewed as the innocent victim of Italian aggression. Nowhere in the Catholic world did sentiment in his favor run higher than in the United States. For years Protestant Nativists had attacked American Catholics precisely because of their loyalty to the pope, and American Catholics had responded in kind by flaunting their allegiance to the successor of St. Peter. Bishops like John Hughes made the temporal power of the popes a litmus text of orthodoxy. "The temporal sovereignty of the Popes is a sequel and consequence of their spiritual supremacy," Hughes declared in a sermon in the old St. Patrick's Cathedral on July 1, 1860.[9] "We do not allow any

9. *Complete Works of the Most Reverend John Hughes*, II, 56. See also the Pastoral

differences on such questions," explained Father Thomas Preston, the chancellor of the Archdiocese of New York. "Whoever maintains contrary opinions cannot be a Catholic."[10] The loss of Rome in 1870, therefore, was a severe blow to the pride of American Catholics and led to protest meetings in many cities. What made the papal defeat all the more galling to American Catholics was the glee with which it was greeted by many American liberals and Protestants.

New York City Hails United Italy

On the evening of Thursday, January 12, 1871, five thousand people gathered in the Academy of Music on East 14th Street to celebrate the Italian occupation of Rome. Another five thousand well-wishers filled the streets outside. The enthusiastic crowd listened to speeches, passed resolutions, and demonstrated their approval that Rome had finally become the capital of a free and united Italy. Much of the evening's rhetoric was focused on the horrors of the papal government from which the inhabitants of Rome had just been liberated. The tone was set by the presiding officer and first speaker, Major General John A. Dix, who said: "United Italy presents to us what we consider all that is most precious in human government, a free church in a free state."

Other speakers included two veteran New York journalists, Horace Greeley, editor of the *New York Tribune,* and William Cullen Bryant, editor of the *New York Evening Post,* both of whom spoke in much the same vein. They took for granted that they were addressing a partisan Protestant audience that would welcome their criticism of the Catholic Church. Bryant spoke passionately of the reli-

Letter issued by Hughes and his suffragan bishops at the conclusion of the Third Provincial Council of New York, January 19, 1860, ibid., 36–48.

10. *New York Times,* November 28, 1870. Twenty years later Preston said that one of the characteristics of the "Americanists" was that they "look upon the temporal power of the Supreme Pontiff as a thing of the past [and] are willing to let it die and feel no obligation to do anything in their power to restore it." Thomas Preston, "American Catholicity," *American Catholic Quarterly Review* 16 (1891): 397. Both Patrick McSweeny and Richard Burtsell openly opposed the temporal power of the papacy. AANY, Burtsell, Diary, November 26,1865; November 4, 1866.

gious intolerance that had prevailed in the Papal States. "Was such a government worthy to exist for even an hour?" he asked. Horace Greeley was more restrained, contrasting more in sorrow than in anger the sad plight of Pope Pius IX in 1871 and his popularity after his election in 1846, when he had been hailed as the champion of liberty throughout Europe and even in faraway New York City.

Another speaker was Henry W. Bellows, for thirty-three years pastor of the First Unitarian Congregationalist Church of New York and the organizing genius behind the U. S. Sanitary Commission during the Civil War. He wandered far from the topic of united Italy. Instead he used the occasion to rehearse many of the standard Nativist objections to Catholicism, such as the alleged incompatibility of Catholic doctrine and democratic institutions. "We must be on the watch!" he thundered from the podium. "When, therefore, bishops and archbishops attempt to govern votes and influence legislation by ecclesiastical consideration, we ought all to take alarm. When any foreign ruler is recognized as having a power in our politics, it is time to look sharply into the theories and practices of those who uphold his right."

Perhaps the most captivating orator of the evening was the Reverend Henry Ward Beecher, one of the best-known Protestant clergyman in the country. A glib speaker who never read a book from cover to cover, he preached to a packed congregation every Sunday at his fashionable Plymouth Church in Brooklyn Heights. He entertained his audience that evening for almost half an hour with a lively talk that was peppered with a mixture of patriotic bromides and appeals to old-fashioned Protestant prejudices. He provoked a round of cheers and applause with a gratuitous reference to the Catholic Church as "the only church in which salvation is sure, registered and prepaid."

For the most part, however, Beecher avoided the standard anti-Catholic rhetoric and reverted instead to a tactic that had been popular with some Nativists twenty years earlier, that of killing Romanism with kindness. He expressed sympathy for Pius IX as an individual "in so far as it can be done in consistency with our well-known Protestant feelings." He assured his listeners that there were Catholic bishops who did not really believe the doctrine of papal infallibility that they had voted for a year earlier at the Vatican Council. He even claimed that there were some bishops who were happy to see the pope shorn of his temporal possessions. "I don't forget," he added, "that within the bosom of the Holy Church itself there are those who are fully in sympathy with us, that there are many Roman Catholics that are not Papists."[11]

The Academy of Music was filled that evening with journalists, clergymen, lawyers, and businessmen, but local politicians were as scarce as hen's teeth, reflecting the newly cemented alliance between Boss Tweed's Tammany Hall and New York's Irish Catholics. Horace Greeley received sustained applause when he said that the mayor "ought to be here tonight." The *New York Times* noted the absence of elected officials and suggested snidely that they would have turned out in force to celebrate a revolution that brought Irish Catholics to power in Dublin. James Raymond, editor of the *New York Times*, explained darkly why no local officials dared to attend the meeting: "There is an established church and a ruling class in New York," said Raymond, "but the Church is not Protestant and the ruling class is not American."[12]

One of the most interested and perceptive observers of the evening's events was James Gordon Bennett, the pugnacious editor of the *New York Herald*. Bennett viewed the proceedings with the practiced eye of a caustic Catholic newspaper editor who had impeccable credentials as a critic of his own church. Bennett dismissed both Bellows and Beecher as hypocrites who judged Catholicism by a different standard than the one that they applied to Protestantism, but he was surprised by the relatively sympathetic treatment that Pius IX received at the hands of the other speakers due to his recent misfortunes.[13]

11. *New York Times*, February 13, 1871.
12. Ibid., January 7, 1871.
13. *New York Herald*, January 13, 1871.

The sympathy was all the more surprising because the basic issue which surfaced again and again in all the speeches was not Italian unity, but the teaching of the Catholic Church on religious freedom. On that issue Pius IX had made himself obnoxious to most of the world only seven years earlier when he had issued the Syllabus of Errors, solemnly condemning religious toleration. Under his rule the Papal States had been a model of religious intolerance that all Catholic countries were supposed to imitate. In theory, this was the system that the United States would be expected to adopt if Catholics ever became the majority of the population. Although such a possibility was infinitely remote in 1871, it was a nightmare that haunted the dreams of many Protestant Americans and was reflected in the speeches in the Academy of Music. "The American Catholic Church has hardly a bond of political and intellectual sympathy with the Liberal Catholic Church in Europe," declared the *New York Times.* "We deeply regret that a Church which controls such masses of ignorant persons should not lead them on to the highest ideas in civil and religious liberty."[14]

Father Farrell's Open Letter

In addition to the featured speakers at the Academy of Music, many prominent political and religious leaders sent congratulatory messages. They included Vice President of the United States Schuyler Colfax and Secretary of State Hamilton Fish. Several other cabinet members, United States senators, and justices of the United States Supreme Court also sent messages of support, as did Ralph Waldo Emerson, William Dean Howells, and William Lloyd Garrison. Public endorsements came from religious leaders as diverse as Philip Schaff, Asa Smith, Horace Bushnell, and James McCosh. However, the last name on the list that was read that evening was perhaps the most surprising of them all. It was the name of a Catholic priest, Father Thomas Farrell.

The news of Farrell's letter to the meeting in the Academy of Mu-

14. *New York Times,* February 19, 1871.

sic spread quickly in the local Catholic community, as did rumors that it contained heretical statements. A week later, on January 21, 1871, the full text appeared in the *New York Sun.* Farrell made no direct criticism of the pope in his letter, and he was more circumspect than he had been in his controversial lecture of eighteen months earlier, but he did not conceal the fact that he was happy to see the end of the Papal States. "I could not wish to see Italy occupied by foreign troops," he wrote, "nor could I consider their presence there as an evidence of the contentment of the people." Moreover, Farrell did not limit himself to the topic of Italian unity. He expressed other political opinions that would have been far too radical for most of the middle-class audience in the Academy of Music. Among other items, he called for the abolition of standing armies and hereditary aristocracy, the latter of which he termed "the greatest curse in the world."

Farrell's views on religious freedom were especially radical for a nineteenth-century Catholic cleric. It is easy to understand why they gave rise to accusations of heresy. Farrell admired the American system of separation of church and state as ardently as any Protestant minister at the meeting in the Academy of Music. Moreover, like the "Americanist" Catholics of a generation later, he wanted the rest of the world to adopt the American system of religious freedom. "The people too of every country and every creed have so long persecuted [others] on account of religion," wrote Farrell, "that they do not understand our theory and practice of civil and religious liberty. When they come to understand and practice it the world over, one of the greatest causes of human misery and oppression will be removed forever." He ended his letter with a flourish: "That all men throughout the world may soon enjoy civil and religious liberty and equality before the law is the sincere wish of yours truly, Thomas Farrell."[15]

Farrell could hardly have chosen a more emotionally charged issue on which to express his opinions than that of the temporal power of the popes. All over the United States, Catholics were holding

15. *New York Sun,* January 21, 1871.

rallies and issuing protests over the spoliation of the Holy Father's territory by the Robber-King, Victor Emmanuel II of Italy. In New York City virtually every Catholic pulpit rang with denunciations of the Italian occupation of Rome. A public address of sympathy, signed by the leading clergy and laity of the archdiocese, was read aloud in the parish churches and sent to the Holy Father. "We repudiate and condemn the lawless injustice which has invaded your lawful dominion as a Sovereign Prince," the signatories assured the Holy Father. Even Farrell's abolitionist comrade-in-arms, Father Sylvester Malone, found it expedient to hold a protest demonstration in the Williamsburg parish where he was the pastor.[16]

Moreover, Farrell could hardly have chosen a worse forum for publicizing his opinions than the meeting at the Academy of Music. To many Catholics, it seemed the height of disloyalty for Farrell to associate himself, even by letter, with a gathering that included so many well-known critics of the Catholic Church. The commendations that he received in the secular press only confirmed the suspicions of many Catholics that Farrell had betrayed the Holy Father in his hour of greatest need. Moreover, for generations Catholics had been led to believe that the temporal power of the pope was not simply a matter of political expediency, but a doctrine of the church, which it would be heretical to repudiate. It was Farrell's special misfortune that he happened to live in the same city with a Catholic newspaper editor who was one of the most outspoken defenders of the temporal power in the whole United States, James Alphonsus McMaster.

Nemesis: James Alphonsus McMaster

McMaster was a convert twice over, first from the Presbyterian Church to the Episcopal Church, and then from the Episcopal Church to the Catholic Church. He was born in upstate New York on April 1, 1820, the son of a Scotch-Irish Presbyterian minister. He

16. The text of the statement was printed in the *New York Times,* December 3, 1870. Father Malone's protest meeting took place on Sunday, February 5, 1871. *New York Herald,* February 6, 1871.

was received into the Catholic Church on May 16, 1845, while studying for the Episcopalian ministry in New York City at General Theological Seminary, which was then the leading center of the Oxford Movement in the United States. Shortly thereafter he was confirmed by Bishop Hughes in St. Joseph's Church. McMaster tried his vocation with the Redemptorists, left their novitiate by mutual agreement after a brief period, married, settled in New York City, and then found his true vocation as a journalist. He bought the *New York Freeman's Journal and Catholic Register* from Bishop John Hughes in 1848 and edited it until his death in 1886. For several decades it was the leading Catholic newspaper in New York City and one of the most important Catholic newspapers in the United States.[17]

A man of strong but narrow opinions, McMaster delighted in controversy, not only with non-Catholic critics, but also with any Catholics who dared to disagree with his own ardently held political and theological positions. During the Civil War, his criticism of President Abraham Lincoln and his defense of states' rights led to accusations of sedition and a brief period of imprisonment by the federal government. McMaster devoted himself with equal passion to the dissemination of his theological opinions. He was among the most ardent American ultramontanes, a champion of papal infallibility conceived in the broadest possible terms, and a diehard apologist for the temporal power of the papacy. "He loved all lost causes," said one of his assistant editors, "and he was a rebel to the core of his heart."[18]

17. On McMaster, the only biographical study is an M.A. thesis, Mary Augustine Kwitchen, *James Alphonsus McMaster: A Study in American Thought* (Washington: The Catholic University of America Press, 1949). See also M. Mildred, "James A. McMaster, Pioneer Journalist," *Records of the American Catholic Historical Society of Philadelphia* 46 (1935): 1–21; and Mary Canisius Minihan, "James A. McMaster, A Pioneer Catholic Journalist," ibid., 47 (1936): 87–131.

18. Maurice Francis Egan, "A Slight Appreciation of James Alphonsus McMaster," *Historical Records and Studies* 15 (1921): 10. "On the matter of the temporal power of the pope," said Egan, "he was an ultra-Montane of the ultra-Montanes. As far as I could understand, he would admit of no compromise." Ibid., 15. John Talbot Smith described the *New York Freeman's Journal and Catholic Register* as "a noisy and pompous sheet, very

If Thomas Farrell was the lonely American counterpart to European liberal Catholics like Dupanloup and Lacordaire, McMaster aspired to be the mirror image of that *enfant terrible* of nineteenth-century French Catholic journalism, Louis Veuillot, whom he admired greatly. Like Veuillot, McMaster had a facile pen which he used like a battering ram against all those whom he regarded as enemies of the true faith. With little sense of history or understanding of the development of doctrine, McMaster exalted papal power virtually to the exclusion of all other sources of authority in the Catholic Church. Like Veuillot, too, he directed some of his most vitriolic outbursts at Catholics who he thought were too ready to compromise with the forces of evil. With regard to the temporal power of the papacy, in the face of incontestable evidence to the contrary, he repeated ad nauseam that the inhabitants of the Papal States were the most contented subjects in Europe.[19]

For McMaster, the question of the temporal power of the papacy had been settled definitively in 1864 by Proposition Seventy-Six of the Syllabus of Errors, which condemned as erroneous the statement that "the abrogation of that civil power, which the Apostolic See possesses, would conduce in the highest degree to the Church's liberty and felicity." As a result, proclaimed McMaster, "no Catholic, without falsifying his Catholic profession, can hold that filthy rag of a depraved liberalism which has carped at the civil dominion by which the personal independence of the Pope has been secured in times past." In McMaster's opinion, Catholics who were unwilling to support the pope's temporal authority should "quit the Church . . . and call themselves Protestants." Six weeks after the fall of Rome to

---

poorly edited, offensive in its defense of orthodoxy, and half the time on the wrong side." Of McMaster himself, Talbot Smith said: "His services to the development of sound thought on public questions were vitiated by his bitter attacks on all opponents. Whoso did not agree with him was heretical and foredamned. On this method he conducted his journal for over thirty years." Smith, *Catholic Church in New York*, II, 395–96. McMaster told Burtsell that three-quarters of the readers of his newspaper bought it for its political views rather than for its religious opinions. AANY, Burtsell, Diary, March 20, 1865.

19. *New York Freeman's Journal and Catholic Register*, December 10, 1870.

the Italian army, McMaster raised the temporal power of the pope to cosmic dimensions when he said: "All the foundations of the earth are out of joint because the Vicar of Christ is disturbed in his abode." He called upon the Catholic youth of America to launch a Grand Crusade to recover the Papal States by force. "It is the glory of youth to die young," the fifty-year old McMaster announced, "when they die in a good cause." Such wild and irresponsible rhetoric was the last thing that Archbishop McCloskey wanted to see printed in a Catholic newspaper published in New York.[20]

If Archbishop McCloskey was unhappy with the firebrand lay journalist in his midst, McMaster was equally unhappy with the cautious prelate who was the Archbishop of New York. Upon his return from the Vatican Council, McCloskey had explained the doctrine of papal infallibility in language that Father Farrell might have endorsed. He assured the welcoming crowd in St. Patrick's Cathedral that "the Vatican Council has made no new doctrine. It has given to the Pope no authority or prerogative which has not existed in him." When the Italians seized Rome on September 20, 1870, and McCloskey authorized a public address of sympathy to the Holy Father, McMaster regarded the archbishop's response as timid and inadequate. "We have been overwhelmed with letters and personal appeals," said McMaster in his newspaper, "asking if this is *all* that is to be done in New York." What McMaster wanted was a monster rally in Central Park that he claimed would bring out 100,000 Catholic men and the mayor of New York. He repeatedly tried to cajole and pressure McCloskey into authorizing such a public demonstration, but the proverbially prudent archbishop simply ignored such transparent efforts to manipulate him.[21]

20. *New York Freeman's Journal and Catholic Register,* October 1, November 5, 1870. Neither McCloskey nor Spalding favored recruiting Americans for the papal army. The Inspector General of the U.S. Army warned Spalding that the U.S. government would not permit recruitment for the papal army. AANY, A-32, Spalding to McCloskey, January 16, March 11, May 22, June 9, 1868.

21. *New York Daily Tribune,* September 1, 1870. *New York Freeman's Journal and Catholic Register,* December 17, December 24, 1870; January 21, February 18, 1871.

Although McMaster regarded Archbishop McCloskey as a woefully tepid defender of the Holy Father, he could hardly criticize him publicly. He felt no such inhibitions, however, when it came to Father Farrell. Shortly before Christmas, McMaster announced that there was one priest in New York who was speaking publicly against the temporal power of the pope. He did not identify him by name, but, in a thinly veiled criticism of Archbishop McCloskey, he mentioned that, when such incidents had occurred in Germany, the offending priests had been censured by their bishops. Frustrated up to this point by McCloskey's well-known prudence, McMaster taunted him with the comment that "the German prelates are too prudent to damn their souls by tolerating other men's sins."[22] Three weeks later Farrell wrote his celebrated letter to the organizers of the rally at the Academy of Music. As the contents became public, a reluctant archbishop was forced to take action.

Canonical Trial and Aftermath

McCloskey confronted Farrell with the published text of his letter to the organizers of the rally at the Academy of Music. Farrell defended himself on the grounds that he was not questioning church doctrine, but only expressing his opinions on European politics and history. In an obvious reference to McMaster, he noted that "others may express without rebuke opinions the most extravagant, not to say absurd." He added: "I am convinced that many things said are placing our religion in a false light." However, Farrell promised to remain silent, if McCloskey ordered him to do so. But, "if I do speak," he warned his archbishop, "I must utter my convictions."[23]

Farrell's response did not mollify McCloskey, and McCloskey removed him as pastor of St. Joseph's Church. Under the canon law then prevailing in the United States, McCloskey had the authority to do so, since American pastors were technically not pastors but only missionary rectors, removable at the pleasure of the bishop. When

22. Ibid., December 24, 1870.

23. AANY, G-58, Farrell to McCloskey, January 20, 1871.

McCloskey refused to reconsider his decision, Farrell invoked the only legal recourse available to him and demanded a canonical trial. "Let it not be said of our Church in the nineteenth century that she allowed a priest to be hung without a trial," he chided the archbishop. "If I have written or spoken anything contrary to the teaching of God's Church, point it out to me, and I will condemn it." A meeting between the two of them failed to resolve the dispute, and a canonical trial was set for February 3 in the Chancery Office on Mulberry Street.[24]

McCloskey appointed six priests to consider the charges against Farrell. Three were members of the Archbishop's Council, William Starrs, Thomas Preston, and Isaac Hecker, and the other three were pastors, Arthur Donnelly, Edward O'Reilly, and Michael Curran. The six priests were all asked the same question: "Has [sic] the teaching and public acts of Rev. F[ather] Farrell in his pastoral charge of St. Joseph's been such as to justify his removal?" All six responded in the affirmative, and Father Isaac Hecker added that "the Archbishop has been very patient and lenient."[25] When informed of the verdict, Farrell replied that he was not surprised and said that he was prepared to leave St. Joseph's rectory before the end of the month. While offering to apologize publicly for any disobedience or "imaginary scandal" that he might have caused, Farrell told McCloskey bluntly: "Neither you nor they have pointed out to me a single falsehood that I have ever uttered unless from the reports of newspapers which have often made me say what I never meant." Although he had previously indicated that he would leave his fate in God's hands, he now changed his mind and announced that he would appeal to Rome for judgment.[26]

24. AANY, G-58, Farrell to McCloskey, January 28, 31, 1871.

25. AANY, G-58, Question of the Archbishop. William Starrs was the vicar general; Thomas Preston, the chancellor, was a former Episcopalian minister whose extravagant views of papal authority rivaled those of McMaster; Isaac Hecker was another convert and the founder of the Paulist Fathers. Arthur Donnelly, Edward O'Reilly, and Michael Curran were pastors respectively of St. Michael's Church, St. Mary's Church on Grand Street, and St. Andrew's Church.

26. AANY, G-58, Farrell to McCloskey, February 9, 1871.

In the meantime, Farrell received support from both priests and laity in New York. Several of the parish societies of St. Joseph's Church and the Sunday School teachers sent petitions to McCloskey asking him to reinstate Farrell as pastor. One parishioner wrote privately to the archbishop, mentioning how Farrell had received his wife into the Church and asking better treatment for a faithful priest who "had not, in his advanced years, a home nor means to obtain one." Fifteen New York priests, including some of the most prominent pastors, sent McCloskey another petition, asking him to restore Farrell to the pastorate of St. Joseph's Church. Without questioning the verdict of the canonical trial, they appealed to McCloskey for leniency on the basis of Farrell's long service to the diocese and because he had already been sufficiently punished. Moreover, they warned the archbishop: "The occasion . . . will be seized, no matter how unreasonably or unjustly, by non-Catholics and enemies of the Church, to malign the Church and ecclesiastical authority."[27]

Some of Farrell's clerical friends hinted that McCloskey was waiting for a written statement from him. He obliged with a declaration that he accepted all the teachings of the Catholic Church, including the decrees of the Vatican Council, and regretted that anyone should have thought otherwise. McCloskey found the statement inadequate and sent Farrell an amended version, which he accepted. In this he stated: "I likewise reject all erroneous opinions which are proscribed and prohibited by the constitutions and decrees of the Apostolic See, and whatever I may have spoken or written in any contrary sense, I hereby retract."[28]

Under orders from McCloskey, Farrell read the statement at Mass

27. AANY, G-58, Petition of St. Joseph's Benevolent Association to McCloskey, February 15, 1871; Petition of St. Joseph's Temperance Society to McCloskey, February 15, 1871; Petition of St. Joseph's Sunday School to McCloskey, February 12, 1871; John Sadin to McCloskey, February 11, 1871; Petition of the Priests of the Diocese [sic]of New York to McCloskey, February 9, 1871. The signatories were Thomas McLoughlin, Felix Farrelly, Richard Burtsell, Edward McGlynn, James Byrne, Patrick Egan, William Everett, William Morrogh, M. Nicot, Patrick McCarthy, John Larkin, Michael McAleer, Gabriel Healy, Thomas Mooney, and M. McNamara.

28. AANY, G-58, Farrell to McCloskey, February 12, 14, 1871.

in St. Joseph's Church on the following Sunday, February 19. It was a highly emotional occasion which left much of the congregation in tears. Farrell thanked his parishioners for their support and reiterated his contention that he had been the victim of "vile calumniations." Without ever mentioning McMaster by name, he attributed much of his difficulty to him. "One little fellow," he said, "who has got charge of a paper, I believe he calls it Catholic, has denounced me in that paper. This little fellow has done more harm than good people can repair in many years." By contrast, Farrell had nothing but praise for McCloskey. He mentioned how the two of them had broken down in tears at their last meeting. "A man must be deeply moved when he cries," Farrell said, "and so was I as deeply moved as you are now." He repeated from the pulpit McCloskey's parting words to him that "I was to be your pastor and would continue to be so until you would get tired of me or I would get tired of you."[29]

Although chastised and contrite, Farrell made it clear that he had not abandoned the basic convictions that had caused him so much grief. "I have loved my religion better than my life," he said, "and I have also loved liberty with a very ardent devotion. Our religion does not forbid, but rather sanctifies it. There is no incompatibility between religion and true liberty any more than there is between religion and true science. While loving my religion more than life, I will ever, under its guidance, hate tyranny, oppression, injustice and wrong, and give my sympathy and assistance to the oppressed and the afflicted the world over."[30]

Farrell's dramatic performance in the pulpit of St. Joseph's Church on February 19 was not what McCloskey had expected. Neither on that occasion nor in his previous correspondence with the archbishop had Farrell ever specifically repudiated his approval of Italian unification. McMaster, who was busy collecting money for the restoration of the Papal States, spotted the omission immediate-

29. AANY, G-83, Farrell, Sermon Notes, n.d. The notes are mistakenly filed with the papers of John Cardinal Farley.

30. *New York Herald*, February 20, 1871; *New York Sun*, February 20, 1871.

ly and heaped abuse upon both Farrell and McCloskey for permitting Farrell's restoration to St. Joseph's Church under such circumstances. He complained bitterly that Farrell was "retracting nothing and denying nothing of the filthy, vile and stupid balderdash of false doctrine that has been publicly attached to his name." With characteristic exaggeration McMaster predicted: "Twenty years or less of this kind of doings will result in the open schism and speedy death of the Catholic Church in America."[31]

The very next day McMaster had his revenge. McCloskey insisted that Farrell specifically accept the temporal power of the papacy, and Farrell capitulated. He signed a statement dictated by McCloskey in which he declared: "I do accept what the Holy Father has affirmed concerning his temporal power or civil princedom and I do not regard it as a free question."[32] It was not Farrell's finest hour, but his surrender appears to have been motivated by gratitude to McCloskey as much as by fear of further punishment. To his credit, McCloskey never made public Farrell's humiliating *volte face.* He may have wanted to spare Farrell's feelings, but he may also have wanted to frustrate McMaster, who was asserting, with transparent insincerity, in his editorial page: "How Mr. Farrell has settled matters with the ordinary of the diocese, we do not know and do not seek to know."[33]

Father Farrell's Legacy

Thomas Farrell never again became the center of a public controversy and spent the last nine years of his life at St. Joseph's Church caring for the needs of his parishioners. Throughout his long tenure in St. Joseph's Church, Farrell was assisted by Father Jerome Nobriga, a refugee Portuguese Franciscan friar, who came to St. Joseph's

31. *New York Freeman's Journal and Catholic Register,* February 25, 1871. With McMaster ideology was stronger than friendship. Less than two years earlier, Farrell had written McMaster a warm and sympathetic letter on the occasion of his son's illness and recovery. AUND, Farrell to McMaster, May 14, 1869.

32. AANY, G-58, Farrell to McCloskey, February 26, 1871.

33. *New York Freeman's Journal and Catholic Register,* March 4, 1871.

six years before Farrell in 1850 and remained as a curate until his death, one year after Farrell's, in 1881.[34] Although Farrell avoided public controversy after 1871, he continued to host the meetings of the Accademia, the liberal "think tank" which, in the opinion of Thomas Spalding, was probably unique in the American Catholic Church at that time.[35] Farrell's relationship with McCloskey remained friendly. When McCloskey was named the first American cardinal in 1875, Farrell gladly accepted an invitation to the formal reception in St. Patrick's Cathedral. He also demonstrated his loyalty to the archdiocese by raising funds for the completion of the new cathedral, which was finally dedicated in 1879.[36]

Farrell cut a lonely figure as a spokesman for liberal Catholicism in the United States in an era of fervid ultramontanism. Lacking both theological expertise and diplomatic finesse, Farrell tried to give instinctive expression to a particularly American understanding of Catholicism that he was able to articulate in only an unsophisticated way. Nevertheless, he realized that he was recovering an earlier tradition in American Catholicism, the colonial Maryland Catholic tradition of religious freedom and respect for the rights of conscience. "He was an Irishman by birth," said one of Farrell's favorite disciples, Edward McGlynn, "but he was as true and thorough an American as anyone who traced his American ancestry back through generations."[37] Later, American Catholic thinkers like Fa-

34. Nobriga was one of three Portuguese priests who fled the anticlerical government in their homeland and found refuge in New York. See Corrigan, "Register of Clergy," *Historical Records and Studies* 6:2 (1913): 170.

35. Thomas W. Spalding, *Martin John Spalding: American Churchman* (Washington: The Catholic University of America Press, 1973), 268–69.

36. AANY, A-27, Farrell to John Farley, April 21, 1875.

37. *New York Times*, July 24, 1880. Both the foes and friends of Father Farrell indicated that he lacked the technical training to defend the adventuresome theological positions that he advocated. "He has an overactive, but not a well-poised brain," said McMaster in his usual slashing style. *New York Freeman's Journal and Catholic Register*, February 25, 1871. On the other hand, immediately after Farrell's death, three of his closest young priest friends, McGlynn, McSweeny, and Burtsell, destroyed all of Farrell's papers and discarded a large number of his books. Burtsell said that the books were "marked with all sorts of queer notes." AANY, Burtsell, Diary, July 24, 1880.

ther Francis P. Duffy and Father John Courtney Murray, S.J., would offer scholarly and nuanced justifications for many of the positions defended by Thomas Farrell. Murray in particular would have the satisfaction of seeing the American Catholic tradition of religious freedom enshrined in the Declaration on Religious Freedom of Vatican Council II.[38]

Farrell's old nemesis, James McMaster, is today a deservedly forgotten figure whose intransigent Catholicism seems as unreal as the political ideology of Joseph de Maistre or the polemics of Louis Veuillot. Unknown to Farrell, however, McCloskey shared his dislike for the incendiary journalist. "Let McMaster alone," McCloskey advised Archbishop Spalding in 1869 in connection with another issue. "He will not fail to bring discredit on this cause as he has done upon almost every other cause that he has undertaken to advocate. His insolence and intemperance of language simply disgust the laity."[39] McCloskey illustrates another enduring clerical type in American Catholic history. Although hardly sympathetic to liberal Catholicism, McCloskey was a pragmatic conservative rather than a reactionary ideologue with the good pastoral sense to keep Thomas Far-

38. On Duffy, see Thomas J. Shelley, "'What the Hell Is an Encyclical?': Governor Alfred E. Smith, Charles C. Marshall, Esq., and Father Francis P. Duffy," *U.S. Catholic Historian* 15:2 (1997): 87–107. On John Courtney Murray, see Donald Pelotte, *John Courtney Murray: Theologian in Conflict* (New York: Paulist Press, 1976); and D. Gonnet, *La liberté religieuse à Vatican II: La contribution de John Courtney Murray* (Paris: Editions du Cerf, 1994).

39. AAB, 36A-N11, McCloskey to Spalding, March 3, 1869. The issue in question was the dispute between priests and bishops over the rights of pastors. McMaster sided with the priests. When McMaster sent McCloskey a donation of $275 in 1868, McCloskey told him: "I am at a loss to reconcile this with the course which as editor of the Freeman's Journal you have thought proper to pursue toward me for these last three years and more." AUND, McCloskey to McMaster, November 20, 1868.

McCloskey also found McMaster's strident advocacy of parochial schools counterproductive. Writing from Rome during the Vatican Council, McCloskey told Preston that "the violent attacks of McMaster" had created sympathy in Rome for Dr. Edward McGlynn in his opposition to parochial schools. "The clergy of New York have reason to say 'non tali auxilio, non defensoribus istis,'" McCloskey said with regard to McMaster. McCloskey to Preston, May 26, 1870, in Farley, *Life of McCloskey,* 283–85. The letter is no longer available in the archives of the Archdiocese of New York.

rell within the fold rather than drive him out of it as McMaster would have wished.

Although Farrell made a humiliating surrender to McCloskey on the issue of the temporal power of the pope in 1871, he evened the score with McCloskey on another issue *d'outre tombe* a decade later. At his death in 1880, Farrell left $5,000 in his will for the establishment of the first black Catholic church in New York City. Knowing McCloskey's lack of enthusiasm for the project, Farrell shrewdly added a codicil to his will that, if the bequest were not used for that purpose within three years, the money should go to a non-Catholic charitable organization for African Americans.[40] McCloskey waited the full three years, weighed the two equally distasteful options, swallowed hard, and then reluctantly used the legacy in 1883 to establish the Church of St. Benedict the Moor for New York's black Catholics. It was a fitting memorial to St. Joseph's intrepid abolitionist pastor, even though he had to pay for it himself.[41]

40. AANY, Burtsell, Diary, July 23, 1880.

41. AANY, C-10, McGlynn to McCloskey, July 18, 1883. On the history of St. Benedict the Moor Church, see Jack M. Arlotta, "Before Harlem: Black Catholics in the Archdiocese of New York and the Church of St. Benedict the Moor," *Dunwoodie Review* 16 (1992–1993): 69–108.

5 *Parish Life at the Turn of the Twentieth Century*

BY THE TIME of Father Farrell's death in 1880, Greenwich Village was a neighborhood in transition. By most economic and social standards, it was also a neighborhood in decline. However, from the perspective of the Catholic Church, the 1880s mark the beginning of a golden age for the Church in Greenwich Village that lasted for about fifty years. It began with the influx into the Village of large numbers of Irish and Italian Catholics, and smaller numbers of French, Spanish, and black Catholics, during the last two decades of the Gilded Age. Catholic Greenwich Village only began to disintegrate after World War I, with urban renewal, gentrification, the flight of middle-class Catholics to the outer boroughs and the suburbs, and the emergence of Greenwich Village as the bohemia of America.

The Three Villages

Like Caesar's Gaul, Greenwich Village in the 1880s and 1890s could be divided into three parts.[1] The smallest part was the exclusive enclave that fronted on Washington Square North and on Lower Fifth Avenue. This was the part of the Village that was to change the least in the late nineteenth

1. "By 1850," said Edmund Delaney, "class structure in the Village had become quite rigid; aristocrats, or old Knickerbockers, lived north of the Square; the middle class concentrated in the West Village and the working class in the South." Edmund Delaney, *New York's Greenwich Village* (Barre, Mass.: Barre Publishers, 1968), 70–71.

century. The old Knickerbocker families and the prosperous mercantile princes clung to their stately town houses, entertained one another in season, dined in the evening at Delmonico's restaurant, went to Newport in August, and worshipped on Sunday perhaps in the Church of the Ascension or the First Presbyterian Church. They included Serena Rhinelander, whose row house at the corner of Washington Square North and Fifth Avenue had been built for her by her father in 1839–1840. Among her neighbors were Edward Cooper, former mayor of New York, who maintained a household staff of sixteen servants; the Reverend Henry C. Potter, the rector of Grace Church and future Episcopal bishop of New York; and Robert W. de Forest, whose Huguenot ancestors settled in New Amsterdam in 1636.[2]

In 1906 the North Villagers formed the Washington Square Association "to maintain the present desirable character of the neighborhood." They expected and usually received deferential treatment from the Irish Catholic politicians in City Hall. "We admonish them to perform [their] duties with an entire absence of the artificial and perfunctory respect that they are accustomed to receive from the [ward] heelers," said the president of the Washington Square Association in 1908 with the pompous self-assurance of a country squire giving directions to his groundskeeper.[3]

For many years, one of the most prominent residents of the North Village was James Lenox, one of the half-dozen richest men in New York City. He was also a generous benefactor of the First Presbyterian Church, and he filled his three-story mansion, located across from the church at the northeast corner of Fifth Avenue and 12th Street, with a priceless collection of books that eventually became the prized possession of the New York Public Library. To the surprise of everyone, however, when Lenox died in 1880, he did not leave a penny to the First Presbyterian Church. Alarmed at the

2. Gerald W. McFarland, *Inside Greenwich Village: A New York City Neighborhood, 1898–1918* (Amherst: University of Massachusetts Press, 2001), 78–87.

3. Frederick W. Whitridge, *Washington Square Association Yearbook* (1908): 21.

looming loss of income, the elders of the church decided to create an endowment fund. Like their fellow religionists in Ulster, these New York Presbyterians knew how to play the Orange card. "Had it not been for Trinity Church and Collegiate Church endowments," they warned the parishioners, "the lower portion of the city would have been given over to Roman Catholics some time ago."[4]

The second part of the Village was the area south of Washington Square Park. A working-class district by 1880, it had deteriorated to such a point that the extension of the Sixth Avenue El was almost constructed on Washington Square South instead of West 3rd Street. The South Village was also the home of the largest African American community in New York City, a declining French community, and a rapidly growing Italian community. After 1880, however, the Italian community was vastly expanded with the arrival of tens of thousands of additional Italian immigrants, many of them poor and uneducated. The main center of Italian settlement in Manhattan was originally located farther south, below Houston Street, concentrated around the notorious Mulberry Bend. However, spurred by the pressure of numbers and the deplorable housing conditions in that area, the Italians soon spilled into the blocks north of Houston Street and transformed the South Village into a heavily Italian area.

In the 1890s and 1900s, the housing stock in the neighborhood was rebuilt with six- and seven-story tenement buildings, which quickly deteriorated into overcrowded slum dwellings. By 1910, more than 80 percent of the residents were either foreign-born or the children of immigrants, more than half of them Italian.[5] In 1915, a newly arrived minister of the Judson Memorial Church on Washington Square South took a walk through the area and was shocked at what he witnessed. Although he later came to revise his harsh judgment, he said publicly, "When I first went south of the Square and saw the people in their filth with their undernourished children

4. Fowler, *A City Church*, 192.

5. Caroline F. Ware, *Greenwich Village, 1920–1930* (Berkeley: University of California Press, 1994), 12–13.

in their dirty halls and unhealthy environment, I said to my wife, 'These people are not humans. They are rats. No human beings would live like this.'"[6]

Such comments help to explain why Protestant proselytism among the Holy Father's kinsmen produced minimal results in Greenwich Village. For example, the University Place Presbyterian Church established the Bethlehem Mission on Bleecker Street and began to offer religious services in Italian in 1899. One wealthy parishioner contributed $190,000 to rescue the Italians from popery. By 1910 the Bethlehem Mission had an Italian congregation of between fifty and sixty and boasted that it acquired six new members that year. By way of contrast, at the nearby Italian national parish of St. Anthony of Padua, 2,644 children were baptized between 1912 and 1914.[7]

The West Village

The third part of Greenwich Village was the West Village, or the Ninth Ward, which formed the core area of St. Joseph's parish. After Father Farrell's death in 1880, Cardinal McCloskey appointed Father Felix H. Farrelly to succeed him. Farrelly was born in Ireland in 1832, and educated at St. Patrick's College, Maynooth, and at the Missionary College of All Hallows in Dublin, where he was ordained on July

6. Reverend A. Jay Petty, Address at the Meeting of the Washington Square Association, January 11, 1921, *Washington Square Association Yearbook* (1921), 24.

7. Fowler, *A City Church*, 119, 183; Donald Tricario, *The Italians of Greenwich Village: The Social Structure and Transformation of an Ethnic Community* (New York: Center for Migration Studies, 1984), 48. In the United States as a whole by 1918 the Presbyterians, Methodists, Baptists, and Episcopalians together had founded 326 churches for the Italians. They claimed a combined membership of thirteen thousand—out of the four million Italians in the United States by that date. Rarely in the course of religious history was so much spent by so many for so few. If Italian immigrants were bad Catholics, at least in the judgment of contemporary Irish American Catholics, that did not mean that they were about to become good Protestants. See F. Aurleio Palmieri, O.S.A., "Italian Protestantism in the United States," *Catholic World* 107 (1918): 177–87. Rudolph Vecoli described Palmieri as "a learned Augustinian who had spent many years in America . . . [and] was probably the most astute commentator on the religious situation of the Italian immigrants." Rudolph J. Vecoli, "Prelates and Peasants: Italian Immigrants and the Catholic Church," *Journal of Social History* 2 (1969): 263.

3, 1854. He left that same year for America, where he held a number of pastoral assignments in the Archdiocese of New York before his appointment as pastor of St. Joseph's Church. In 1871 Farrelly was one of fifteen priests who signed the petition to McCloskey on behalf of Father Farrell. By 1880, unfortunately, Farrelly's health was already beginning to decline and he died after only two years at St. Joseph's. He in turn was succeeded by Father John B. Salter, who had been a curate at St. Joseph's since 1876.[8]

In the late nineteenth century, the West Village or Ninth Ward was still a solidly middle-class neighborhood that the older residents liked to call the American Ward. In 1886 Father Salter reminded Archbishop Corrigan that the area was the old Know-Nothing Ward, and he said that the majority of the population was still Protestant. Anti-Catholic prejudice flared occasionally, as in 1889 when the owner of property on Waverly Place withdrew it from sale when he discovered that St. Joseph's Church was interested in purchasing it. As late as 1893 an observer who would have endeared himself to the Know-Nothings of the 1850s commented on "the moral and physical cleanliness" of the West Village, which he attributed to the fact that it was inhabited by "a humanity of the better sort," unlike the Lower East Side, "where even the bad smells have foreign names." "It really does one's heart good," said this same gentleman, "on the 4th of July or the 22nd of February to see the way the owners of the roomy comfortable houses which here abound proclaim their nationality by setting the trim streets of Greenwich ablaze with American flags."[9]

By the turn of the twentieth century, however, Irish Catholics had replaced American-born Protestants as the dominant ethnic element in the local population. On Christopher Street, for example,

8. Shea, *Catholic Churches of New York,* 403–4. Farrelly is not listed in the comprehensive list of graduates of All Hallows College prepared by Kevin Condon, C.M., *The Missionary College of All Hallows, 1842–1891* (Dublin: All Hallows College, 1986), 290–364.

9. AANY, Salter to Corrigan, November 20, 1886; Edward McGuire to Corrigan, February 14, 1889. Thomas A. Janvier, "Greenwich Village," *Harper's New Monthly Magazine* 87 (August 1893): 356–57.

the majority of the residents had English surnames as late as 1890, but a decade later, 40 percent of the residents were of Irish ancestry, 24 percent were of American ancestry, and 16 percent were of German ancestry. When Mary Kingsbury Simkhovitch, the founder of Greenwich House, moved into the West Village in 1902, she said that the area was mainly Irish Catholic.[10] The days were long past, however, when the Irish could all be lumped together indiscriminately as poor immigrants. Perhaps a few of the Irish in the Village could trace their roots as far back as the opening of St. Joseph's Church in 1834. Many more were the descendants of the Famine Irish, who were just climbing into middle-class respectability and assuming the status of community leaders. Still others were more recent immigrants or the children of immigrants, often enough refugees from the South Village, from which they had been displaced by the Italians. Inevitably this group occupied the lowest rung on the neighborhood economic ladder.[11]

One result of the heavy Irish presence was the emergence of Greenwich Village as a solid bastion of the Democratic Party. Together with the Catholic Church and the Irish county societies, the local Tammany clubs were the most influential neighborhood institutions. In the era before the New Deal, these clubs dispensed political patronage, found jobs for the unemployed, distributed coal to the needy during the winter, provided them with turkeys at Thanksgiving and Christmas, and served as rudimentary social welfare agencies. Three of the clubs that were organized in the 1890s were flourishing forty years later, two of them still controlled by the members of the same family.[12]

The social gradations among the Village Irish were discernible

10. Christine Boyer, "Straight Down Christopher Street," in *Greenwich Village: Culture and Counterculture,* 47. Mary Kingsbury Simkhovitch, *Neighborhood, My Story of Greenwich House* (New York: Norton, 1938), 107.

11. The classifications are those of Caroline Ware, *Greenwich Village,* 203–4. Writing in 1935, she said that not one of fifty Irish people interviewed had any recollection of the descendants of the original Irish settlers in Greenwich Village.

12. McFarland, *Inside Greenwich Village,* 38; Ware, *Greenwich Village,* 270–71.

geographically. Generally speaking, the farther west one went from Sixth Avenue and the closer to the Hudson River, the poorer the Irish families were likely to be. Many of the men worked as longshoremen on the docks, or in the coal and lumber yards, or in the Empire Brewery, a colossal building that occupied a whole city block on the waterfront between West 10th Street and Charles Street. The waterfront itself was expanded west an extra block from Washington Street to West Street on landfill over the river. The tracks of the New York Central Railroad's west side freight line were then extended south at grade level down the center of West Street to the freight terminal at St. John's Park. Small factories, warehouses, breweries, and loft buildings completed the commercialization of the once residential Ninth Ward.

Real estate values on the waterfront skyrocketed after the Hudson River docks replaced those on the East River as the favored moorings for the big transatlantic steamships. "The land is too valuable for tenements or dwellings of any kind," said Father Salter in 1886. "There is not a residence along West Street nor on the west side of Washington Street from Houston to Christopher Street, and the same may be said of Greenwich and the transverse streets. Whole squares are occupied by storage warehouses, factories, coal yards, breweries, etc." Hudson Street was three blocks from the river, but most of the old houses between Hudson Street and the river were built on property leased from either Trinity Church or the Astor estate. "As fast as these leases run out," Salter observed, "the land is used for business purposes solely."[13]

The housing stock in the West Village deteriorated as one got closer to the Hudson River. Many private homes were converted into lodging houses or subdivided into workers' flats. For the first time too, tenement houses were built in considerable numbers in the West Village. By 1903 there were 2,283 tenement houses in the Ninth Ward, with 51,577 residents.[14] Fortunately, most of these

13. AANY, Salter to Corrigan, November 20, 1886.

14. A housing survey published in 1903 noted that "in former years [the Ninth Ward]

buildings were erected after the housing reform act of 1879, which required minimum standards of light and sanitation that were absent in the tenements erected earlier in the century. The older tenements built before 1879 contained "railroad flats" with windows only in the front and rear of the building. The newer tenements were commonly called "dumb-bell tenements" because of the air shaft that narrowed their width at the center of the building. Thanks at least in part to this tenement house legislation, housing in the Village did not deteriorate to the extent that it did in the slums of the Lower East Side.[15]

Nonetheless, even in these "dumb-bell tenements" living conditions were hardly attractive. "In these houses, built on lots twenty-five feet wide, the rooms were small, and, on the lower floors of six-story buildings, dark," said Caroline Ware in her classic study of Greenwich Village in the 1920s. "Typically each floor contained four flats, two four-room flats in the front, and two three-room flats in the rear. A toilet at one or both ends of the hall was shared by four or two families. There were no baths, and the only running water was in the kitchen sink. The largest room in each flat was at most eleven feet wide by twelve to fourteen feet deep, often less. The other rooms were from nine to six feet wide and less than ten feet deep. Closet space was almost never provided, and every room was habitually used for sleeping."[16]

Changes in transportation also played a role in the transformation of the West Village. For decades the area had been more or less

---

was not distinctly a tenement house district. It has, however, recently become so, and this tendency is fast increasing." By contrast, the neighboring Fifteenth Ward, which was located east of Sixth Avenue, contained only 596 tenement houses. Lawrence Veiller, "A Statistical Study of New York's Tenement Houses," in *The Tenement House Problem*, ed. Robert W. DeForest and Lawrence Veiller (New York: Macmillan, 1903), I, 201, 205.

15. In 1890 the population density in the Ninth Ward was 169.0 people per acre and only 122.3 people per acre in the Fifteenth Ward. On the Lower East Side, the population density was 384.3 people per acre in the Eleventh Ward, and in the Tenth Ward, the so-called Jewish Quarter between Norfolk Street and the Bowery, the population density rose to 523.6 people per acre. *Report of the New York State Legislative Assembly Tenement House Committee* (Albany: James R. Lyon, 1895), 273.

16. Ware, *Greenwich Village*, 26.

isolated from the main north-south commercial thoroughfares in the city because of the diagonal layout of its streets. "Uptowners did not know their way about south of Fourteenth Street on the West Side," said Mary Kingsbury Simkhovitch, "and hence travel was principally down Broadway and east of Sixth Avenue." That blissful isolation came to an abrupt end in the 1870s, however, with the construction of the first two successful elevated railways in Manhattan. In 1872 the Ninth Avenue El began regular operations along Greenwich Street to South Ferry. The Sixth Avenue El was in full service six years later. It ran down Sixth Avenue to West 3rd Street (close to where Sixth Avenue ended in those days), then swung east for four blocks along West 3rd Street, and continued south on South Fifth Avenue to South Ferry. By 1898 both lines had been electrified and they remained the main rapid transit facilities in the neighborhood until the extension of the West Side IRT subway from Times Square to South Ferry in 1917. For over sixty years the Sixth Avenue El trains rattled past the front steps of St. Joseph's Church, providing cheap and efficient transportation for New Yorkers, but blighting the street below and drowning out all but the most powerful preachers in St. Joseph's pulpit.[17]

St. Veronica's Parish

In view of the increasing Catholic population in the West Village, the archdiocesan authorities decided in 1886 that the time was ripe for a new parish that would be located somewhere between Sixth Avenue and the Hudson River. Predictably, Father Salter objected strenuously to the proposal and offered every possible objection to it. He claimed that the Catholic population in Greenwich Village was actually declining, that many Catholics in the area already went to Mass at other churches on Sunday, and that the establishment of

17. Simkhovitch, *Neighborhood,* 113. An advertisement for the West Side Elevated Railway Company, the unsuccessful predecessor of the Ninth Avenue El, stated in 1863 that "this method of rapid transit between the extremities of Manhattan Island has become a public necessity and is loudly demanded by the popular vote." *New York Daily Tribune,* October 23, 1863.

a new parish would place an impossible financial burden on his own diminished congregation. He also claimed (inaccurately) that St. Joseph's was no farther from the Hudson River than St. Bernard's at West 14th Street or St. Michael's at West 32nd Street. "There is not now a sufficient population between St. Joseph's and the river to support another church, much less a school," he said, "and the population is yearly decreasing." However, Salter indicated to Archbishop Corrigan that he would be happy to get rid of the portion of the parish lying east of Sixth Avenue, Carmine Street, and Varick Street, since most of the Catholics in that area attended other churches, "if they go to church at all."[18]

Archbishop Corrigan was adamant that a new parish should be established *west* of Sixth Avenue rather than *east* of it. His diocesan consultors warned him that the division of the parish proposed by Father Salter was pastorally irresponsible, because it would leave St. Joseph's Church at the eastern edge of the parish boundaries and three-quarters of a mile from many of his parishioners, especially those who lived near the waterfront. The archbishop left the delicate negotiations with Father Salter in the hands of two of the diocesan consultors, Father John Farley, the vicar general and pastor of St. Gabriel's Church, and Father Arthur Donnelly, the pastor of St. Michael's Church.[19]

On a rainy evening late in November 1886, Farley and Donnelly called upon Salter at his rectory to break the unpleasant news to him. Salter reacted so badly that Donnelly, a no-nonsense individual known for his "grit," left and went home. However, the more genial Farley tried to sooth Salter's wounded feelings by agreeing to his request that they should walk through the neighborhood together to conduct an on-site inspection. As they tramped through the darkened streets of the West Village in the rain, Salter made his case that there were only a couple of hundred Catholic families in the whole area and very few Catholics west of Hudson Street near the waterfront. (Farley had earlier calculated that there were in fact 17,000

18. AANY, Salter to Corrigan, September 22, November 20, 1886.
19. AANY, Farley to Corrigan, October 10, 1886.

Catholics in St. Joseph's parish.) Feigning shock at the paucity of Catholics near the river, Farley said that the obvious solution was to give the new parish an even larger portion of St. Joseph's territory by drawing the dividing line farther east at Bleecker Street rather than at Hudson Street. Salter then did an abrupt verbal somersault and conceded that perhaps there really were more Catholics west of Hudson Street than he had suspected. "I allowed myself to be convinced of this," said Farley with a chuckle, "and fell back on Hudson [Street], to which he by this time had become more than reconciled; in fact, [he] asked me to see that the eastern boundary would not be other than Hudson."[20]

The new parish of St. Veronica was established in January 1887, embracing thirty square blocks from Hudson Street to the river, and from Bank Street in the north to Houston Street in the south. The first pastor was Father John F. Fitzharris, who had been a curate at St. Joseph's Church since 1876 and was recommended for the post by Father Salter. Father Fitzharris leased an old warehouse and stable at 626 Washington Street for $2,000 per year, spent $6,000 on renovations, and celebrated the first Mass there on Palm Sunday, April 3, 1887. He raised much of the funds by taking up collections in the neighboring churches, St. Joseph's, St. Bernard's, St. Francis Xavier's, and St. Peter's Church on Barclay Street, whose pastor, Father James McGean, had been born in the West Village. Three years later, on March 16, 1890, the cornerstone was blessed for the present Church of St. Veronica on Christopher Street between Greenwich and Washington Streets. Christopher Street was a busy commercial thoroughfare because the ferry to Hoboken docked at the foot of the street, and it was also a stop on the Ninth Avenue El. In October 1890, Mass was celebrated for the first time in the basement of St. Veronica's

20. AANY, Farley to Corrigan, December 1, 1886. Salter seems to have been a querulous individual who was often a thorn in Corrigan's side. When one of Salter's curates called him a liar, he demanded that Corrigan "compel him to make reparation." AANY, C-12, Salter to Corrigan, October 15, 1887. When Salter resigned as pastor of St. Joseph's for reasons of ill health in 1892, Bishop Charles McDonnell of Brooklyn commented to Corrigan, "This must be a relief to you." AANY, C-33, McDonnell to Corrigan, November 6, 1892.

Church. It took another thirteen years to complete the upper church, which was dedicated by Archbishop John Farley on June 7, 1903.[21]

The journal that was published for the dedication of St. Veronica's Church is a good indication of the character of the neighborhood. In addition to the usual full-page advertisements from undertakers, there were numerous advertisements for stables, horse dealers, truckers and forwarders, scrap metal dealers, and even a horse and dog hospital, all located within the confines of the parish and mostly owned by proprietors with Irish names. The advertisers of these modest establishments represented the more affluent residents, but the bulk of St. Veronica's parishioners were employed in even more humble occupations, many of them as longshoremen and teamsters. The fact that it took thirteen years to complete the construction of the church is a fair indication of the poverty of the parish. Indeed, almost half of the money for the church came from exceptionally successful parish fairs in 1890 and 1902. Parish fairs were the nineteenth-century equivalent of bingo games. Organized by the women of the parish, they usually lasted several weeks and featured games of chance in a carnival-like atmosphere accompanied by music, entertainment, and refreshments. The two parish fairs at St. Veronica's together raised over $33,000.[22]

The parishioners of St. Joseph's regarded themselves as the social superiors of their poor cousins on Christopher Street, since their parish was far older and larger, and included the wealthier areas of the Village. In 1908 the principal of St. Veronica's School reported that almost half of the fathers of the students were unemployed.[23] Even after the establishment of St. Veronica's parish in 1887, St.

21. *Church of St. Veronica* (New York: Church of St. Veronica, 1903).

22. Ibid. At the fair held at St. Francis Xavier Church in November 1880, the prizes featured "Indian Curiosities" from the Camp of Sitting Bull, including a full set of bow and arrows and a tomahawk said to belong to Rain-in-the-Face. This was only four years after the battle of Little Big Horn. *The Journal of the Fair to Aid in the Completion of the New St. Francis Xavier Church,* November 13, 1880, 6–7.

23. Greenwich House Papers (hereafter GHP), Tamiment Institute Library, New York University, Mary Kingsbury Simkhovitch, Report of the Director, January 21, 1908.

Joseph's was still quite large in area, comprising eighty-one square blocks, with a Catholic population of perhaps ten thousand. The parish boundaries extended from West 14th Street on the north to Houston Street on the south, and from Hudson Street on the west to University Place and South Fifth Avenue on the east. In 1895–1896, St. Joseph's Church reported an income of $27,773.60, almost half of which ($12,023.58) came from pew rent and seat rent, two sources which indicated a relatively stable and prosperous congregation. Another $6,873.48 was derived from the Sunday collection, and the remaining money came from special collections and donations. Unlike St. Veronica's, St. Joseph's did not have to resort to a parish fair to raise money until it embarked on the construction of a new school.[24]

Sacramental Life

Then as now, the celebration of the Eucharist was the central act of Catholic worship, and St. Joseph's provided its parishioners with Mass on Sunday every hour on the hour from 6:00 A.M. until 11:00 A.M., including a children's Mass at 9:00 and a sung High Mass with sermon at 11:00. The last Mass was at the relatively early hour of 11:00, which was the rule in New York's Catholic churches. A notable exception was St. Stephen's Church on East 28th Street where, in the late 1880s, the pastor, Father Edward McGlynn, introduced a noon Mass that drew 2,500 worshippers to his church every week.

"Churches are for the people, and not the people for the churches," McGlynn informed Archbishop Corrigan. He mentioned that the noonday Mass had brought back to the practice of the faith many Catholics who had ceased to attend Mass on Sunday, but McGlynn had to defend himself from the complaints of other pastors who called the noonday Mass "the Mass of the Weak" and accused him of encouraging sloth among his parishioners. Such accusations, he said, "come with poor grace from any who have so much leisure every day of the week and are so generously supported by

24. AANY, Financial Report of St. Joseph's Church, January 1, 1895, to January 1, 1896.

our hard-working people, whether of the laboring, trading or professional class. Surely we should not grudge them such additional rest as they might be able to take . . . on their one day of much needed rest," he argued. "[F]or so many of them," he explained, "[it] is by no means a day of total rest from labor. Very many have to work all night or from 3 or 4 o'clock in the morning of Sundays as well as other days."[25]

A full decade after McGlynn introduced the noonday Mass at St. Stephen's Church with such obvious success, neither St. Joseph's nor St. Veronica's had done so. If all ten thousand Catholics residing in St. Joseph's parish attended Mass every Sunday, there would have been almost 1,700 people at each Mass. That number of people did show up once a year for the parish mission, but it is improbable that there were that many present at each Mass on Sunday. A more likely explanation is that, although St. Joseph's Church had several thousand faithful parishioners, there were many other Catholics in the neighborhood who were not regular churchgoers. As in every parish, many came to church only at Christmas and Easter, and on Ash Wednesday and Palm Sunday. However, the more devout parishioners not only attended Mass every Sunday morning but returned to St. Joseph's Church on Sunday evening at 7:30 for vespers, a sermon, and Benediction of the Blessed Sacrament, a Eucharistic service which concluded with a blessing of the congregation by the priest holding the consecrated host in a special glass-and-gold liturgical vessel called a monstrance.[26]

There were eight Protestant churches in the Village proper and another seven Protestant churches in the vicinity. Their congregations began to dwindle after the turn of the century, and they limited their activities largely to Sunday services. By contrast, St. Joseph's Church had four scheduled Masses every weekday between 6:30 and 9:00 A.M., which were attended by both housewives and men on their way to work. Special attention was given to the First Friday of

25. AANY, C-10, McGlynn to Corrigan, March 11, 1886.

26. AANY, Rules and Regulations of St. Joseph's Church, 1896.

each month, when the 9:00 Mass was celebrated as a High Mass.

The Catholic piety of that era placed great stress on the First Friday of the month as a day for Eucharistic devotion. Catholics were encouraged to receive Holy Communion on that day as a way of combating the Jansenist spirituality that discouraged frequent reception of Holy Communion for all except the most devout. At St. Joseph's Church, in addition to the High Mass, the consecrated host was placed in a monstrance and left on the altar all day for the adoration of the people. This particular type of Eucharistic piety was associated with a theology of expiation. Catholics were encouraged to spend some time in silent prayer and adoration before the Blessed Sacrament as a way of making reparation for sins of impiety and sacrilege. When Father Joseph McMahon wanted to introduce this practice at St. Patrick's Cathedral in 1897, he told Archbishop Corrigan that "this act of reparation . . . already is very generally practiced throughout the diocese and in other dioceses." At St. Joseph's, the First Friday devotions concluded with an evening service consisting of a sermon and Benediction of the Blessed Sacrament.[27]

The administration of the sacraments at St. Joseph's Church reflected the standard Catholic practice of that era. Confessions were heard after every weekday Mass, but Saturday was the traditional day for Catholics to go to confession in preparation for Sunday Mass. All five priests heard confessions on that day from 4:00 P.M. until late in the evening, with a brief break for supper. The same was true on the eve of holy days and the eve of the First Friday of the month. Many Catholics would never have dared to receive Holy Communion without first going to confession, although there was no church law that obliged them to do so.

On Saturdays every priest could expect to spend long hours in the confessional. The diary of Richard Burtsell is filled with references to occasions when he heard confessions for four or five hours at a stretch or even longer. One of the topics debated by Burtsell and

27. AANY, G-2, McMahon to Corrigan, December 12, 1897.

the other members of the Accademia at their sessions in St. Joseph's rectory was the wisdom of encouraging frequent confession on the part of devout lay people who had no serious sins to confess. Even Dr. Burtsell seem surprised, however, when Father Farrell once suggested that teenage boys were too young to go to confession.

In striking contrast to the meticulous attention given to confession, baptism and marriage were treated in an almost nonchalant fashion. There was no pre-baptismal catechesis or even an interview with the parents. Parents were simply advised to present their children for baptism any Thursday evening from 7:00 to 9:00, or on Sundays from 4:00 to 5:00 P.M. and again in the evening from 7:00 to 9:00. It was presumed that any parent requesting baptism would raise the child as a Catholic. In the case of weddings, which were usually celebrated in the morning at Mass time, there was a three-week waiting period, but only to allow sufficient time for the reading of the banns at Mass on three successive Sundays, a relic from a rural society where such announcements were made to forestall bigamous unions. There was no spiritual preparation for the sacrament other than an exhortation to the bride and groom to receive Holy Communion on their wedding day.

The visitation of the sick was a major pastoral responsibility in an era when many people avoided hospitals and died at home. Parishioners were urged to inform the rectory by 10:00 A.M. if they wished a priest to visit a sick person in their home. Office hours in the rectory lasted only from 8:00 to 10:00 A.M., and again from 6:00 to 9:00 P.M., leaving the priest on duty free to make house calls in the middle of the day. Many Catholics deferred asking for the sacrament of the sick until the last minute, since even the contemporary name, Extreme Unction, implied that it was a sacrament for the dying rather than for the aged and the ill. At St. Joseph's, the printed instructions for sick calls pointedly called attention to the fact that "one effect of the Sacrament of Extreme Unction is to heal."[28]

Parish missions—the Catholic equivalent of a Protestant re-

28. AANY, Rules and Regulations of St. Joseph's Church, 1896.

vival—were an integral feature of the parish life of that era. A large urban parish like St. Joseph's might sponsor a mission every year, especially during Lent. As mentioned earlier, the first English-language parish mission ever given by the Redemptorist Fathers took place at St. Joseph's Church in 1851. The mission at St. Joseph's in 1897 was unusual in that it was not conducted by priests from a religious community like the Redemptorists, but by the Archdiocesan Mission Band, a group of New York diocesan priests who specialized in that work.

Three diocesan priests, Fathers Cusack, Guinon, and Goggin, assisted by Father Walter Elliott, a well-known Paulist mission preacher, conducted a mission that lasted four weeks. As was customary, each week was set aside for a specific group of parishioners. The first week was reserved for married women, because they were the ones who were most likely to attend in large numbers and set the tone for the next three weeks. The second week was reserved for young women; the third week for married men; and the fourth week for the hardest catch of all, the young men of the parish. The technique worked at St. Joseph's, at least for the first week, when almost 1,700 married women filled the church to capacity for the morning Mass and evening sermon, and flocked to the confessionals throughout the day. One newspaper reporter was especially impressed with the congregational singing at the services. Such popular participation was uncommon in Irish American parishes of that era, but it was said to be a long-established feature of worship in St. Joseph's Church. Another unusual aspect of this parish mission, due perhaps to Father Walter Elliott, was that it concluded with a series of lectures on the Catholic Church for prospective converts.[29]

Parish Societies

In the heyday of big city Catholicism in the United States, which coincided with the golden age of the Catholic Church in Greenwich Village, churches like St. Joseph's were not only religious centers, but

29. New York *Catholic News*, December 5, 1897.

also educational, cultural, and social centers for their parishioners. A dense network of sodalities, confraternities, and parish societies created strong bonds between the parishioners and the parish, and among the parishioners themselves. These organizations served different age groups, and they all had their own officers and a priest moderator. They held regularly scheduled meetings and performed specific functions in the parish, many of which would be described today as lay ministries.

One of the smallest but most valuable organizations in St. Joseph's Church was the local conference (chapter) of the St. Vincent de Paul Society, which was the principal means of bringing material assistance to the needy of the parish. It was the local branch of an international organization founded in France in the 1840s for Catholic laymen who were dedicated to helping the poor. Unlike some of the bigger parish societies, it was a highly structured, no-nonsense organization. Members were required to attend a weekly meeting and to visit the poor in their homes at least once a week. At St. Joseph's Church, the Vincentians, as they called themselves, had their own meeting room. They met each Sunday with the pastor after the 11:00 Mass to consider requests for financial assistance. In 1895 they distributed $501.17 to poor parishioners on their visits to their homes.

The guiding force behind the St. Vincent de Paul Society in New York City in the 1890s was Thomas Mulry, the secretary of the Supreme Council of New York, whose headquarters were located only a few blocks east of St. Joseph's Church at Two Lafayette Place. "There is no room in our society for drones," he warned the members in 1893. "The man who does not earnestly enter into this work had better retire at once." That same year Mulry proudly pointed out to Archbishop Corrigan that, in the previous year, the Society had aided needy families with 11,000 children, 5,000 of whom would probably have been sent to institutions without the help provided by the Vincentians on their home visits.[30]

The two largest parish organizations were the Holy Name Society

30. AANY, G-2, Mulry to Sirs and Dear Brothers, August 29, 1893; Mulry to Corrigan,

for the men and the Rosary Society for the women, each of which held a monthly meeting. For the younger parishioners there were the Sodality of the Children of Mary and the Sodality of the Holy Angels. St. Joseph's Lyceum, located next to the church on Sixth Avenue on the site of the present rectory, was the cultural and social center of the parish. There was also a parish library, but it was open only on Thursday and Sunday evenings at 7:30. The League of the Sacred Heart was the local branch of a national organization sponsored by the Jesuits to promote devotion to the Sacred Heart and the Eucharist, especially in connection with the First Friday of the month. The Sisters of Charity and the Christian Brothers provided religious instruction every Sunday afternoon at 2:30, but this was regarded as a poor substitute for the enrollment of children in the parochial school. In fact, the purpose of still another parish society, St. Joseph's Parochial School Guild, was to raise additional funds for the parish school. Membership was open to anyone who pledged the payment of ten cents per week, but in 1895 it collected only the paltry sum of $208.40.[31]

Catholic Education

Despite the poor showing of St. Joseph's Parochial School Guild, the school itself was flourishing in the 1890s. In 1893 the building was almost forty years old, but the diocesan inspector of schools reported that the classrooms were well ventilated and lighted, and that the academic standards were excellent. In 1895 there were 715 students in the school, with a teaching staff of nine Sisters of Charity,

---

November 18, 1893. Mrs. Josephine Shaw Lowell, a well-known Protestant social reformer, paid Mulry a handsome tribute in 1897 when she asked Archbishop Corrigan to recommend Mulry for the post of Commissioner of Charities of the Borough of Manhattan. She did so, she said, "not because Mr. Mulry wishes the appointment, for I do not know whether he does or not, but because the ten thousand helpless and suffering men, women and children in our public institutions need the protection and care of a man of his character and capacity." AANY, G-14, Lowell to Corrigan, November 10, 1897. Mrs. Lowell was an early advocate of placing children in foster care rather than in institutions. She admired the practice of the St. Vincent de Paul Society of providing assistance to needy people in their own homes.

31. AANY, Rules and Regulations of the Church of St. Joseph, 1896.

seven Christian Brothers, and one lay teacher. The total expenses that year were $7,978.45, which meant that the per capita cost of educating the children came to $11.16.[32]

However, the location of the school, on Leroy Street, one-quarter mile distant from the church, was a major inconvenience. To make matters worse, when St. Veronica's Church was established in 1887, St. Joseph's School wound up within the boundaries of the new parish. As far back as 1886, Father Salter—and later his successor, Father Denis O'Flynn, who served as pastor from 1892 to 1906—attempted to purchase property for a new school adjacent to the church. Nothing came of their efforts, however, until 1897, when Father O'Flynn erected the new St. Joseph's School on Washington Place and also a new rectory on Waverly Place. The combined cost of the two buildings was $108,000, a cost overrun of $26,316 on the original estimate of $81,864.[33] The cornerstone of the new school was laid on March 7, 1897, and construction proceeded so rapidly that the building was ready for occupancy by the following September. It was a five-story limestone and brick structure with terra cotta trimmings surmounted by a massive copper cornice. It included not only classroom space for a thousand students, but also an auditorium for 550 people with a stage that could be used for parish social functions.

At the laying of the cornerstone, the guest speaker was Father James McGean, whose address on the evolution of public and Catholic education in New York City provides a good insight into contemporary Catholic opinion on the subject. As a native of Greenwich Village, McGean first paid a handsome tribute to the old public school teachers whom he had known as a youth, several of whom he mentioned by name. "Such teachers are remembered by the old people of this part of the city as able, impartial, kindly men," he said,

32. AANY, G-83, M. J. Considine, Report of the Parish School Inspector, July 10, 1893; Financial Report of St. Joseph's Church, January 1, 1895, to January 1, 1896.

33. AANY, C-12, Salter to Preston, February 5, 1886; AANY, G-15, Estimate for St. Joseph's School, October 6, 1896; AANY, O'Flynn to Connolly, September 4, 1895; O'Flynn to Corrigan, October 6, 1896; AANY, Minutes of the Meetings of the Archdiocesan Consultors, December 4, 1889; June 5, 1895; September 4, 1895; September 2, 1896.

"and I feel it a privilege that on this occasion I can give testimony to the worth of the old schoolmasters." He also acknowledged with affection the religious atmosphere that prevailed in the public schools in Greenwich Village and throughout New York City. "I remember," he declared, "when in the common schools the name of God was mentioned on every page of the reading book." However, McGean also diplomatically pointed out why Catholics had found this religious atmosphere objectionable. "Unfortunately for ourselves," he added, "there was a positive opposition in many of the lessons that were given inside the old schools to what we claim to be the religion of Almighty God. . . . On this account, there were those who were willing that their children should be from day to day in the basement of this old church that they might receive the religious instruction which they could not have in the common school."

McGean went on to deplore the subsequent secularization of the public schools in New York City, although he carefully refrained from mentioning Archbishop John Hughes' unintentional contribution to that development. He also touched on a theme that was dear to Father O'Flynn, the injustice in the law that forced Catholics to pay taxes for the public schools while denying them any share of those taxes for their own schools. Nevertheless, McGean closed on an irenic and optimistic note that would have warmed the Americanist heart of Father Farrell's ghost: "I believe that the spirit of fairness that is characteristic of the American mind will ultimately give to the Catholic minority their rights." In the meantime, while waiting for that happy day (which has yet to arrive), McGean urged his listeners to support the building of their new school both as good Catholics and good Americans.[34]

Even after the opening of the new St. Joseph's School, the problem still remained of what to do with the old school on Leroy Street. Father O'Flynn, who still held the legal title to the building, wanted to sell it to help pay for the construction of his new school. On the other hand, Father McCormick, the pastor of St. Veronica's Church,

34. New York *Catholic News,* March 10, 1897.

who was strapped for cash, with a debt of $58,000 and a weekly income of $240, wanted to get title to it so that he could sell it to reduce his debt. Neither solution was acceptable to Archbishop Corrigan or the diocesan consultors, who wanted the school kept open. Father McGean, one of the consultors, sounded a rather different note at the meeting than he had done at the laying of the cornerstone of the new St. Joseph's School. He remarked that a second Catholic school was needed in the West Village because the two local public schools were still "Protestant schools." The result was a decision by the archbishop that the old school on Leroy Street should be given to St. Veronica's Church, but with the stipulation that it be kept open as that parish's parochial school. Meanwhile, the new school in St. Joseph's parish flourished. Within seven years of its opening, attendance shot up from 800 to 1,500.[35]

The Irish Village

Although the enrollment in St. Joseph's School practically doubled between 1897 and 1904, Father O'Flynn initially had fears that he would not be able to fill the new school because of an influx of Jews and Italians into his parish. In 1896 he wondered how Catholic the parish would be ten or fifteen years hence. What he really meant, of course, was how Irish the parish would be. His identification of Italian as well as Jewish immigrants as outsiders was an unconscious reflection of how O'Flynn took for granted that St. Joseph's was an Irish parish. In 1889, for example, two years before O'Flynn came to St. Joseph's, Father Salter published the list of parishioners who contributed to the special collection for new pews and a new floor for

35. From 1887 to 1896, the total cost of maintaining the school on Leroy Street had been borne by St. Joseph's Church, although nearly half of the students were residents of St. Veronica's parish. AANY, O'Flynn to Corrigan, October 6, 1896; AANY, Minutes of the Meetings of the Archdiocesan Consultors, October 6, November 4, 1896; May 5, 1897, February 2, 1898. The cagey O'Flynn offered to split the profits of the sale of the Leroy Street school with McCormick and to allow the children of St. Veronica's parish to attend St. Joseph's School. When challenged by Farley to put the latter promise in writing, he declined to do so. Ibid. For the enrollment in the new school, see AANY, O'Flynn to Farley, December 6, 1904.

the church. Of the 720 names listed, 98 percent of them were Irish, with an abundance of Kellys, Murphys, and O'Briens. There was a small sprinkling of German names, but not a single Italian name. Incidentally, only 38 of the 720 contributors gave more than $5, an indication that it was still a working-class parish, albeit a few notches higher on the social ladder than St. Veronica's. The ethnic makeup of the parish changed little during the fifteen years of O'Flynn's pastorate. When the women of the parish organized a fair for the benefit of the new school in 1897, virtually every member of the coordinating committee was Irish and one of the prizes was a trip to Ireland (another prize was one share of stock in the New York Central Railroad).[36]

Father O'Flynn's identification of St. Joseph's parish with its Irish parishioners was all the more surprising in view of his own cosmopolitan background. Born in County Cork around 1848, O'Flynn received his initial higher education at St. Colman's College, Fermoy, but then he received all of his seminary education on the continent, first in Paris at the Seminary of St. Sulpice, and then in Belgium at the Catholic University of Louvain. After ordination, he remained at Louvain for an additional two years, earning a licentiate in theology, an achievement that would have made him one of the best-educated priests in the archdiocese. On first coming to New York, he served for three years as a curate in Immaculate Conception Church on East 14th Street and then as pastor of St. Mary of the Snow Church in Saugerties, New York. The latter assignment, one hundred miles north of New York City, was not a coveted position in the archdiocese. O'Flynn remained there from 1878 to 1892, with a brief interruption in 1889–1890 when he served in the Bahama Islands, which were then under the jurisdiction of the Archdiocese of New York. O'Flynn obviously did not place himself in the category of what he called "that numerous class of priests who think that any place outside of the city is not a fit appointment for them."[37]

36. AANY, O'Flynn to Corrigan, October 6, 1896; A Special Collection, October 20, 1889; New York *Catholic News*, October 31, 1897.

37. AANY, C-11, O'Flynn to Corrigan, February 4, 1886.

At St. Joseph's he proved to be an able administrator as well as a popular pastor. In 1892 Archbishop Corrigan made him the Permanent Rector of St. Joseph's Church, an honor that was reserved for the senior pastors of the most important parishes in the archdiocese. When he died in 1906, two thousand people turned out for his funeral and seventy-five carriages accompanied the funeral cortège to Calvary Cemetery. However, he seems to have confined his pastoral interest to the Irish, unlike some other Irish American priests of that era who displayed an admirable concern for the Italian immigrants arriving in New York in ever greater numbers during that era. Monsignor Michael Lavelle said with unconscious irony in his funeral eulogy that O'Flynn's building achievements would keep his memory "green" among his parishioners. Archbishop Corrigan could not attend O'Flynn's funeral because he was away from the archdiocese on a visit to Ireland.[38]

In 1896, Father O'Flynn grew alarmed because "the Italians and the others" were "encroaching" upon his parish. By the time of O'Flynn's death ten years later, the majority of the population of Greenwich Village was probably Catholic, but that was due not only to the Irish, but also to the Italians and "the others," especially the French, Spanish, and black Catholics who lived in the Village. Few, if any of them, attended St. Joseph's Church. In June 1898, at the monthly meeting of the archdiocesan consultors, Bishop Farley mentioned that there were now probably 300,000 Italians in New York City. He stressed the "need to impose upon rectors their duties to *all* the souls in their parish," and he complained especially about the fact that "some seem to feel that they are not responsible for the Italians."[39] Unfortunately, that seems to have been the situation at St. Joseph's Church at the turn of the twentieth century. In many respects, it was a model parish for the Irish Catholics of Greenwich Village. However, those Village Catholics who were not Irish had to look elsewhere to find a Catholic church where they felt welcome.

38. New York *Catholic News*, August 25, September 1, 1906.

39. AANY, Minutes of the Meetings of the Archdiocesan Consultors, June 3, 1898.

6 *Catholic Greenwich Village*

The Centenary of the Diocese

IN 1908 the Catholics of New York celebrated the centenary of their diocese with a week-long series of ceremonies that began with a Solemn High Mass in every parish on Sunday, April 26th. The observance of the centenary was officially a religious event, but it was also a demonstration of Catholic political power in New York at a time when it was reaching its apogee. The archbishop's residence at 452 Madison Avenue was commonly referred to as "the Powerhouse" in recognition of the fact that local politicians—or at least the Democrats, and they were the ones who usually mattered—paid careful attention to the wishes of the Archbishop of New York. In 1904 the newly elected mayor, George McClellan, a reform Democrat who was not a Catholic, called upon Archbishop Farley at 452 Madison Avenue to inquire if he had any candidates for city commissioners. Farley won high praise from McClellan as a "very broad-minded, liberal, fine old man" when he replied that he would prefer to have McClellan appoint fair-minded Protestants. "All that the Church wants," Farley said, "is a square deal."[1]

The centenary observance of the diocese was not only a demonstration of Catholic power in New York, but also a demonstration of Irish Catholic power. The tone was set on Monday, April 27, with the arrival from Ireland of Michael

1. George B. McClellan, Jr., *The Gentleman and the Tiger*, ed. Harold C. Syrett (Philadelphia: J. B. Lippincott Co., 1956), 237–38.

Cardinal Logue, the Archbishop of Armagh and Primate of All Ireland. His Cunard liner, the R.M.S. *Lucania,* was serenaded by a brass band composed of orphans from the Mission of the Immaculate Virgin on Staten Island. They greeted him with a rousing rendition of "The Wearing of the Green," possibly the first and last time a Cunard liner has received such a welcome. Everywhere in New York that the Irish cardinal went, he was inevitably hailed as "the 114th successor of St. Patrick." Father O'Flynn would have felt very much at home. Judging by the Celtic character of the celebration, one would never have suspected the ethnic diversity of the archdiocese. In New York City alone by that date, 42 of the 136 parishes were national parishes, representing no fewer than eleven different ethnic groups.

Ethnically speaking, Greenwich Village was a religious microcosm of the archdiocese. There were eight Catholic churches or chapels in the Village. Four of them were territorial parishes, which meant that, in effect, they were largely Irish in ethnic composition. St. Joseph's, of course, was the oldest and most important parish. Even a non-Catholic observer like Mary Kingsbury Simkhovitch noticed that only the pastor of St. Joseph's Church enjoyed the distinction of being a Permanent Rector. However, there were also substantial congregations at the other three territorial parishes, St. Bernard's on West 14th Street, St. Veronica's on Christopher Street, and St. Alphonsus on South Fifth Avenue. St. Alphonsus had been founded as a German national parish, but it had long since become predominantly Irish.

The four national parishes were parishes without territorial boundaries that had been founded for Catholics of a specific ethnic group. The dates of their founding reflected the history of Catholic immigration in New York. The oldest was the Church of St. Vincent de Paul, founded as a French national parish in 1841. From 1888 until 1947 St. Vincent de Paul maintained a chapel in the heart of Greenwich Village on Washington Square South. Of the two Italian national parishes, the older, St. Anthony of Padua on West Houston

Street, was the first permanent Italian national parish in New York, dating from 1866. The newer Italian parish, Our Lady of Pompei, dated only from 1892, when the flood of Italian immigrants necessitated the immediate building of more churches for them. The newest of the four, the Church of Our Lady of Guadalupe on West 14th Street, founded in 1902, catered to the still numerically insignificant Spanish-speaking Catholic population which was concentrated in the northwest corner of the Village. For fifteen years there had been a fifth "national" parish, St. Benedict the Moor on Bleecker Street, the first black parish in New York. Established in 1883 as a result of Father Thomas Farrell's benefaction, the church remained at the Bleecker Street location until 1898, when it moved uptown. In one way or another, each of these national parishes, and the ethnic groups they served, interacted with St. Joseph's Church as the mother church of the Catholics of Greenwich Village.

The French Village

St. Vincent de Paul is the oldest national parish still functioning in the archdiocese. Located on Canal Street near Broadway when it was founded in 1841, the clergy followed the northward migration of the congregation in 1856 and built the present parish church on West 23rd Street between Sixth and Seventh Avenues. The parish was founded and administered by the Fathers of Mercy, a small French religious congregation that came to New York at the invitation of Archbishop John Hughes. From its inception the parish was plagued by chronic financial difficulties because the French Catholic community in New York was so small and dispersed throughout the city.

In order to provide the Fathers of Mercy with an additional source of revenue, in 1888 the archdiocese took the unusual step of making St. Vincent de Paul a territorial parish as well as the national parish for all French-speaking Catholics in the archdiocese. The territorial parish comprised a tiny twelve-block area between West 23rd Street and West 28th Street from Seventh Avenue to Broadway.

However, making St. Vincent de Paul a territorial parish failed to solve the parish's financial difficulties or to end the repeated requests from the Fathers of Mercy to relocate the church farther uptown. The trustees of the church complained in 1894 that the area assigned to them was made up "largely of business men, negroes and an undue proportion of disreputable resorts." They also estimated that fewer than 5 percent of the French-speaking people who came to Mass on Sunday lived south of 23rd Street.[2]

The problem was not the lack of French-speaking Catholics south of 23rd Street, but the fact that the Church of St. Vincent de Paul was too far north for many of them to attend Mass there conveniently on Sunday. In fact, in the 1890s the area of Greenwich Village south of Washington Square was known as the French Quarter and was famous for its French restaurants. The Fathers of Mercy recognized that, ever since the transfer of the Church of St. Vincent de Paul from Canal Street to West 23rd Street, they had lost contact with much of this French-speaking population. In order to rectify the situation, in 1888 they opened Our Lady of Mercy School and a day nursery (they called it a "crèche") at 69 West 4th Street (Washington Square South), a location that was within the boundaries of St. Joseph's parish. They did so, they stated, with the encouragement of Archbishop Corrigan, in response to complaints about the lack of a parochial school for children of French-speaking parents in lower Manhattan. The Marianite Sisters of the Holy Cross took charge of Our Lady of Mercy School. They charged no tuition, ran bilingual classes, and welcomed not only French children but also Alsatians, French Canadians, Belgians, and Swiss. In the early 1890s the enrollment averaged around three hundred students. It is not likely that Father O'Flynn would have raised any objections to this school, when his own parochial school was bursting at the seams.[3]

2. AANY, Preston to Rev. G. Septier, June 16, 1888, typed copy; Memorandum Concerning the Church of St. Vincent de Paul, May 1, 1894.

3. AANY, H. L. Hoguet and Rev. G. Septier to Preston, March 8, 1888. The desire of the Fathers of Mercy for an uptown church was partially satisfied in 1910 with the establishment of the Mission Chapel of Notre Dame at Morningside Drive and 114th Street.

At the same time, the Fathers of Mercy also opened a small chapel in Our Lady of Mercy School, a step which could easily have led to friction with the pastor of St. Joseph's Church if the chapel drew parishioners away from his church. However, there is no indication that this happened, perhaps because the Fathers of Mercy restricted their apostolate to a French-speaking congregation—unlike the situation at the Church of St. Vincent de Paul, where they offered services in both French and English. The benefactors of Our Lady of Mercy Chapel included the cream of New York's French-speaking Catholic community, such as the Bouviers, Couderts, Hoguets, Binsses, and Delmonicos, as well as Archbishop Corrigan, who contributed $100. The archbishop's patronage would have quashed any thoughts that Father Salter or Father O'Flynn might have had of protesting the existence of this chapel in their parish. Our Lady of Mercy School and Chapel continued to exist until 1947, by which time the French Quarter of Greenwich Village was only a memory. The chapel's closing was hardly noticed because it had never become an integral part of the Catholic community in Greenwich Village. The 112 children in Our Lady of Mercy School were distributed among the parochial schools of St. Joseph, St. Anthony, and Our Lady of Pompei, without a whimper of protest from the parents.[4]

The African American Village

In the 1880s the area of the South Village around Bleecker and MacDougal Streets was known as "the Plantation" or "Little Africa," because it was home to the highest concentration of African Americans in New York City. The few Catholics among them were unlikely to frequent St. Joseph's (after the death of Father Farrell) or any oth-

---

The chapel later became an independent parish. As late as 1916, the Fathers of Mercy were still seeking permission from the archdiocese to move the Church of St. Vincent de Paul "out of this deserted part of the city." AANY, Pastor of St. Vincent de Paul Church to Farley, February 28, 1916.

4. AANY, Financial Statement, Church of St. Vincent-de-Paul, New York, for the Year 1888; Edward Gaffney to James Francis McIntyre, January 22, 1947.

er Catholic church, in view of the shameful treatment that black Catholics in New York had received from white Catholics. In 1846 Father Alphonse LaFont, the pastor of St. Vincent de Paul Church, had opened a French and English school for black children, but he closed it a few years later, apparently under pressure from Archbishop Hughes. A black Catholic lay woman, Harriet Thompson, wrote to Pope Pius IX in 1853 to tell him that "it [was] well known by both white and black that the Most Reverend Archbishop Hughes . . . hates the black race so much that he cannot bear them to come near him." She added: "If Your Holiness's Nuncio were to condescend while he is here to inquire about the colored people he would find many families with the parents Catholic and the children Protestant, overwhelmed with the belief that the name of Catholic amongst the black race will in a few years pass away."[5] An anonymous New Yorker, writing in February 1867 in the *Catholic Mirror,* the Baltimore Catholic newspaper, claimed that there were 1,500 black Catholics in New York City, but that "not one hundred attend Catholic worship."[6]

The author of the letter to the *Catholic Mirror* may well have been Father Thomas Farrell, one New York priest who made no secret of his sympathy for African Americans. He did more for black Catholics in the archdiocese than any other priest since Father LaFont. It is hard to imagine that a dedicated abolitionist like Farrell would not have welcomed black Catholics to St. Joseph's Church during his tenure as pastor. However, even he must have realized that, in the segregated world of that day, the only practical way to provide for the pastoral needs of black Catholics on a long-term basis was to give them a separate black parish modeled on the national parishes that had been established for the French, Germans, and other Catholic ethnic groups. As mentioned already, in his will Farrell left $5,000, in Alabama state bonds, precisely for this purpose.

5. Cited in Davis, *History of Black Catholics,* 95–96. The "nuncio" in question was Archbishop Gaetano Bedini, who visited the United States in 1853 to explore the possibility of establishing diplomatic relations between the Holy See and the United States.

6. Jack M. Arlotta, "Before Harlem: Black Catholics in the Archdiocese of New York and the Church of St. Benedict the Moor," *Dunwoodie Review* 16 (1992–1993): 73–75.

His dream of a black parish might never have been realized, however, without the dedicated efforts of two of his closest young priest disciples, Edward McGlynn and Richard Burtsell.

Farrell's will contained a stipulation that, if the $5,000 were not used to build a church for black Catholics within three years, the money should go to the Colored Orphan Asylum, a non-Catholic institution. Three years elapsed without any action on the part of the archdiocese. Just as the time limit was about to expire, Edward McGlynn pleaded with Cardinal McCloskey not to let slip this golden opportunity.[7]

Richard Burtsell took even more decisive action. Alerted indirectly by Monsignor William Quinn that a Protestant church on Bleecker Street was for sale, he asked for an interview with Cardinal McCloskey. He did not get to see McCloskey, but he outlined his proposal to Father John Farley, who was then McCloskey's secretary. "I explained," he confided to his diary, "that I was willing to undertake the experimental scheme of a colored church on my own responsibility." As a sweetener, he added: "If the scheme was a success, I would be glad to turn it over to the ecclesiastical authorities. If it turned out a failure, the loss would be upon me." Two days later McCloskey accepted Burtsell's proposal.[8]

Armed with McCloskey's carefully hedged permission, Burtsell used his own money for a mortgage to buy the former Third Universalist Church on Bleecker Street for the price of $40,000. He renamed it the Church of St. Benedict the Moor. It was not only the first black Catholic church in New York City, but the first black Catholic church north of the Mason-Dixon line. The blessing of the church on November 18, 1883, was such an unusual event that it attracted a large number of curious bystanders, who blocked traffic on Bleecker Street. The church itself was so crowded for the occasion that, with the exception of the clergy, choir, and reporters, admission was restricted to African Americans.[9]

7. AANY, McGlynn to McCloskey, July 18, 1883.

8. AANY, Burtsell, Diary, September 5, 7, 1883.

9. *New York Times,* November 19, 1883.

The congregation on Sunday included black Catholics not only from Greenwich Village and the rest of Manhattan, but from as far away as Brooklyn, Queens, and New Jersey. By January 1885 there were 510 parishioners "on record" and seventy-six children in the Sunday school. During those first thirteen months of the parish's existence, there were seventy-four baptisms, thirty-five First Communions, fifty-eight confirmations, and four marriages. It may be surmised that most parishioners were working people, but at least two, Washington Parker and Robert N. Wood, were prominent figures in local politics and instrumental in the organization of the four Colored Catholic Congresses that were held between 1887 and 1891. Still another parishioner, Dr. John E. W. Thompson, served as the U.S. minister to Haiti from 1885 to 1891. He sent a gift of fifty dollars to the church from Haiti in 1886. Not all of the worshippers were black. Both Father Burke and Father Salter mention that whites frequently attended Sunday Mass at St. Benedict the Moor. In fact Salter complained that the congregation was mainly white, which must have made it one of the few integrated churches of any denomination in New York City.[10]

Although Burtsell was the founder of the new church, he remained pastor of his own Church of the Epiphany. The first pastor of St. Benedict the Moor was Burtsell's curate, Father John E. Burke, who was to spend the next forty-two years working in ministry to black Catholics. In 1887 Burke prevailed upon the archdiocese to send him a curate, Father Thomas F. O'Keefe, a newly ordained priest who had been his altar boy in Epiphany Church. Like Burke, O'Keefe was to devote the rest of his life to the black apostolate and succeeded Burke as pastor of St. Benedict the Moor in 1907. One of John Burke's most impressive accomplishments at St. Benedict the Moor was the establishment of St. Benedict's Home, an orphan asylum for black Catholic children whom other Catholic institutions would not accept. St. Benedict's Home was originally located in the

10. AANY, Financial Report of the Church of St. Benedict the Moor, 1885; AANY, C-29, Burke to Corrigan, June 12, 1892; AANY, Salter to Corrigan, November 20, 1886.

former rectory at 120 MacDougal Street and was operated by the Dominican Sisters of Sparkill, New York. In 1890 it moved to Rye, New York, where a new building was constructed the following year. By that time St. Benedict's Home was caring for 125 children and had a staff of eleven Sparkill Dominicans.[11]

The debt on St. Benedict's Church was reduced to $14,000 in 1885, but it shot up again to $30,000 after the opening of St. Benedict's Home. Father Burke had a difficult task in meeting expenses. In 1884 a parish fair brought in $10,637.34, and collections in twenty-seven parishes raised another $8,634.24, including $400 from St. Joseph's Church and $1,131.98 from Burtsell's Church of the Epiphany. Burtsell was especially generous; in addition to the collection from his church, he contributed $1,000 of his own money to St. Benedict's in 1884 and another $200 in 1886. Other New York priests were generous also. John Drumgoole, Edward McGlynn, and Arthur Donnelly all gave $100. The laity also showed their interest in this unique parish. Eugene Kelly, the banker, contributed $500, Mrs. Adrian Iselin gave $250, and William Grace, New York's first Catholic Mayor, sent $50. Last but not least, Father Farrell's legacy was finally released from litigation, yielding $4,531.25.[12]

Nevertheless, finances remained a constant worry for Father Burke. In 1892 he explained to Archbishop Corrigan why neither he nor his parishioners had made any contribution to the archbishop's favorite building project, the new archdiocesan seminary at Dunwoodie. "I have done nothing personally," he explained, "because I have no money." He received fewer than twenty-five Mass stipends per year and gave half of his salary to charity. "Connected with my mission," he added, "the calls for help are surprisingly constant and quickly drain my scant purse. It is simply out of the question for me to give money to the new seminary." As for raising money for the seminary from his parishioners, he said, "I have done nothing

11. Arlotta, "Before Harlem," 85–90.

12. AANY, Financial Statements of the Church of St. Benedict the Moor, 1883, 1885, 1887.

through others because the 'others' are colored people scattered over the city who are unable to assist."[13]

In the 1890s the center of New York's black population shifted north from Greenwich Village to the area of Manhattan in the West 50s. Father Burke decided that the Church of St. Benedict the Moor should follow its people. Accordingly he purchased a former Protestant church on West 53rd Street and made it the new home of St. Benedict the Moor. The last service in the old church was a baptism that took place on May 1, 1898, bringing to an end one chapter of Catholic life in Greenwich Village. However, the building on Bleecker Street was not vacant long. It was quickly taken over by Italian Catholics who renamed it the Church of Our Lady of Pompei. By 1930 all that remained of "Little Africa" in Greenwich Village were two dilapidated tenement houses on West 3rd Street in the shadow of the Sixth Avenue El.[14]

The Italian Village

In 1880 there were only 12,223 Italians in New York City. In 1900 they numbered 225,024, and ten years later their numbers had doubled to 554,449. Not since the days of the Great Famine in Ireland had so many Catholic immigrants from one country descended upon New York in such a short period of time. Not all of the Italians remained in the Archdiocese of New York; many settled across the East River in the Diocese of Brooklyn. However, Bishop Farley's estimate of 300,000 Italians in the archdiocese in 1898 seems reasonable.[15] This massive influx of hundreds of thousands of Italian immigrants was the single biggest pastoral challenge faced by the Archdiocese of New York during the administrations of Archbishop Michael Corrigan (1885–1902) and John Cardinal Farley (1902–1918).[16]

13. AANY, C-29, Burke to Corrigan, June 12, 1892.

14. Ware, *Greenwich Village,* 128.

15. Mary Elizabeth Brown, "Italian Immigrants and the Catholic Church in the Archdiocese of New York, 1880–1950," Ph.D. dissertation, Columbia University, 1967, 66. AANY, Minutes of the Meetings of the Archdiocesan Consultors, June 3, 1898.

16. On Corrigan and the Italian immigration, see Stephen M. DiGiovanni, *Archbish-*

By 1900 there were at least three "Little Italys" in Manhattan. The largest was in Lower Manhattan, centered around Mulberry Street in the formerly Irish Sixth Ward. The second, made famous by Robert Orsi's book, *The Madonna of 115th Street,* was located uptown in East Harlem. The third and oldest "Little Italy" was in the South Village between Washington Square South and Houston Street. It was smaller in both area and population than the other two "Little Italys," but the number of Italians would continue to increase until, by 1930 at the latest, they constituted half the population of Greenwich Village. The first Italian settlers in Greenwich Village were mainly immigrants from northern Italy, first from Genoa, later from Piedmont and Tuscany. Not until after 1900 did southern Italians move into Greenwich Village in any considerable numbers, and even then leadership in the community remained firmly in the hands of northern Italians.[17]

Greenwich Village was also the site of the oldest permanent Italian national parish in the archdiocese, St. Anthony of Padua. The parish dates from 1866, when Italian Franciscans from upstate New York answered Archbishop McCloskey's appeal to minister to the Italian immigrants in New York City. Unlike the Neapolitans and Sicilians, the Genoese parishioners of St. Anthony's had no tradition of an annual *festa.* The first one was introduced by an enterprising pastor in the 1950s as a way of raising money from tourists.[18]

From 1866 until 1883, the Franciscans were the only religious

---

op Corrigan and the Italian Immigrants (Huntington, Ind.: Our Sunday Visitor Press, 1994). On Farley and the Italian immigration, see Mary Elizabeth Brown, *Churches, Communities and Children: Italian Immigrants in the Archdiocese of New York, 1880–1945* (New York: Center for Migration Studies, 1995).

17. Ware, *Greenwich Village,* 127, 152–53.

18. *St. Anthony of Padua Church, New York City* (South Hackensack, N.J.: Custombook, 1967). There was an earlier Italian church in New York dedicated to St. Anthony of Padua. It was founded in 1857 by Father Antonio Sanguinetti, an Italian priest, in the former Church of St. Vincent de Paul on Canal Street. However, due to Sanguinetti's difficulties with his own parishioners and with Archbishop Hughes, the church did not last. "He lacks judgment," said Father Jeremiah Cummings, the pastor of St. Stephen's Church on East 28th Street. Silvano Tomasi, *Piety and Power: The Role of Italian Parishes in the New York Metropolitan Area* (New York: Center for Migration Studies, 1975), 68–71.

community in New York caring for the Italians. However, from the beginning, their ministry was not limited to Italians. The first sacramental act recorded in the parish was the baptism of a child named Elizabeth Kelly, on March 23, 1866. Like the Fathers of Mercy at the Church of St. Vincent de Paul, the Franciscans complained they did not receive sufficient financial support from their immigrant congregation. The archdiocese accommodated the Franciscans in 1882 as they had done earlier with the Fathers of Mercy, by making St. Anthony a territorial parish as well as the national parish for all the Italians in New York City. The boundaries of the parish ran from Houston Street on the north to Broome Street on the south, and from South Fifth Avenue (present-day West Broadway) on the east to West Street on the west. Like the German Redemptorists at St. Alphonsus Church a half-century earlier, the Italian friars also discovered that the Irish were more generous contributors than their own countrymen. Predictably the reaction among the parishioners was also the same as it had been at St. Alphonsus. The Italians promptly complained that they were being neglected in favor of the Irish.[19]

Among the early pastors of St. Anthony's the outstanding figure was Father Anacletus DeAngelis. In 1888 he replaced the original St. Anthony's Church, a former Methodist church on Sullivan Street, with the present large Romanesque church on Houston Street. Father Anacletus' luck was legendary. The property on Houston Street that he wanted for the site of his new church was scheduled to be sold at auction on January 31, 1882. That day a sudden blizzard left New York City paralyzed by snow drifts. Father Anacletus was the sole bidder to show up at the auction. He got the property at the price he wanted. Despite such feats, Father John Farley, who knew the diocese as well as anyone, expressed unhappiness with the friars' management of the Italian apostolate. He told Archbishop Corrigan in 1883: "Something more must be done for these poor unfortunate people: the children are being swallowed up everyday by heretics—

19. DiGiovanni, *Archbishop Corrigan and the Italian Immigrants*, 114.

and the Franciscans are utterly inefficient." Corrigan agreed with Farley's criticism and reported to Rome in 1885 that only one of the friars at St. Anthony's took any interest in the Italians.[20]

Archbishop Corrigan's solution was to request other religious congregations, such as the Pallottines, Salesians, and Jesuits, to send Italian-speaking priests to New York. He was especially interested in bringing to New York the Pious Society of St. Charles (the Scalabrinians), a religious community founded by Bishop Giovanni Battista Scalabrini of Piacenza in 1887 specifically for missionary work among Italian immigrants. Bishop Scalabrini was also instrumental in establishing the Italian Saint Raphael Society for the protection of these immigrants. By 1892 the Scalabrinians had opened three parishes in New York. Two of them, St. Joachim and Most Precious Blood, were situated in the heart of "Little Italy" in Lower Manhattan. The third, which would prove to be the most successful, was located in Greenwich Village, only a stone's throw from St. Joseph's Church.

The Scalabrinian church in Greenwich Village had a modest beginning in a private house. The founder of the parish was an Italian Scalabrinian priest, Father Pietro Bandini, who came to New York in 1891 to serve as director of the Italian St. Raphael Society. Father Bandini, who ministered every day to the Italian immigrants on Ellis Island, established the headquarters of the St. Raphael Society in a private residence at 113 Waverly Place. With the help of Pallottine Sisters, Bandini used the house to provide temporary lodging for women and children, and he opened a labor bureau for the men. He also fitted out a room on the first floor as a chapel, which he dedicated to Our Lady of Pompei. He celebrated the first Mass there on May 8, 1892, the day which is regarded as the founding date of Our Lady of Pompei Church. The church would move twice in the next

20. AANY, C-2, Farley to Corrigan, November 1, 1883, cit. in DiGiovanni, *Archbishop Corrigan and the Italian Immigrants*, 114–15. Farley's letter is no longer available in the archives of the Archdiocese of New York. Donald Tricario's criticism that St. Anthony's apostolate to the Italians was "constrained by the policies of an Irish archdiocese" is simply not true and ignores the complaints of both Corrigan and Farley about the friars. Tricario, *Italians of Greenwich Village*, 12.

six years, first to a former Protestant church on Sullivan Street, and then to the former church of St. Benedict the Moor at Bleecker and Downing Streets. It finally found a permanent home in 1928 in the magnificent building that was erected one block west of the old church at the corner of Carmine and Bleecker Streets.[21]

The pastoral care of the Italians in New York was not left entirely in the hands of the religious communities. In 1889 Archbishop Corrigan issued a pastoral letter in Italian welcoming the new immigrants to the archdiocese and listing the names and churches of thirty-six Italian-speaking diocesan priests who were eager to serve them. At the head of the list was St. Patrick's Cathedral and *noi stessi* ("we ourselves"). Almost all of the priests on the list were Irish Americans with names like Burke and Flynn and McSweeny, many of whom had spent their seminary years in Rome, as Corrigan himself had. The attitude of the Irish American New York clergy to the Italians varied greatly. There was a huge cultural gap between what Walter Elliott once called the "catacombical public worship" favored by most Celtic Americans and the warm emotional flavor of Italian devotional practices.[22] The standard thirty-minute silent Latin Mass seemed like a low church Protestant service to many Italian immigrants. Reciprocally, some manifestations of Italian popular religion, like the annual *festa,* seemed little better than pagan superstition to Irish American pastors. One of them, Father Thomas F. Lynch, commented, "The fact is that the Catholic Church in America is to the mass of Italians almost like a new religion."[23]

21. Mary Elizabeth Brown, *From Italian Villages to Greenwich Village: Our Lady of Pompei, 1892–1992* (New York: Center for Migration Studies, 1992), 15–16.

22. Archives of the Ryan Memorial Library and Historical Collections, St. Charles Borromeo Seminary, Philadelphia, Elliott to Herman Heuser, June 6, 1909. Elliott had in mind particularly Archbishop John Ireland of St. Paul, but he also told Heuser that Archbishop Corrigan "simply foamed at the bare mention of vernacularity" in the liturgy.

23. Bernard [sic] J. Lynch, "The Italians in New York," *The Catholic World* 47 (1888), 72. It is obvious from internal evidence that the author of the article was Thomas F. Lynch, the pastor of Transfiguration Church on Mott Street, a parish that was undergoing a rapid transformation from an Irish parish to an Italian parish at that time.

Many New York pastors complained that the Italians did not support the Church as generously as did the Irish. At Transfiguration Church, Father Lynch said: "These people would hardly be able by themselves to erect and support a church in New York, but they could certainly share in the support of any church which is in a tolerably good financial condition."[24] As a result of such advice, Archbishop Corrigan hesitated to establish independent Italian national parishes for fear that they would not be financially viable. Instead, he frequently created "annex parishes," that is, Italian parishes that were attached to already existing territorial parishes.[25]

Unfortunately, what this often meant in practice was that the Italians were relegated to the basement of the "Irish" church for Sunday Mass, a practice which many of them found insensitive and demeaning. One Irish American curate at St. Jerome's Church in the Bronx, Father Patrick J. Mahoney, tried to explain the lack of financial support from the Italians. He told Archbishop Corrigan: "*Andare alla chiesa e pagare* [Go to church and pay] is something very harsh to a poor Italian. They have been brought up in Italy where they had to pay little or nothing. . . . If we treat the present generation generously, I believe that their children will pay nearly as well as other Catholics when they shall have been rightly instructed."[26]

By the early twentieth century the Italians of Greenwich Village could boast of two flourishing churches, St. Anthony of Padua and Our Lady of Pompei. In 1903 St. Anthony's claimed to have eight thousand parishioners and a parochial school with fifteen sisters

24. AANY, G-33, Thomas F. Lynch, Some Facts Concerning the Italian Congregation of the Church of the Transfiguration, Mott Street, n.d

25. "This is called an annex congregation," explained Lynch, "because it is so; and it must be so. This is proved, first, by the total breakdown of every autonomous Italian church in this section of the country. It begins Italian and ends Irish—except in the personnel of the clergy—who, like the Normans in Ireland, sometimes become *Hiberniores Hiberniis*. It is further proved by experience. For with careful prudence, with every known appliance of raising funds applicable to them, this Italian congregation, two thousand strong, being a fair average of the whole population, give a revenue every week of but about forty-five dollars." Lynch, "Italians in New York," 71.

26. AANY, G-59, Mahoney to Corrigan, May 5, 1893.

and 887 children. There were seven priests assigned to the parish, which was not an excessive number in view of the fact that, during the previous year, there had been 999 baptisms and 258 marriages, and some of the friars celebrated Mass in other parishes on Sunday. The sisters who staffed the school were not Italians, but Irish Americans. Our Lady of Pompei Church claimed an even larger number of parishioners, 8,500. There was no parochial school until 1929, but there were 777 children in the Sunday school. Since there were only seven teachers, one wonders what kind of religious instruction the children received. The Scalabrinians had three priests assigned to the parish. They must have been kept busy with the 547 baptisms and 196 marriages that were recorded in 1902.

Although the sacramental statistics in these two parishes were impressive, they pale in comparison with the numbers recorded in some other Italian parishes. The Scalabrinian Church of St. Joachim on Roosevelt Street claimed 23,300 "souls," and the "annex parish" at St. Patrick's Old Cathedral claimed 28,000 "souls." Obviously these figures are only estimates of the number of Italians residing within the parish, not regular churchgoers. However, the sacramental statistics give a clearer picture of the heavy pastoral demands made upon the clergy in these Italian parishes. In 1902 the Pallottine priests at Our Lady of Mount Carmel Church in East Harlem baptized 2,721 children, and the Jesuits at the Sicilian Church of Our Lady of Loretto on Elizabeth Street baptized 1,188 children. At the Church of the Most Precious Blood on Baxter Street, which the Franciscans had taken over from the Scalabrinians, the friars baptized 1,914 children and witnessed 488 marriages in 1902.[27]

There are indications that the close proximity of the two Italian parishes in Greenwich Village created a certain friction between them and that the Scalabrinians were more popular than the Fran-

27. Thomas F. Meehan, "Evangelizing the Italians," *The Messenger* 39 (1903): 16–17. Meehan obtained the statistics on the Italian parishes from Father Patrick J. Hayes, the secretary to Archbishop Farley and future Cardinal Archbishop of New York, who had access to the annual *cura animarum* reports submitted to the Chancery Office by every pastor.

ciscans. When both churches were assigned the same evening for their Lenten devotions in 1899, Father Anacletus asked the Chancery Office to change the day assigned to St. Anthony's from Thursday to Monday so that his parish would not have to compete with Our Lady of Pompei. Father Thomas Lynch claimed that his Italian parishioners at Transfiguration Church disliked the Franciscans at St. Anthony's and stayed away in droves when they conducted a mission in his parish. An attempt to organize the St. Vincent de Paul Society in St. Anthony's for the benefit of poor Italians was unsuccessful because the men of the parish failed to respond. As late as 1898 Archbishop Corrigan was still expressing unhappiness with the work of the friars at St. Anthony's. The fact that, within ten years of its founding, the Church of Our Lady of Pompei had as many parishioners as the much older Church of St. Anthony may well indicate that, like Archbishop Corrigan, the Italians of Greenwich Village preferred the Scalabrinians to the Franciscans.[28]

In the 1880s, before Our Lady of Pompei Church was founded, several of the Irish American churches in Greenwich Village made efforts to reach out to the Italians. Among the Italian-speaking priests on the list published by Archbishop Corrigan in 1889 were Father John Milo at St. Veronica's, Father T. F. McManus at St. Bernard's, and Father John Burke at St. Benedict the Moor.[29] St. Joseph's Church, with four priests, is notable by its absence from the list. Neither Father Salter nor Father O'Flynn seems to have taken any initiative in providing for the Italian immigrants living within the parish boundaries. In fact, both expressed fears that the Italian national parishes might attract some parishioners away from St. Joseph's.

Back in 1886, Salter complained to Archbishop Corrigan: "The parish is now surrounded by churches, each one drawing a large

28. AANY, G-23, Anacletus to Rev. Dear Father, January 12, 1899; Anacletus to Corrigan, January 14, 1898; AANY, G-33, Lynch, Some Facts Concerning the Italian Congregation of the Church of the Transfiguration, Mott Street, n.d.

29. AANY, Michele Agostino Corrigan Ai Cattolici Italiani dimoranti in questa Diocesi, January 15, 1889.

percentage of communicants from us." He mentioned specifically that most of the Irish American longshoremen had transferred their allegiance from St. Joseph's to St. Anthony's when that parish received territorial boundaries in 1882. He also claimed that most of the people attending the Church of St. Benedict the Moor were whites, who should have been coming to his church. Salter's claims cannot be taken at face value, since at the time he was deliberately minimizing the number of his parishioners in the hope of forestalling the establishment of a new parish in Greenwich Village. What is clear, however, is that he did not express any sense of responsibility for the Italians. He regarded them as foreigners who belonged somewhere else on Sunday morning.[30]

Before Father Bandini opened his little chapel on Waverly Place in 1892, he told the archdiocesan authorities: "I did all what [*sic*] human prudence could suggest to me." He called upon Father O'Flynn to assure him that his little chapel would not be in competition with St. Joseph's Church. The response that he got from O'Flynn was a tirade against the Jesuits at St. Francis Xavier for stealing his parishioners, a long-standing grievance with pastors of St. Joseph's. Bandini promised that this would not happen at his "microscopical Church." He even posted a sign on the door of the chapel announcing that admission was restricted to Italians. Father Bandini's caution and courtesy were no match, however, for the paranoia that seems to have been rampant on the subject in St. Joseph's rectory. Within three months O'Flynn reported Bandini to the Chancery Office for stealing his parishioners. When Bandini denied the accusation, Father James F. McLaughlin, a curate at St. Joseph's Church, practically called him a liar.[31]

It is small wonder that Bandini was happy to leave New York when the opportunity arose in 1896 for him to serve as chaplain to an Italian agricultural colony in Arkansas. Bandini was also a poor

30. AANY, Salter to Corrigan, November 20, 1886.

31. AANY, G-77, Bandini to Reverend Dear Father, August 11, 1892; McLaughlin to Rev Dear Sir, August 22, 1892.

financial manager. After his departure, Archbishop Corrigan came under pressure from his real estate agent and from some unidentified priests to close Our Lady of Pompei Church. Happily Corrigan resisted the pressure, and the parish survived under Bandini's successor, Father Francesco Zaboglio, thanks to two Irish American New Yorkers who showed a more enlightened attitude to the Italians than Father O'Flynn. One was Miss Annie Leary, a wealthy heiress who became a generous benefactor. The other was John Farley, who was then auxiliary bishop and vicar general. He told Archbishop Corrigan that the priests who were criticizing Our Lady of Pompei were "neither capable nor interested in the success of the work there." He expressed confidence in Father Zaboglio as a pious and honest man, and sent him a check for $750 to supplement the money that he had received from Miss Leary. He warned Archbishop Corrigan that it would be a mistake to close even one Italian parish at a time when "we must provide churches for these Italians who are pouring in at an unusually rapid rate now."[32] Our Lady of Pompei stayed open.

The Spanish Village

By the turn of the twentieth century a small colony of Spanish Catholics had established themselves in the northwest corner of Greenwich Village, in the area along the Hudson River south of West 14th Street. It was minuscule in size compared with the Italian community and proved to be ephemeral. By 1930 it had virtually disappeared. In 1902, however, the Spanish presence in Greenwich Village was sufficiently strong to lead to the establishment of still another national parish, Our Lady of Guadalupe. Located in a former private residence on the north side of West 14th Street, the church itself was just outside the northern boundary of Greenwich Village. The Spanish population that it served was made up mostly of immigrants from Galicia, who worked as seamen, longshoremen, or laborers. As was the case with the Italians, the women were more

32. AANY, G-15, Farley to Corrigan, April 25, May 28, 1896.

faithful churchgoers than the men. Even more than the Italians, the Spanish formed an isolated, tightly knit community with their own grocery stores, barber shops, and taverns. When the women traveled the five or six blocks from their home to the stores on West 14th Street, they regarded it as a major adventure.[33]

Archbishop Corrigan established Our Lady of Guadalupe Church as the national parish for all the Spanish-speaking Catholics in the Archdiocese of New York. The building was blessed on February 23, 1902, and confided to the care of a small religious community, the Augustinians of the Assumption. Although French in origin, the Assumptionists included a number of Spanish-speaking priests. After their recent expulsion from France because of their notorious role in the Dreyfus affair (their Paris daily, *La Croix*, was rabidly anti-Semitic), the Assumptionists had a surplus of priests available to staff parishes like Our Lady of Guadalupe. From the beginning, they were unhappy with the small size of the church, which was little bigger than a convent chapel. In 1903 the pastor told the new archbishop, John Farley, that they could only hope to attract Spanish Catholics to Mass if they had a "*vrai temple*" (real church) that would appeal to their pride. He seemed to expect the archdiocese to provide it for them.[34]

Archbishop Farley did not provide the Assumptionists with the *vrai temple* they desired, but he did give them permission to enlarge their little church in 1905. He also gave them some unsolicited paternal advice based on his own long experience in dealing with both the diocesan clergy and various ethnic groups in the archdiocese. He predicted that the Irish in New York would be more generous to them than the Spanish. However, he warned them not to recruit the Irish to Our Lady of Guadalupe Church, but to let them come on their own initiative, so that neighboring pastors could not accuse them of stealing their parishioners. It proved to be wise advice in both respects. The Assumptionists soon discovered that the Irish

33. Ware, *Greenwich Village*, 227–31.

34. AANY, Thomas Darbois, A.A., to Farley, April 26, 1903; Paul Journet, A.A., to Hayes, February 23, 1927.

came unsolicited to Mass at Our Lady of Guadalupe and contributed more to the upkeep of the church than the Spanish for whom the parish had been founded. As Farley anticipated, however, this development did not escape the notice of Father Clark, the pastor of the Jesuit Church of St. Francis Xavier on West 16th Street, who complained that the Assumptionists were poaching on his territory. He voiced his complaints in almost the same terms that the pastors of St. Joseph's had been using about the pastors of St. Francis Xavier for several decades.[35]

For almost forty years Our Lady of Guadalupe Church advertised itself as "the parish for all Spanish-speaking people in New York," where they had the right to be baptized, married, and buried. This role gave the parish its raison d'être even after the disappearance of the local Spanish community in Greenwich Village. The pastor told Auxiliary Bishop John J. Dunn in 1926: "Our parish being a Spanish-American parish, comprises all the faithful coming from these parts of America and [the] Ancient [sic] World where the Spanish tongue is in common use." The Assumptionists provided a full range of pastoral services, including six Masses on Sundays, four Masses on weekdays, and confessions and baptisms every day of the year. Despite its status as the official Spanish parish for the whole archdiocese, the Irish from the local neighborhood were very much in evidence. Most of the members of the boys' championship basketball team in 1937 had names like Reilly, McLoughlin, and McGee, and the Irish Emigrant Society advertised trips to Ireland in the bilingual parish bulletin.[36]

The Catholic Village in an Irish Church

By the turn of the twentieth century, if not before, the population of Greenwich Village had become predominantly Catholic.[37] The

35. AANY, Zachary Saint-Martin, A.A., to John J. Dunn, February 28, 1926.

36. Ibid., and *Church Bulletin o Calendario Mensual,* Our Lady of Guadalupe Church, March 1937, October 1938, June 1939.

37. In addition to the ethnic groups already mentioned, there was a small community of Lithuanian Catholics who, after many years of effort, erected the Church of Our

anonymous author of the WPA *New York City Guide* wrote condescendingly: "By 1910 the transformation of Greenwich Village had been completed. The American Ward had become Ward 9, a foreign ward, leading its life of pushcart, café, fiesta, and bar, its land values as cheap as in nearly any settled section of the city, its people faithful followers of the Roman Catholic Church and of Tammany."[38]

Catholic Greenwich Village was hardly a homogeneous religious community, however, for ethnic divisions ran as deep as the common religious bonds. The one exception was the relationship between the two oldest Catholic ethnic groups in the Village, the Germans and the Irish. The old animosities that had marked their relationship at St. Alphonsus Church earlier in the nineteenth century were now largely forgotten. The Germans and Irish were easily the two most assimilated Catholic ethnic groups. Since the Irish vastly outnumbered the Germans, however, they virtually absorbed the remnants of the once flourishing German Catholic community. St. Alphonsus preserved only the barest traces of its origins as a German national parish, and it is significant that the Germans were the one ethnic group that felt comfortable in the heavily Irish atmosphere of St. Joseph's Church.

The smaller Catholic ethnic groups, the French, Spanish, and African Americans (if one may use that designation for a multiethnic black community), remained largely isolated from the rest of the religious and civic community in Greenwich Village. Their churches also tended to draw worshippers from outside the Village to a greater extent than the other churches, since the African American and Spanish churches were the only ones in New York City for their

---

Lady of Vilna on Broome Street in 1905. The church never became part of the Catholic life of the Village and in 1930 had an average Sunday Mass attendance of only three hundred. Back in 1910, when Greenwich House organized a cooking class for Lithuanian girls, the director noted that the pastor, Father Joseph Shestokas, "is much pleased to think that anyone is interested in his people." AANY, Our Lady of Vilna Parish File, *Cura Animarum* Report, 1933; Ware, *Greenwich Village*, 128, 318; GHP, Mary Kingsbury Simkhovitch, Report of the Director, November 16, 1910.

38. *New York City Guide* (New York: Random House, 1956), 128. The *Guide* was first published in 1939.

respective ethnic groups. The African Americans were pretty well gone by the turn of the century, as was their Church of St. Benedict the Moor, which had moved uptown. The French and Spanish enclaves in the Village also disappeared after World War I, although, as mentioned earlier, the Church of Our Lady of Guadalupe found a new purpose as the religious center for the increasing number of Portuguese, Puerto Rican, and Cuban immigrants who were spreading throughout New York City.

The most important factor in the shaping of the Catholic community in Greenwich Village was the relationship between the two largest Catholic ethnic groups, the Irish and the Italians. They still lived in separate worlds at the turn of the twentieth century. Cultural differences were often exacerbated by competition for the same jobs, especially on the Hudson River docks. They only began to intermingle (integrate would be too strong a word) after World War I, when members of both groups moved up the economic ladder and into some of the better housing on the same streets.[39]

In view of the structure of the Catholic Church, the role of the clergy was bound to be crucial in giving direction to the Catholic community. Unfortunately, St. Joseph's Church, which might have been expected to take the lead as the oldest, largest, and wealthiest Catholic church in Greenwich Village, provided no leadership at all. After the death of Father Thomas Farrell in 1880, his successors retreated from involvement in the affairs of the larger Catholic community in the Village and displayed a narrow concern for protecting their own turf from other Catholic ethnic groups. Father John Salter even opposed the creation of a new parish in Greenwich Village that was intended to provide additional pastoral care for the Irish.

On the other hand, some Irish American clerics showed admirable concern for the plight of their Italian co-religionists. Father John Burke did extraordinary work not only as the first pastor of St. Benedict the Moor, but also in making himself available to the Italians. The pastor of St. Veronica's added an Italian-speaking priest to

39. Ware, *Greenwich Village*, 130.

his staff, and the Italian-speaking pastor of St. Bernard's volunteered to assist in the ministry to Italians. On the diocesan level, both Archbishop Corrigan and Cardinal Farley have rightly been praised by historians for their efforts on behalf of the Italian immigrants. What also emerges from a study of the Church in Greenwich Village is the unexpectedly positive role played by John Farley for a quarter-century before he became the Archbishop of New York, first as secretary to Cardinal McCloskey and then as vicar general under Archbishop Corrigan. Farley called attention to the inadequate pastoral care provided by the Franciscans at St. Anthony's in the 1880s, saved Our Lady of Pompei from suppression in the 1890s, and was a consistent advocate of an expanded apostolate to the Italians at the meetings of the archdiocesan consultors throughout this period.[40]

Finally, one should not overlook the role of the Irish American laity. Whatever their economic rivalry with the Italians and their social antipathy toward them, they showed a willingness to worship with their fellow Italian Catholics in their churches. Not only did they frequent their churches, but they provided them (and black, French, and Spanish Catholics) with indispensable financial support.[41] Professor Lawrence McCaffrey once said that only the Irish

40. Farley was incensed in 1903 when *La Civiltà Cattolica*, the Roman Jesuit periodical, called upon American Catholics to do more for the Italian immigrants. He wrote an uncharacteristically blunt letter to the editor, Father Salvatore Brandi, S.J., referring him to the recent article by Thomas F. Meehan in *The Messenger* [39 (1903):16–32]. In that article, Farley told Brandi, "[It] is pointed out very clearly and statistically what has been done by the late Archbishop for the salvation of the Italians, under circumstances unprecedented, perhaps, in the history of the Church; hundreds of thousands of poor people, our co-religionists, without money, and, I am sorry to say, many thousands of them without any knowledge of the Faith; and these coming within the short space of a few years, untrained in the ways of providing financially for their religious wants."

"I should like to know," Farley asked in a parting shot, "how such a condition of things would be met in Italy, if the case were reversed." AANY, I-6, Farley to Brandi, March 20, 1903. Farley's letter produced the desired results. Shortly thereafter *La Civiltà Cattolica* published a glowing account of the way that the Archdiocese of New York cared for Italian immigrants. "Gli Emigranti Italiani a Nuova York, *La Civiltà Cattolica* 55 (April 4, 1904): 172–79.

41. For a survey of the contribution made by Irish Americans to other Catholic ethnic groups in the Archdiocese of New York, see Thomas J. Shelley, "'Only One Class of

could have provided the leadership for the multiethnic community that constituted the Catholic Church in the United States.[42] Whether or not his thesis is true about the Catholic Church in the United States as a whole, it was certainly true of the Catholic Church in Greenwich Village during that half-century that it was a predominantly Catholic Village.

People to Draw Upon for Support': Irish-Americans and the Archdiocese of New York," *American Catholic Studies* 112 (2001): 1–22.

42. Lawrence J. McCaffrey, *The Irish Diaspora in America* (Bloomington: Indiana University Press, 1976), 9. See also Philip Gleason, "Thanks to the Irish," *America*, May 14, 1966, 696–98.

7 Et in Bohemia Ego

Long-Haired Men and Short-Haired Women

IN THE FIRST DECADES of the twentieth century, Greenwich Village became nationally famous as the bohemia of the United States. A combination of low rents, quaint surroundings, and a tolerance for unconventional lifestyles and radical politics attracted writers, artists, dramatists, and poets to the area. It was not an altogether new development. Throughout the nineteenth century, writers as different as Thomas Paine, James Fenimore Cooper, Herman Melville, Edgar Allan Poe, and Mark Twain all made their home in Greenwich Village for more or less extended periods, but the presence of these individuals never turned the area into a literary quarter. After 1900, however, a major change took place when the Village became a magnet for avant-garde intellectuals and would-be intellectuals from all across the country. Greenwich Village became New York's equivalent of the Latin Quarter in Paris, as aspiring writers and artists congregated close to one another in converted rookeries, mingled in the tea rooms and restaurants that catered to them, and supported a half-dozen short-lived political and literary journals.

Although the literati never constituted more than a tiny percentage of the total population, they gave the Village its reputation as a hotbed of nonconformity. The luminaries included Max Eastman, the editor of the *Masses*, the most famous of the Village magazines, which, as Alfred Kazin pointed out, "the masses notoriously never read." Founded in 1913, the magazine's offices were located at 91 Greenwich Street. It numbered among its staff a young poet named John Reed, who was to become an ardent admirer of the Bolshevik revolution, and a young journalist from the Midwest named Dorothy Day, whose spiritual odyssey was to lead her in the opposite direction, to the Catholic Church. Even in her radical days Dorothy Day occasionally visited St. Joseph's Church, sitting in a back row gazing at the altar.[1] Lincoln Steffens, the muckraking journalist, and Theodore Dreiser, the controversial novelist, both made their home in the Village. As Dreiser's material fortunes improved, he moved from a flophouse on Bleecker Street to an elegant apartment on St. Luke's Place. The painter John Sloan, the novelist Willa Cather, the poets E.E. Cummings, Floyd Dell, Marianne Moore, and Edna St. Vincent Millay (who won the Pulitzer Prize for poetry in 1923), the literary critics Edmund Wilson and Van Wyck Brooks, and the novelist Sherwood Anderson were all residents of the Village at one time or another.

Eugene O'Neill did much of his serious drinking at the Golden Swan (a.k.a. the Hell Hole), a vintage neighborhood Irish bar at the corner of Sixth Avenue and West 4th Street with an eclectic clientele that ranged from neighborhood widows to the Hudson Dusters, a notorious local gang. There O'Neill discovered many of the characters who would appear in *The Iceman Cometh* a quarter of a century later.[2] Long before that, O'Neill's earliest plays were produced at the Provincetown Playhouse at 139 MacDougal Street. Polly's restaurant, located next door to the Provincetown Playhouse, became a favorite gathering place for Village bohemians, as did the Liberal Club and the adjoining Washington Square Book Shop. Not all of the habitués of the Village were poor refugees from small town America. Gertrude Vanderbilt Whitney, a wealthy New York heiress,

1. William D. Miller, *Dorothy Day: A Biography* (New York: Harper and Row, 1982), 113. After the baptism of her daughter and her own baptism in 1927, Dorothy Day moved to an apartment on West 14th Street "in order to be near the Church of Our Lady of Guadalupe," where she found a sympathetic confessor in the person of Father Zachary Saint-Martin, A.A. Robert Coles, *Dorothy Day: A Radical Devotion* (Reading, Mass.: Addison-Wesley Publishing Company, 1987), 9.

2. Arthur and Barbara Gelb, *O'Neill* (New York: Harper and Row, 1962), 285.

opened a studio in a remodeled stable in MacDougal Alley in 1907 and later used her considerable fortune to establish an art museum on West 8th Street. Likewise, Mabel Dodge turned her fancy apartment at 23 Fifth Avenue into a salon where society people from uptown could rub shoulders with raffish Village types.[3]

More typical was the experience of Malcolm Cowley, a native of Pennsylvania who became the literary editor of *The New Republic.* He described how, after World War I, he and other like-minded young writers "drifted to Manhattan, to the crooked streets south of Fourteenth, where you could rent a furnished hall-bedroom for two or three dollars weekly or the top floor of a rickety house for 30 dollars a month." "We came," he said, "because living was cheap, because friends of ours had come already . . . because it seemed that New York was the only city where a young writer could be published." Edmund Wilson had one of his fictional characters describe Greenwich Village as a place where "those heroes of my youth, the artists and prophets of the Village [had come] from the American factories and farms, from the farthest towns and prairies . . . [where] they had lived with their own imaginations and followed their own thought." Still another writer remembered Greenwich Village in those days as a place where "there was an inexhaustible supply of young men and women from the provinces seeking to escape from having to enter the family business in some place about which Sinclair Lewis was writing."[4]

From her vantage point at Greenwich House, Mary Kingsbury Simkhovitch noted the willingness of gullible newcomers to the neighborhood to pay exorbitant rents for the substandard housing that she had been criticizing for years. In an often-quoted comment,

3. "'Bourgeoisie and Bohemians': Village Peoples," in *Greenwich Village, Culture and Counterculture,* 93–109.

4. Malcolm Cowley, quoted in Alfred Kazin, "Greenwich Village Writers," in *Greenwich Village, Culture and Counterculture,* 299. Edmund Wilson, quoted in Martin Green, *New York 1913: The Armory Show and the Paterson Strike Pageant* (New York: Collier Books, 1988), 16; Kenneth Campbell, "The Village of Other Days," *New York Times,* March 27, 1965.

she said, "It was certainly amusing to us who had fought against cellar lodgings as unhealthy, damp and unfit for human habitation, as they were, to see them revived as 'one-room studios' and let at often six times the price of the former rentals."[5]

In popular estimation, all the residents of Greenwich Village came to be identified with the most radical causes espoused by the disaffected activists who lived there. Somewhere in the Village at sometime or another, someone was advocating socialism, communism, syndicalism, anarchism, feminism, eugenics, free love, birth control, cubism, fauvism, imagist poetry, Freudian psychology, modern art, or some combination of the above. Two events in 1913 brought the radicalism of the Village to the attention of a wider public. One was the so-called Armory Show, the International Exhibition of Modern Art, held at the Sixty-Ninth Regiment Armory on Lexington Avenue between 25th and 26th Streets from February 17 to March 15. Although far removed in locale from Greenwich Village, the Armory Show gave many New Yorkers their first taste of the modern art that was popular with the Village artists and the patrons who frequented Gertrude Vanderbilt Whitney's studios or Mabel Dodge's salon. Mabel Dodge told Gertrude Stein, "I was going to dynamite New York and nothing would stop me." The Armory Show had a profound impact on the American art world, but another event three months later had an even more disturbing effect on a much wider circle of New Yorkers.[6]

On the evening of June 7, Mabel Dodge, John Reed, John Sloan, and other Village radicals staged a "pageant" in Madison Square Garden that reenacted some of the events in the long and bitter strike that was still in progress in Paterson, New Jersey, between silk workers and factory owners. Although the *Masses* gave the strike extensive coverage, most of the New York press had deliberately ignored it because it had been organized by the International Workers of the World, the most radical labor union in the United States. On

5. Simkhovitch, *Greenwich House*,110–11.
6. Green, *New York 1913*, 288.

June 7, 1913, more than a thousand strikers participated as actors in the pageant; they marched through the streets of lower Manhattan from the Lackawana Railroad Ferry Terminal to Madison Square Garden singing the Marseillaise. Inside the Garden itself not a single American flag was to be seen that evening. The strike collapsed the following month, but the sympathetic publicity that it received at the pageant only confirmed the worst suspicions of many New Yorkers that Greenwich Village was a hotbed of subversive radicals. The *New York Times* accused the organizers of the pageant of "stimulating mad passion against law and order and promulgating a gospel of discontent."[7]

In December 1919 an article appeared in the *New York Times Magazine* recounting the adventures in Greenwich Village of a Dr. I. L. Nascher, a physician who was said to specialize in nervous disorders. According to the article, Dr. Nascher spent several months in the Village incognito, disguised in "velveteens, sandals and a smock," observing the lifestyle of the natives. He allegedly reported in a medical journal that the real bohemians were suffering from a disease called "esthesiomania," which he classified as a form of insanity. The author of the article characterized this disease as "marked by erratic moral opinions which happen not to be yours or mine or Miss Ella's." Miss Ella was Ella Froeligh, a veteran schoolteacher, who declared that, after fifty years in the classroom at Public School 3, she was completely oblivious to her nonconformist neighbors in the Village and did not have the slightest curiosity to learn more about them. It is impossible to tell whether the satirical article was fact or fiction, but, in either case, it indicated New Yorkers' general estimation of Greenwich Village.[8]

The onset of Prohibition added another dimension to the sinister reputation of Greenwich Village. Rightly or wrongly, it was regarded as one of the easiest places in the city to obtain illegal alcohol because of the prevalence of restaurants with ready access to home-

7. *New York Times,* June 8, 9, 1913: Green, *New York 1913,* 288.
8. *New York Times Magazine,* December 21, 1919.

made wine and bootleg whiskey. As a consequence, Greenwich Village was also associated with the proliferation of organized crime, which was one of the unanticipated side effects of "the experiment noble in purpose," as President Herbert Hoover once called Prohibition. Perhaps the least publicized of all the underground activities that flourished in the Village were the gay and lesbian relationships that were quietly formed and occasionally surfaced in events like the costume balls at Webster Hall on East 11th Street near Third Avenue. The frequent mention in the press of "long-haired men" and "short-haired women" in the Village may have been a veiled reference to gays and lesbians. Needless to say, neither of these words was ever used in print. In fact, the *New York Times* did not even allow the use of the word "homosexual" until 1926.[9]

In 1924 Sister Manuella, the superior of St. Joseph's Convent, complained to a reporter about the deterioration that she had observed in the Village during her thirty years of residence there. When she first arrived in the Village, she said, "There was none of the gay life that one hears of in the Village today. Waverly Place was a quiet old street, full of respectable people." Obviously Sister Manuella was not using the word "gay" with the connotation that it would have fifty years later. No woman of her background would have dared to mention such a taboo topic to a newspaper reporter. Even some Village residents with otherwise impeccably radical credentials drew the line at homosexuality. As recently as 1961, an English professor at New York University could publicly associate homosexuality with narcotics as "the obviously reprehensible elements of Village life." According to George Chauncey, however, "by the twenties the presence of both gay men and lesbians in the Village was firmly established."[10]

9. Charles Kaiser, *The Gay Metropolis* (New York: Harcourt Brace, 1997), 19.

10. Rose Lee, "A Convent in Greenwich Village," *New York Times Magazine*, August 17, 1924. David Boroff, "An Appeal to Save the Village," *New York Times Magazine*, May 7, 1961, 78. Boroff used the word "gay" in the same sense as Sister Manuella. George Chauncey, "Long-Haired Men and Short-Haired Women," *Greenwich Village, Culture and Counterculture*, 160.

By that time the political radicalism of the Village was a spent force, but the Village itself loomed larger than ever in the popular imagination as America's bohemia and became a popular tourist attraction. New York journalists poked fun at unwary visitors from Kansas who came to the Village to see the real bohemians and only discovered other Kansans pretending to be real bohemians. The double-decker buses of the Fifth Avenue Coach Company, which were popular with many sightseers from out of town, ended their southbound runs at the Washington Arch, leaving the passengers within easy walking distance of notorious tourist traps like Bruno's Garrett or one of "Romany Marie's" taverns. Guido Bruno was an alias for Kurt Josef Kisch, an enterprising gentleman who commuted to the Village every day from his home in Yonkers. He happened to be born near Prague, making him by the accident of birth one of the few authentic Bohemians in the Village. Romany Marie claimed to be the daughter of a Romanian gypsy chief, but her dubious pedigree provoked the editor of *The Quill*, a popular Village magazine, to say: "I've heard Delancey Street called a lot of things but this is the first time I've heard it called Romania."[11]

"The Ninth-Warders and the Villagers"

The older established residents of the Village resented the influx of both the bohemians, authentic and otherwise, and the tourists whom they attracted to the neighborhood. The patrician Washington Square Association complained that the cabarets, tea rooms, and dance halls brought to the Village "a vicious and sometimes criminal element which [is] a constant menace to the peace and property of the neighborhood." The old-timers found a sympathetic spokesman in Justice John M. Tierney of the Bronx Supreme Court. In presiding over a messy divorce case in 1919 that involved a "love nest" in Greenwich Village, Justice Tierney said, "This section some years ago was one of the most delightful in the city. . . . I am aston-

11. Jan Seidler Ramirez, "The Tourist Trade Takes Hold," *Greenwich Village, Culture and Counterculture*, 376, 384.

ished at the people and the change of character that the neighborhood has undergone." The judge especially deplored the proliferation of cabarets. "I cannot understand why people go to these cabarets to dine and dance," he said. "They order expensive food and then begin dancing and kick dust into it."[12]

Some of the older residents now distinguished themselves from the newcomers, the Villagers, by resurrecting the old political name for the area and describing themselves as Ninth Warders. One of them was a local judge named House. He announced in Traffic Court: "I lived for a great many years in the old Ninth Ward, and we were very proud of it because it was known as the old American Ward." He added an incautious comment that today would cost him his job: "In the old days," he said, "if one wanted to find real aristocracy or a real Christian, you could depend on this section of the city." Still another member of the lesser judiciary who shared those sentiments was Municipal Court Judge William J. A. Caffrey, a prominent Catholic resident in the Village. Speaking at a dinner in Greenwich House in May 1922, Judge Caffrey said, "The types of people who have come to this locality in droves in recent times have not added to the good name and fame of the neighborhood." In order to reverse the trend, he called upon his receptive audience "to fight for it so that the very foundation of the old Ninth Ward will not crumble." What seemed to upset Judge Caffrey the most was the sight of women smoking cigarettes on the streets, which drew the following retort from the Health Commissioner: "Will you tell me why in Heaven's name the women shall not smoke cigarettes on the streets if a man does?"[13]

By the time that Judge Caffrey delivered his address, the battle lines between the two sides had been clearly drawn. A delegation that included Father Joseph Breslin, a curate at St. Joseph's Church, appealed to Mayor John F. Hylan in June 1921 to clean up the dance

12. Washington Square Association, Report of the Executive Committee, *Washington Square Association Yearbook* (1923–1924), 11; *New York Times*, September 14, 1919.

13. *New York Times*, June 3, May 12, 1922.

halls in Greenwich Village. "If your Honor will pass along 6th Avenue from 4th Street to Washington Place any night," the attorney for the Ninth Warders informed the Mayor, "the first thing that will impress you is how in the world the people ever got permission to operate dance halls in these filthy cellars." Within a week this protest produced a counter petition from an eclectic assortment of writers, clergymen, and real estate agents who defended the changes in the Village. "The Village is perhaps the most important creative center in America," they declared.[14]

The *New York Times* noted with some amusement that "the whole human race might be divided into the Ninth-Warders and the Villagers." The *Times* also pointed out that the biggest winners in the Greenwich Village cultural wars were the real estate operators, who had converted old dwellings into two-room studio apartments and rented them at rates that old-timers regarded as exorbitant. One ironic consequence of the rise in rents was the flight of the real bohemian element from the Village to less expensive parts of the city. The *Times* editorial writer was not much impressed with the bohemians who were still left in the Village. "To the unpartisan eye," he said, "they look pretty much like the concessionaires who pick up a living around the edges of the county fair." The same writer put the best possible spin on the tea rooms whose presence was so annoying to the Ninth Warders. "The most that can be said for them is that they furnish occupation for persons who, if they couldn't keep tea rooms, might inflict themselves on the arts."[15]

In the 1920s only a small minority of even the newcomers to the Village could be classified as bohemians. Most were solid middle-class and upper-middle-class citizens. They settled in the Village because of its proximity to the downtown business and financial district rather than from any desire to patronize the cabarets and tea houses. The construction of the West Side IRT subway under Seventh Avenue accelerated the gentrification of the Village by making

14. *New York Times,* June 3, 8, 1921.
15. *New York Times,* June 4, 1921.

it more accessible than ever before. However, progress came at a price. The extension of Seventh Avenue south of West 12th Street bulldozed a one-hundred-foot-wide path through the heart of the Village and resulted in the destruction of two hundred old houses. One of the casualties was the apartment house on Bank Street where Willa Cather lived. She at least had the means to move to a hotel on Fifth Avenue, where she continued to hold her Friday afternoon literary teas with the assistance of her French cook.[16]

The poorer residents in Greenwich Village had fewer options than Willa Cather. They often found themselves squeezed out of the neighborhood completely by the improvements taking place around them. In addition to the extension of Seventh Avenue, the construction of the Holland Tunnel, with its extensive feeder roads, wreaked havoc with the housing stock in the lower part of the Village. Anticipating the changes to come, Mary Kingsbury Simkhovitch wrote in November 1920: "Eight blocks of this neighborhood will be destroyed by the construction of the vehicular tunnel between Spring and Canal Streets. The old residents are very much disturbed by the middle class invasion of our neighborhood. They have lived here all their lives and they want to stay. We should make every effort to assist them to do so."[17]

Hitherto Greenwich Village had escaped the skyscraper age, lying like a low valley between the tall towers of Wall Street and those of midtown Manhattan. Beginning in the 1920s, however, real estate developers dotted the Village with high-rise, luxury apartment buildings and residence hotels like the one at 51 Fifth Avenue, where former Governor Alfred E. Smith made his home. Even the Washington Square Association, which had been founded in 1906 by the local bluebloods "to maintain the present desirable character of the neighborhood," conceded in 1925 that it was hopeless to try to ban apartment buildings from the Village. Gustavus Kirby, the president of the association, told his fellow members that year: "Some of us

16. Ware, *Greenwich Village,* 298, 267.

17. GHP, Report of the Director, November 18, 1920.

... wish that we could go back to the old times of nothing but the private house, but you cannot keep the tide of progress and desire back, and inasmuch as we must have apartment houses, let's do what we can to have them of the right type and properly maintained, which means that the right kind of people will come into our neighborhood."[18]

If the proliferation of luxury apartment buildings threatened to alter the landscape of the old Village, another menace was the construction of tall loft buildings for commercial and industrial use, especially in the western part of the Village near the Hudson River. The Trinity Corporation, the largest landowner in the West Village, systematically replaced old tenement buildings with new lofts that displaced still more of the old residents. "If the factories come, we the residents must go," Alderman Henry A. Curran told the Washington Square Association at a meeting on January 11, 1921. "It cannot be avoided. And today they are still coming in." A few months earlier the *New York Times* had noted with regret that "Old Greenwich Village has been so thoroughly cut up within the past few years ... that that interesting section of Manhattan Island is rapidly becoming little more than a memory of what it was in its palmy days of comfortable domesticity."[19]

Organized Religion in the Land of Whoopee

For a variety of reasons, Greenwich Village was changing in the 1920s. Sheridan Square with its fine new apartment buildings came to symbolize the new Greenwich Village just as the town houses on Washington Square North had once been synonymous with the Old Village. The older residents, largely conservative Irish and Italian Catholics, found the changes as unwelcome to them as the influx of the Irish and Italians had been to the WASP Ninth Warders at the turn of the twentieth century. The raffish bohemian element with

18. Gustavus Kirby, Report of the Executive Committee, *Washington Square Association Yearbook* (1925), 9.

19. Henry A. Curran, *Washington Square Association Yearbook* (1920–1921), 16. *New York Times,* October 31, 1920.

their dance halls and tea houses was the most noticeable irritant to those who now considered themselves the true Ninth Warders. However, the old-timers soon discovered that they also had little in common with the eminently respectable new Villagers who moved into the new apartment buildings, residence hotels, and renovated town houses.

Caroline Ware noticed how the Ninth Warders and the Villagers studiously ignored one another. "They were strikingly unconscious of each other," she discovered, even when they lived on the same block, or, more rarely, in the same apartment building. She attributed the gulf to "difference of education, social background, wealth, and social standards." "Each of these factors in turn," she emphasized, "reinforced the others." Religion was also a major differentiating factor between the two groups. Political radicals like Emma Goldman and Max Eastman shared Karl Marx's view that religion was the opiate of the people, and they expressed their views in no uncertain terms. Eastman's remark that "the Roman Catholic Church is the most tragically stupendous swindle that human and animal nature ever combined to produce" would have given great offense to Catholics, except that none of them ever read the *Masses.* One local priest described the surprise of tourists when they spotted him as they were piling out of their tour buses. "The guides have just told them what a den of iniquity Greenwich Village is," he explained.[20]

The middle-class businessmen and professional people who lived in the new apartment buildings were not shocked at the presence of priests in the street and they were too well bred to criticize religion as vituperatively as Max Eastman had done. However, for the most part, religion was not an important factor in their lives. The clergy in the Village, Protestant as well as Catholic, described the new Villagers as mostly a "godless crowd." Among the Villagers whom Caro-

20. Ware, *Greenwich Village*, 106, 96. Max Eastman, "Jesus Christ," *Masses* 5 (December 1913): 5, cited in Leslie Fishbein, *Rebels in Bohemia: The Radicals of the Masses* (Chapel Hill: University of North Carolina Press, 1982), 114.

line Ware interviewed, she discovered that 71 percent admitted that they did not attend any church. Few of the newcomers were Catholics. Almost invariably the Catholics among them went to St. Joseph's Church rather than to any of the other Catholic churches, but they rarely became active in the affairs of the parish.[21]

The statistical information leaves a bleak picture of the state of the Protestant churches in the Village in the 1920s. There were eight Protestant churches, two Episcopalian, two Presbyterian, two Baptist, one Methodist, and one Lutheran. By 1929 their combined membership was only 58 percent of what it had been in 1900. Even more ominous for the future, in 1929 their combined Sunday school population was only 29 percent of what it had been in 1900, and it had declined a full 45 percent in the 1920s. Only two of the eight Protestant ministers in the Village reported that a majority of their congregation actually lived in the Village.[22]

One of the most outspoken local Protestant ministers, Dr. John L. Davis, the pastor of the Washington Square Methodist Episcopal Church on West 4th Street, gave an address titled "Religion and What It Means to a Neighborhood" in the Village in 1931. His own congregation had dwindled to a mere 150 members. Understandably, he emphasized the contributions that the Protestant churches had made to the Village in the past, "a heritage which money cannot buy." As for the future, without ever mentioning God by name, he declared: "It is the business of the ministers of the churches of this community to breathe into the rebellious hearts a spirit of love and devotion toward that great Power that is over all of us." He raised a minor commotion a few months later when, in a Sunday morning sermon, he declared that most of the Protestant churches in the Village would have gone out of business twenty years earlier if they had not received financial support from congregations outside the Village.[23]

21. Ware, *Greenwich Village,* 113, 118.

22. Ibid., 294–96.

23. Reverend Dr. John Davis, "Religion and What It Means to a Neighborhood," *Washington Square Association Yearbook* (1930–1931), 9. *New York Times,* April 25, 1932.

Mary Kingsbury Simkhovitch, who knew Greenwich Village as well as anyone alive in the 1930s, remarked on the contrast between the moribund state of the Protestant churches in the Village and the vitality of the Catholic churches. "These churches hold their own against all change," she declared. "Go to any prayer meeting or weekday service in a local Protestant church," she said, "and then drop in at Benediction in Our Lady of Pompei's and see the difference in attendance and interest." An active member of the Episcopal Church herself, Simkhovitch attributed the difference to the fact that "the Catholic claims have a substance and power unknown to Protestantism, which tends to become a society dependent upon the personality of the clergy." She also faulted the Protestant churches for the high turnover in their clergy. It was the result, she thought, of the fact that many ministers regarded a church in Greenwich Village as only a stepping stone to a better assignment elsewhere.[24]

The End of the Salad Years at St. Joseph's Church

That criticism could certainly not be made of the pastors of St. Joseph's Church in that era. Between 1906 and 1943 the church had only two pastors, John Edwards and John J. Hickey. Both men were veteran priests who came to St. Joseph's Church after many years of service elsewhere in the archdiocese and remained at St. Joseph's until their death. Both they and the archbishop of New York who appointed them would have regarded their assignment to Greenwich Village as a reward and even a sign of special favor. Far from being a stepping stone to a better assignment, an appointment to St. Joseph's Church meant that a New York diocesan priest would end his days as the pastor of one of the most prestigious parishes in the archdiocese.

The curates at St. Joseph's Church also seemed to be remarkably content with their assignment. It is noteworthy how little turnover there was in their ranks in the first half of the twentieth century, as they slowly climbed the ladder of parochial preferment (such as it

24. Simkhovitch, *Greenwich House*, 117, 120.

was) from third assistant to second assistant to the prized position of first assistant. Both George B. Fagan and John P. Fitzgerald remained at St. Joseph's for twenty years, while Charles Fitzgerald stayed for seventeen years and John A. Grogan for thirteen years. Later in the century John J. Casserly was to establish the record for longevity by remaining as a curate at St. Joseph's for all of his thirty-four years as a priest.

The first of St. Joseph's twentieth-century pastors was Monsignor John Edwards, who succeeded Father Denis O'Flynn in 1906. Even in that uncritical age, Edwards' appointment must have raised a few clerical eyebrows. Edwards was seventy-three years old and had been pastor of Immaculate Conception Church on East 14th Street for thirty-two years. He was the Permanent Rector of that church, which means that he must have agreed to his transfer to St. Joseph's Church. Edwards was also one of the three vicars general of the archdiocese and he had served for many years as a member of the Board of Archdiocesan Consultors, a select group of senior clergy that was the most important advisory body to the archbishop.

Born in Ireland in 1833, Edwards had emigrated to America in 1849 and was ordained a priest in 1866. As a diocesan consultor he had done yeomen work over the years for both Archbishop Corrigan and Archbishop Farley, most notably in the planning and financing of St. Joseph's Seminary at Dunwoodie. In the stilted language of the day, the diocesan press described him as a strict disciplinarian but one who "leaned to the side of tolerance and consideration for human frailty." However, at the age of seventy-three, his productive years were largely behind him. A priest ordained the year after the end of the Civil War could hardly be expected to cope effectively with the physical and cultural changes that took place in Greenwich Village during the first two decades of the twentieth century.

Monsignor Edwards remained pastor of St. Joseph's Church for sixteen years, until his death on August 30, 1922, at the age of ninety, by which time he was the oldest priest in the archdiocese. While he remained active both as a pastor and as a diocesan consultor and continued to serve as a confessor to several communities of sisters,

Edwards does not appear to have played any role in the community that was changing rapidly under his nose. Mary Kingsbury Simkhovitch never mentions him as having any connection with Greenwich House. Nonetheless, at his death, Edwards left behind a thriving parish that had not yet experienced the full impact of the changes that were beginning to transform the Village. In 1921 there were 279 baptisms and 189 weddings, statistics which indicate the presence of many young families. Unfortunately the *status animarum* reports for the 1920s have not been preserved in the archdiocesan archives, and so it is impossible to give the statistics on Mass attendance. However, one newspaper reporter observed that on Sundays and holy days at St. Joseph's Church, "the crowds press about the altar at Communion time requiring often the service of three priests to give the sacrament in order that one Mass may be finished in time for the next."[25]

Monsignor Edwards' funeral on September 4, 1922, was a grand rally of the cream of New York Catholic society, both clerical and lay. Archbishop Patrick Hayes celebrated the Mass in the presence of four bishops and more than 150 priests. Despite a heavy rain, several hundred people who were unable to enter the packed church waited patiently in the streets outside. The honorary pallbearers included Charles F. Murphy, the powerful leader of Tammany Hall, Martin J. Conboy, the president of the Catholic Club of New York, former State Supreme Court Justice Morgan J. O'Brien, Judge Alfred J. Talley, and George Gillespie, the archdiocesan attorney. Like the celebration of the centenary of the diocese in 1908, the funeral of Monsignor Edwards was a demonstration on a smaller scale of Catholic political power in New York City, more specifically Irish Catholic political power. Virtually all of the clergy and prominent laymen in attendance had unmistakably Irish names.

Edwards' funeral also explains why he and contemporary Catholic pastors for the most part felt little need or responsibility to in-

25. AANY, Financial Report of St. Joseph's Church, 1921, 1922. New York *Catholic News*, September 2, 1922.

volve themselves in the concerns of the wider community in which they resided. They lived securely and contentedly in their own self-contained world. Their churches were filled for Mass several times every Sunday with devout and generous parishioners, many of them immigrants or the children of immigrants. There was a seemingly inexhaustible supply of diocesan priests. In 1923 thirty-six priests were ordained for the archdiocese. Their numbers were so bountiful that it became standard practice to assign four priests to every city parish; before long the rector of the seminary would alert the archbishop to the problem of the oversupply of vocations.[26] The reason that Monsignor Edwards and many other priests of that era could continue to function as pastors well into their eighties was not only the abundance of younger clergy, but also the role of the first assistant, the senior curate who did most of the routine work while waiting patiently to receive his own parish.

In most parishes the parochial school required little attention from the pastor. He might make a ceremonial appearance occasionally to distribute report cards to awe-struck students, but, for the most part, he could leave the day-to-day management in the capable hands of the sisters and brothers. In 1921 St. Joseph's School was filled to capacity with 1,276 children. The faculty consisted of twelve sisters, five brothers, and eleven lay women. By the standards of that day, the percentage of lay teachers was abnormally high, but the cost of their salaries was not likely to be a financial burden in view of the abysmally low wages that they (and also the public school teachers) received. Moreover, there was a plentiful supply of sisters and brothers waiting in the wings to replace them, since the religious communities of men and women were experiencing the same boom in vocations as the diocesan clergy.

On the diocesan level, the Catholic Church reached the apogee of its political influence in New York City in the 1920s, when the Archbishop's residence at 452 Madison Avenue was commonly called the

26. Archives of St. Joseph's Seminary, Dunwoodie, Arthur Scanlan to Hayes, Annual Report, 1932–1933.

Powerhouse. The cozy relationship between the Church and Tammany Hall, which dated from the 1870s, continued into the early years of Cardinal Hayes' administration in the 1920s and only came to an end with the election of Fiorello LaGuardia in 1933.

Father John J. Hickey

Monsignor Edwards' successor as pastor of St. Joseph's Church was Father John J. Hickey, only the third American-born pastor in almost a century and the first native of the parish to become the pastor. After his ordination in 1895, he spent twenty-seven years in several different upstate assignments, the last ten years as the pastor of St. Mary's Church in Kingston. He was a seminary classmate of Archbishop Hayes and was deeply touched when Hayes offered him an opportunity to return not only to the city but also to his native parish and, as he phrased it, to the people "from whom I sprang."[27] Despite the combination of bohemian invasion, public works projects, and gentrification, St. Joseph's was still a highly desirable parish, and Archbishop Hayes was doing his classmate a favor when he appointed him pastor. Despite the adverse conditions mentioned above, the financial condition of the parish actually improved steadily throughout the 1920s. Annual income increased from $69,489.08 in 1920 to $127,105,29 in 1924, and then leveled off at around $100,000 per year for the rest of the decade.[28]

In the 1920s St. Joseph's Church shared the prosperity of the rest of the country. At a meeting with Hickey in the spring of 1923, Archbishop Hayes expressed his disappointment that the annual Peter's Pence collection for the pope that year had raised only $49,000 from the whole archdiocese. Hickey had postponed the collection at St. Joseph's Church because the date coincided with a parish mission. However, he promptly wrote out a check for $1,000 and sent it to Hayes as "an anticipated expression of loyalty of our generous people that they will manifest at a more convenient time." He had al-

27. AANY, Hickey to Hayes, September 8, 1922.
28. AANY, Financial Reports of St. Joseph's Parish, 1920–1930.

Graduation of St. Joseph's School (Girls).

Celebration of Monsignor Hickey's 35th Anniversary, Hotel Astor—June 10, 1930.

Graduation of St. Joseph's School (Boys).

ready sent Hayes a check for $5,000 to establish a parish burse at St. Joseph's Seminary. That same year, when a nearby former private school building on Christopher Street became available, Hickey promptly purchased it for $210,000. He made it the girls' school and made the school building on Washington Place the boys' school.[29]

Unlike the aged Monsignor Edwards, Father Hickey took an interest in community affairs. He served as a chaplain at the women's prison in Greenwich Village and established a good working relationship with Mary Kingsbury Simkhovitch at Greenwich House. He was also the first priest to serve on the executive board of the Washington Square Association and remained an honorary member thereafter, a position that previously had been the exclusive preserve of the local Protestant clergy. In November 1927, when Cardinal Hayes (he received the Red hot in 1924) came to St. Joseph's Church to celebrate confirmation, one of the guests was Mayor James J. ("Jimmy") Walker, a native and longtime resident of the Village whose parents had first met at Mass in St. Joseph's Church.[30]

When Cardinal Hayes returned to the Village in 1932 to dedicate St. Veronica's new parochial school, one of the speakers at the dedication was Judge William Caffrey, who expressed mock surprise that the Cardinal would come to a neighborhood with such a bad reputation. The Cardinal responded in kind. "Had I stayed around down here alone tongues might have begun to wag," said Hayes. Knowing how sensitive many residents were about the Village's reputation, the Cardinal ended on a serious note. "The last time I was in Greenwich Village," he said, "it was for a confirmation. It was a weekday and I walked around among the people. I realized I was among people who loved God. And today I have not been disappointed."[31]

Despite the surface prosperity of St. Joseph's parish in the 1920s, the gentrification of the area slowly but relentlessly drove many

29. AANY, Q-3, Hayes to Hickey, January 11, 1923; AANY, Hickey to Hayes, March 21, 1923; AANY, V-10, Hickey to Hayes, August 21, 1923.

30. AANY, V-5, Hickey to Hayes, October 10, 1929; Q-16, Hickey to Hayes, November 10, 1927.

31. *New York Times*, May 2, 1932.

Catholics from the neighborhood. During that decade, in addition to the demolition of many older buildings, approximately 10 percent of the tenements were modernized, allowing landlords to increase rents from $5 to $25 or more per room. The construction of new luxury apartment buildings as well as the remodeling of single-family dwellings and lodging houses added to the stock of high-priced dwellings. However, affordable lower-middle-class housing became increasingly scarce, polarizing the Village into a neighborhood of the poor and the affluent, who often lived next to one another in very different kinds of buildings. As a result of these changes, some twenty thousand tenement dwellers left Greenwich Village in the course of the 1920s. A considerable number of them must have been Catholics and parishioners of St. Joseph's Church. They were replaced by some four thousand newcomers, who could afford to pay the upscale rents, but relatively few of them were Catholics. One curious consequence of the shifting population pattern in the Village was that the percentage of native-born Americans rose from 17.7 percent in 1920 to 28.7 percent in 1930. The Village was reclaiming its status as the American Ward, but this time American was no longer synonymous with Protestant.[32]

The Great Depression and the Village

The Great Depression had a devastating impact in New York City. By 1932 a third of the city's factories had closed, a quarter of the population was unemployed, and the municipal debt of almost two billion dollars was equal to that of all the forty-eight states combined. On May Day, May 1, 1933, in Union Square Park, one former resident of the Village offered her modest and unorthodox solution to the economic crisis that had engulfed the nation. That day Dorothy Day began to sell her newspaper, *The Catholic Worker,* for one penny a copy.

In the Village itself the Depression accentuated and accelerated the widening gap between the working-class poor and the prosper-

32. Ware, *Greenwich Village,* 21–22, 31, 35.

ous middle class that had been taking place for well over a decade. Unlike the situation almost everywhere else in the city, in the Village new construction continued unabated well after the onset of the Depression. A close observer of the Village estimated that "the Depression that ended the boom of the twenties probably caused less misery in the Village than in most American communities." A full year after the stock market collapse of 1929, the *New York Times* reported that "there is hardly a street, alley or row of rear houses—of which there are still many—that has not known the hand of the wrecker, seen new buildings rise, or witnessed the remodeling of houses that for many years had little value." The same article reported a mass exodus of poor people from the Village to other parts of Manhattan and even to Brooklyn.[33]

In the 1930s, despite the Depression, Greenwich Village was one of the most affluent neighborhoods in Manhattan. A local booster, Walter Gregory Bryan, used the columns and editorials of *The Villager,* a weekly newspaper that he founded in 1933, to dispel the notion that the Village was "a playground for uptown New York" and the "Land of Whoopee." He claimed that the only wealthier areas of New York City were Murray Hill, Park Avenue, Fifth Avenue, Central Park West, West End Avenue, Riverside Drive, and Riverdale. He further claimed that Washington, D.C., was the only city in the United States with a higher per capita income and expenditure than Greenwich Village.[34]

The enthusiastic editor of *The Villager* found confirmation for his boosterism a decade later from an unlikely source, one of the last survivors of the bohemian Village, none other than Romany Marie, who decried the disappearance of the Village tea rooms. "Did you notice," she asked, "no more tearooms in the Village? The new places all open with an uptown policy: eat, pay and out you go." One of her regular customers, a self-styled avant-garde architect, agreed with

33. *New York Times,* October 19, 1930. William Barrett, "New Designs on Our Bohemia," *New York Times Magazine,* August 20, 1950, 20.

34. *The Villager,* April 13, 1933.

her gloomy assessment of the social changes that had overtaken the Village. "The Village has become a bourgeois community," he complained. "Today's Villager is indistinguishable from a resident of Park Avenue."[35]

The new Villagers produced articulate and resourceful leaders who were intensely proud of their unique neighborhood and were determined to protect it from unwanted improvements. They waxed eloquent over the "homelike picturesqueness" of Christopher Street and "the air of comfort, congeniality and warm welcome" that surrounded West 4th Street. "With the possible exception of Quebec in Canada, of New Orleans, of one or two places in California and particularly Old San Francisco," declared one enthusiast, "there is no spot in the United States richer in historic and romantic interest than Greenwich Village." At least one person even came to cherish the grimy sheet-metal stations of the Sixth and Ninth Avenue Els. "They are fearfully and wonderfully made, these old stations," said Edward C. Caswell, the staff artist of *The Villager,* who wrote that he had never come across anything quite like them in his extensive travels through Europe.[36]

An index of the feistiness of the new Villagers was the fact that in 1935 they challenged and defeated Robert Moses' plans to remodel Washington Square Park. It was not often that the imperious Moses lost a fight with anyone. After dealing with the Villagers, however, Moses told Mary Kingsbury Simkhovitch that "the filling in of Orchard Beach in the Bronx, the development of Jones Beach or of Marine Park in Brooklyn and the building of the Triboro and Henry Hudson bridges are child's play in comparison." "There is no other section of the city," he sniffed, "where there are so many ideas per person, and where ideas are so tenaciously maintained." Tongue in

35. Al Hersfeld, "Counter Revolution in the Village," *New York Times Magazine,* April 23, 1944, 18.

36. *The Villager,* July 13, August 31, October 12, November 16, 1933. For the anonymous writer of the *New York City Guide* sponsored by the WPA, the fact that the *Villager* had replaced the erratic, 'villagy' *Quill* was sufficient proof of the *embourgeoisement* of Greenwich Village. *New York City Guide* (New York: Random House, 1939, rep. 1956), 131.

cheek, he threatened to move the Central Park Zoo to Greenwich Village. "But, I am sure," he added, "no cages ever invented would hold in the animals, if we sent them down to Greenwich Village, once they had made up their minds to get out and see the sights."[37]

The Centennial of St. Joseph's Church

In contrast to many of the new Villagers, the Catholic community at St. Joseph's Church was hard hit by the Depression. The financial reports of the church tell the story. The annual income fell by over 50 percent, from $96,508.17 in 1928 to $60,094,17 in 1932 and to $45,182.39 in 1939. There was also an abrupt decline in the number of marriages, from 189 in 1921 to 73 in 1932. The same trend was apparent with baptisms, which fell from 279 in 1921 to 85 in 1932. In 1932 Father Hickey estimated that there were still three thousand Catholic families in his parish, and Sunday Mass attendance at St. Joseph's still outstripped by far the attendance at any of the local Protestant churches. Some 2,200 people came to the six Sunday morning Masses and perhaps another thousand attended Mass in one of the neighboring Catholic churches. Father Hickey also noted that there were "very many Italians" in the parish, but it is not clear from his report whether they attended Mass at St. Joseph's Church or at the two nearby Italian churches.[38]

Curiously, both the centenary of the founding of the parish in 1929 and the centenary of the dedication of the church building in 1934 passed without any celebration or formal recognition. However, in 1934, in the middle of the Depression, Hickey embarked upon a major renovation of the church, which included the installation of a new main altar, an enlarged sanctuary with a new terrazzo floor, and a new altar rail. It was a renovation that he did not want and did not need, but he was forced into it when, in 1930, a wealthy parishioner, Mrs. Margaret Kieley, left the parish $50,000 in her will. For

37. Robert Moses to Mary Kingsbury Simkhovitch, *The Villager,* May 23, 1935.

38. AANY, Financial Reports of St. Joseph's Church, 1928, 1932, 1939; *Status Animarum* Report of St. Joseph's Church, 1932.

four years Hickey did nothing with the bequest, hoping that eventually he could use the money for his school.[39]

However, the executor of Mrs. Kieley's will, Joseph O'Connor, who also happened to be Kieley's nephew, objected to the proposal and insisted that his aunt's money should be used to build a suitable memorial for her in the church. He appealed to Cardinal Hayes, and Hayes suggested that half of the money be used to build a new main altar and the rest of the legacy be given to the poor of the parish. "It is my judgment," Hayes told Hickey, "that you will not satisfy them except by doing something in the nature of an altar." The result was a new neoclassical main altar, flanked by two marble columns that framed the large oil painting of the Crucifixion that had formed the backdrop to the old main altar. The new altar was consecrated by Auxiliary Bishop Stephen J. Donahue in a two-and-a-half-hour ceremony on the morning of March 15, 1937.[40]

Now that he had a newly refurbished sanctuary to show off, Hickey decided to celebrate the centenary of the parish despite the Depression. The date that he set was Sunday, June 13, 1937. It was actually 108 years since the founding of the parish, and 103 years since the dedication of the church. June 13th had no particular significance in the parish's history, but it may have been a convenient date for Cardinal Hayes, who presided at the solemn pontifical Mass of Thanksgiving that Bishop Donahue celebrated that morning at 11:00. Having finally decided to celebrate the parish centennial, albeit a bit late, Father Hickey pulled out all the stops. Some 150 cadets from Xavier High School and the band of De La Salle Institute greeted Cardinal Hayes outside the church, and a color guard of the Knights of Columbus escorted him inside. The preacher was Father Michael A. Reilly, the pastor of St. Barnabas Church in the Bronx, who devoted much of his sermon to a topic that had little relevance to the occasion, the threat that totalitarian regimes posed to the

39. AANY, Hickey to Executors of Estate of Margaret Kieley, December 1932; Hickey to Hayes, December 6, 1932.

40. AANY, O'Connor to Hayes, October 23, 1934; Hayes to Hickey, November 27, 1934.

Church. He called attention especially to the growing aggressiveness of the Nazi regime in Germany and praised Pius XI's recently issued encyclical on Nazism, *Mit Brennender Sorge.* "Pius XI has flung his defiance to the German dictator," Father O'Reilly declared.

In his remarks at the Mass, Cardinal Hayes concentrated on events closer to home, especially the history of St. Joseph's Church. "As I sat here this morning," said the Cardinal, "I could not but sense the presence of some of the great figures whose names are written large in the history of St. Joseph's Church." He mentioned in particular Cardinal McCloskey. "I have often heard the late Cardinal Farley tell the story of Cardinal McCloskey and of his pastoral years at St. Joseph's. He had trying times at the beginning, but gradually his kindness and fairness won the admiration of those who were causing trouble." The Cardinal ended his remarks by paying tribute to the generosity of Mrs. Kieley and turned it into a gracious compliment to all the people of the parish. "Her generosity is typical of the people of St. Joseph's," said Hayes. "While they have not her wealth, they have her spirit, and, if they were possessed of wealth, they too would give generously."[41]

The celebration of the centenary of the church in 1937 was probably the highlight of Father Hickey's tenure at St. Joseph's. An earlier historian of St. Joseph's Church, Father Stephen M. Ryan, a native of the parish writing in the 1980s, noted that it was never again possible to stage a similar celebration on the same scale.[42] Early in 1938 Father Hickey was made a monsignor and he remained as pastor for another five years, until his death on November 22, 1943. For most of that period he was in failing health and much of the responsibility of administering the parish fell upon the shoulders of his first assistant, Father George B. Fagan.

Monsignor Hickey's funeral was a low-key affair quite unlike the lavish sendoff that Monsignor Edwards had received a quarter of a century earlier. The difference reflected the changed status of St.

41. New York *Catholic News,* June 19, 1937; *New York Times,* June 14, 1937.

42. Stephen M. Ryan, "An Historical Look at the Parish of St. Joseph, Greenwich Village," unpublished paper, 1984, 93.

Joseph's Church within the Archdiocese of New York. The salad years were over. When Monsignor Edwards came to St. Joseph's Church in 1906, the parish could still bask in the long afterglow of the era of Immigrant Church in New York City and benefit from all the advantages that residual ethnic loyalties brought to religious practice. By the time that Monsignor Hickey died in 1937, however, not only was the neighborhood changing, but the nature of American Catholicism was beginning to change as well, although the changes would not become fully apparent until the 1960s.

With the demise of the Immigrant Church and the assimilation of Catholics into the American mainstream, cultural conformity in religious matters gave way to personal religious commitment or to no commitment at all. This sea change in the attitude of many American Catholics toward their faith posed a major pastoral challenge to the clergy throughout the archdiocese. That challenge proved to be particularly acute in St. Joseph's Church because of the unique nature of Greenwich Village. Over the next sixty years, the priests who succeeded Monsignor Edwards and Monsignor Hickey responded to that challenge in various ways and with varying degrees of success.

8 *From World War II to Vatican II*

Postwar Manhattan

"ASK ALMOST anyone who remembers Manhattan then," wrote the British writer Jan Morris about New York in 1945, "and they recall it with proud nostalgia, even if they were poor and lonely." A Gallup poll taken at the end of World War II revealed that 90 percent of New Yorkers considered themselves happy. The old capitals of Europe were either lying in ruins or slowly and painfully recovering from the ravages of war. New York was different. "Few cities in the history of the world can have stood so consciously at a moment of fulfillment," added Morris, "looking into a future that seemed so full of reward."[1]

In 1945 Jan Morris (who was James Morris then) found New Yorkers a well-dressed, prosperous-looking bunch and thought that they seemed more distinctively American in manners, dress, and stature than they would appear to be three or four decades later. It was a city where the men still wore hats and immediately doffed them in an elevator if a woman entered. It was a city where women worried about the appearance of their stockings now that skirts were shorter and were constantly asking one another, "Are my seams straight?" It was a city where the word "graffiti" was unknown and where the newspapers used quotation marks when they referred to "muggings." The courtesy of New

1. Jan Morris, *Manhattan '45* (Baltimore: The Johns Hopkins University Press, 1998), 11. The book was originally published by Oxford University Press in 1986.

Yorkers impressed Morris, which she attributed, at least partially, to "the ruling caste of Manhattan, a powerful alliance of Anglo-Saxon and Liberal Jewish whose courtly manners, often disguising uncourtly aspirations, seemed to most New Yorkers the criterion by which all manners should be judged."[2]

Mimi Sheraton, the future restaurant critic of the *New York Times*, was a sophomore at New York University in 1945 who had just moved into a tiny apartment in the Village. It was the closest that she could get to the Latin Quarter of Paris, and she sometimes preferred to wander through the streets of Greenwich Village rather than attend class. "I prowled its winding cobblestone streets and secret gardens," she recalled fifty years later, "shopped its second-hand bookstores, enticing bakeries and junk shops, saw foreign films in art movie houses that poured free coffee from silver urns, and found true meaning in the lines poets read from their own works in Washington Square Park and in the San Remo bar on the northwest corner of MacDougal and Bleecker Streets." Her mother warned her against associating with "mixed" couples, artists, and communists; her father commented with wry amusement, "So you want to be a bohemian?"[3]

Another observer, who painted a less favorable picture of life in postwar New York, was E. B. White, the veteran writer for *The New Yorker*. He preferred small town New England to the charms of the big city and groused in 1949 that New York City "neither looks nor feels the way it did twenty-five years ago." He declared that "the city has never been so uncomfortable, so crowded, so tense." One minor irritation that he deplored was the proliferation of cutesy neighborhood names like NoHo and Carnegie Hill. He also complained that there were fewer daily newspapers, that it was more difficult to find an empty taxi cab, that the policemen no longer patrolled their beat on foot, and that the traffic was worse than ever. "A single run of a cross-town bus contains for the driver," he said, "enough frustration

2. Ibid., 26, 32.

3. Mimi Sheraton, "In the Village, 50-Year Affair for a Walker Still in Love," *New York Times*, January 10, 1997.

and annoyance to carry him over the edge of sanity." He also lamented that "rich men nowadays don't live in houses. They live in the attics of big apartment buildings and plant trees on the setbacks." He thought that even the bars had contributed to lowering the quality of life. "Men go to saloons to gaze at televised events instead of to think long thoughts. It is all very disconcerting."[4]

One New Yorker who agreed with Morris rather than with White was Robert Moses, the city's master planner and builder. In fact Moses would have considered Morris' encomium much too tepid. "We are just too damned sophisticated, hypercritical and ashamed of vaunting ourselves to claim credit where credit is due," he said. Despite Moses' heady optimism, the city fathers received a shock when the U.S. Bureau of the Census reported in July 1950 that the city's population was 7,841,610, which was 400,000 fewer people than the city's Health Department had estimated. "Seemingly," said the *New York Times,* "the city's congested traffic cannot compete with the beckoning fingers of the Palisades, the soft Connecticut countryside, or the broad, flat reaches of Long Island."[5]

The flight of the middle class to the suburbs was already under way. In the former potato farms of Long Island, Levitt houses were selling for $7,990, with monthly carrying charges of only $58. Robert Moses, who never learned to drive a car, was busy constructing bridges, parkways, and expressways to provide easy access to the Levitt houses by automobile. By May 1950 he had completed ninety-seven miles of parkway on Long Island alone. For prospective suburbanites with upscale tastes and pocketbooks, especially those who wanted to avoid the social stigma of a Levittown address, new four-bedroom homes were available in River Edge, New Jersey, for $13,990. For those who had their heart set on moving to "dear old Westchester," as Moses derisively called New York's wealthy northern suburb, new colonial-style homes were selling for as low as

4. E. B. White, *Here is New York* (New York: The Little Book Room, 1999), 50–54. White's book was originally published by Harper and Brothers c. 1949.

5. Robert Moses, "New York *Has* a Future," *New York Times Magazine,* January 30, 1955, 22.

$11,500 in northern Yonkers (without a Yonkers address). The builder advertised the location as "rural."

In 1950 no one as yet realized the devastating social effects that the flight of the middle class to the suburbs would have on cities all across America. The impact was to be felt especially in the old ethnic neighborhoods like Greenwich Village that once had been the strongholds of American Catholicism. Many of the new suburbanites were Catholics, often the first members of their families to go to college or buy their own home, thanks to the G.I. Bill of Rights and low-cost veterans' mortgages. At St. Jerome's Church in the Bronx, once the center of a bustling Irish American parish, Sunday Mass attendance plummeted from 5,000 in 1945 to 795 in 1975. Highbridge, another thriving Irish American neighborhood in the South Bronx, suffered a similar fate in the 1950s. A former resident who made periodic visits to the area in the 1980s was appalled at the changes. "Apartment houses on Woodycrest Avenue that used to sing with the life of bustling families had become burnt-out tombs," he reported.[6]

The Changing Village

Greenwich Village never experienced anything remotely comparable to the almost total devastation that swept through the South Bronx and made it a national symbol of urban decay. However, the Village continued to change as it had been doing throughout its history. Perhaps the most noticeable feature of the postwar Village was the diversity that was to be found among its 85,000 residents in an area no bigger than Central Park. "It is, in fact, a congeries of communities," said one N.Y.U. professor, "whose citizenry ranges from unimpeachable middle-class types to real Bohemians." In the decade after the end of World War II, more than a dozen new large luxury apartment buildings were erected, dwarfing their older neighbors. Nonetheless, right around the corner from the busy

6. AANY, *Status Animarum* Report of St. Jerome's Church, 1945, 1975. Michael Scanlon, "Return to Highbridge," *Catholic New York,* October 7, 1993.

commercial strip of Sixth Avenue, on Washington Square South and West 3rd Street, were rows of renovated town houses with secluded backyards. In the West Village many of the brownstones on the tree-lined streets had been divided into small apartments, but nearly 1,400 of them survived as one-family residences.[7]

One of the main agents of change in the postwar Village was New York University, whose enrollment mushroomed after the war, necessitating additional classroom space and residential housing. The university' s expansion plans found an ardent supporter in Robert Moses, who, as chairman of the City Committee on Slum Clearance, welcomed the opportunity to demolish the substandard housing in the South Village. His original plans would have virtually wiped out the parish of St. Anthony of Padua, but protests from influential Italian politicians and neighborhood leaders forced Moses to scale back his plan. In its abbreviated form, Moses replaced nine square blocks of old factory buildings and lofts with two new classroom buildings and nine fourteen-story apartment buildings. Indirectly, the university was also responsible for the first new Catholic church to be built in the Village in many years. Thanks to the generosity of the Generoso Pope family and the ingenuity of Father Andrew O'Reilly, the charismatic Catholic chaplain at N.Y.U., a chapel and center for the Catholic students were erected on Washington Square South on the site of the former school and French mission church of Our Lady of Mercy.[8]

If Robert Moses had had his way, he would also have constructed a four-lane extension of Fifth Avenue through the center of Washington Square Park to West Broadway. Howls of protests from neighborhood residents, and opposition from Carmine G. De Sapio, a Village resident and the powerful leader of Tammany Hall, forced him to abandon the plan. However, in the new apartment buildings that arose in the South Village under Moses' auspices,

7. *New York Times,* May 12, 1957; June 24, 1955; David Boroff, "An Appeal To Save the Village," *New York Times Magazine,* May 7, 1961, 32.

8. William Barrett, "The Village Gone Bourgeois," *New York Times Magazine,* April 4, 1954, 19.

rents averaged $50 per room, well beyond the means of many long-time residents of the Village, as real estate developers freely admitted. An elderly woman sunning herself on the front stoop of a tenement house that had seen better days summed up her impressions of the impact of gentrification in Greenwich Village. "There is only one bad thing about this neighborhood," she said. "There is no place to live." A committee appointed by New York University to study housing conditions in the Village came to the same conclusion and reported in the summer of 1954 that the proliferation of upscale housing was "squeezing" the middle class out of the Village.[9]

The West Village escaped the large-scale urban renewal that forced many poorer residents to leave the South Village. As a result, St. Joseph's Church did not experience the same massive decline in numbers as did the two neighboring Italian churches, St. Anthony's and Our Lady of Pompei, which drew many of their parishioners from the heavily Italian South Village. St. Anthony's was particularly hard hit. Between 1960 and 1968 the total Catholic population of the parish dwindled from seven thousand to two thousand.[10] In the late 1960s, St. Joseph's began to experience the same phenomenon in a more attenuated form. Throughout the late 1940s and 1950s, however, Mass attendance at St. Joseph's remained remarkably stable, with approximately two thousand people attending Mass every Sunday. It was a far cry, of course, from the ten thousand parishioners that the parish boasted of at the turn of the twentieth century, but the Sunday Mass attendance was virtually the same in the late 1950s as it had been in the early 1930s. However, a more telltale sign was the sharp drop in the number of baptisms, from 150 per year in the depths of

9. *New York Times*, June 24, 1955; May 13, 1954; December 8, 20, 1957.

10. AANY, *Status Animarum* Reports of St. Anthony of Padua Church, 1960, 1968. According to Donald Tricario, the Scalabrinians at Our Lady of Pompei were more successful than the Franciscans at St. Anthony of Padua in preserving the Italian character of the parish and maintaining ties with former parishioners. By the mid-1970s, the *festa* at St. Anthony's attracted a half-million visitors and was extended from seven days to two weeks. However, it was geared to outsiders, not the parishioners. "Italians sardonically point out that only a stranger would pay $2.50 for a sausage sandwich," noted Tricario. *Italians of Greenwich Village*, 113–16.

the Depression, when few couples were having babies, to only 86 in 1960, when the American birthrate was soaring. As in many other Manhattan parishes, young families had joined the flight to the suburbs, leaving St. Joseph's with an aging population.[11]

Father John P. McCaffrey

The pastor of St. Joseph's Church in the postwar years was Father John P. McCaffrey, who served there for almost a quarter of a century, from 1944 until his death from a heart attack in St. Vincent's Hospital on August 4, 1967. A native New Yorker and a graduate of St. Francis Xavier College on West 16th Street, he had previously been pastor of St. Joseph's Church in Kingston. Prior to that assignment, in 1924, at the age of twenty-eight, he had been appointed the chaplain at Sing Sing prison, a maximum security facility in Ossining, New York. Over the next sixteen years he received widespread praise for his devotion to the inmates at Sing Sing, both Catholic and non-Catholic, especially those on death row. He walked the last mile with 167 men and women, probably more than any other chaplain in the history of the prison. One prisoner, Sam Wong, became a Christian on the morning of his execution. After every execution, McCaffrey said, "I could never sleep afterwards. I would walk through the country, on and on, until I knew I had to sleep from sheer physical exhaustion."[12]

Although McCaffrey never questioned the legitimacy of the death penalty, he was an outspoken critic of New York's felony murder law, which made all the participants in a felony subject to the death penalty if a person was killed in the commission of the crime. In 1932 he said: "The two most important things for the prevention of crime are education and religion, and it is these two things that receive the least stress in prison." When McCaffrey celebrated his last Mass in Sing Sing in 1939, a thousand inmates, many non-Catholic, attended the service. In a highly unusual editorial tribute, the

11. *Status Animarum* Reports of St. Joseph's Church, 1932, 1945, 1960.
12. *New York Times,* August 4, 1967.

New York Times commented: "The last moments before death are not easy to watch in any case. One hundred and fifty men and women about to make that last faltering walk from the death house received their final words of comfort on this earth from Father McCaffrey. . . . [He] set up no distinction of creed or race when his services were wanted. He gave what he could of himself to Catholic, Jew, Buddhist or Protestant in the re-shaping of crooked lives, or, when the hour for that was too late, the tending of the spirit."[13]

Some years after he left the prison ministry, McCaffrey came to the defense of another prison chaplain who had ruffled some feathers by helping to establish the innocence of an inmate. McCaffrey admired what the chaplain had done and told Auxiliary Bishop James Francis McIntyre, the archdiocesan chancellor, "At any rate don't be too hard on him." Reflecting on his own experience, he explained, "I had a fellow go who I am sure was innocent. I did all I could to help him, but no one paid any attention until it was all over." McCaffrey may have been describing himself, when he added, "A prison chaplain needs great prudence and, when he does slip, it is generally on the side of some poor devil who is getting a rough deal."[14]

Shortly after his arrival in Greenwich Village, Father McCaffrey reactivated the former school building on Washington Place that had been built at the turn of the century. During the Depression, as school enrollment dropped, Father Hickey had closed the building and consolidated all the classes in the school annex on Christopher Street. Father McCaffrey found a new use for the facility by offering it to the archdiocese as a branch of Cathedral High School for Girls. Despite wartime shortages of materials, he managed to renovate the interior with a new electrical system and new plumbing, and even to

13. *New York Times*, March 7, 8, 20, 1939.

14. AANY, McCaffrey to McIntyre, n.d. [early 1940s]. In 1932 McCaffrey wrote an article contesting allegations that a disproportionately high number of prison inmates were Catholics. He referred the critics to the parable of the Pharisee and the publican. "The fact is we have perhaps a few more publicans and sinners," he admitted, "but as for the Pharisees, that is another matter." *Commonweal* 17 (October 14, 1932), 176.

The Interior of St. Joseph's Church

1937

1965

1972

sandblast the exterior, in a mere sixty days. The building was ready for occupancy in September 1944, staffed by the Missionary Sisters of the Third Order of St. Francis, and was blessed by Archbishop Francis J. Spellman on November 19, 1944.[15]

In the 1950s McCaffrey embarked upon a more ambitious building project when he decided to replace the rectory with a new and larger structure. The original plans called for a brick-and-limestone building that would include not only living quarters for the priests, but also a sacristy, youth center, information center, and a "liturgical baptistry." The initial goal was to raise $100,000, and there was no lack of volunteers to launch the campaign. In February 1954 no fewer than 150 parishioners—all men—fanned out across the parish ringing doorbells and soliciting contributions for the building that now stands on Sixth Avenue adjacent to the church. The successful completion of the project was indicative of the continuing vitality of the parish and the effectiveness of old-fashioned door-to-door fund-raising. Shortly thereafter McCaffrey was made a monsignor, which was the customary way for Cardinal Spellman to honor successful builders among his clergy. However, a decade later, by the time of Monsignor McCaffrey's death in August 1967, the halcyon postwar years had given way to the turmoil and tumult of the 1960s.[16]

The 1960s: Sturm und Drang

The 1960s began on a reassuring note, especially for American Catholics, with the election of the first Catholic president of the United States. Within a few years, however, the romantic vision of Camelot on the Potomac quickly faded as the nation was plunged into deep internal divisions over the civil rights movement, the Vietnam War, and in the early 1970s, the Watergate scandal. The assassi-

15. New York *Catholic News,* November 18, 1944. The rental was a bargain for the archdiocese. The archdiocese paid the parish $300 per month, but the parish had to pay the cost of lighting and heating the building. By 1971 the expenses exceeded the income from the rental. AANY, George J. Lyons, State of St. Joseph's Parish, April 1971.

16. New York *Catholic News,* February 13, 1954.

nations of President John F. Kennedy, Robert F. Kennedy, and Dr. Martin Luther King, Jr., intensified the sense of national crisis. Although President Lyndon B. Johnson eased racial tensions by sponsoring landmark civil rights legislation and pushing it through the Congress, his escalation of the American involvement in the Vietnam War unleashed widespread opposition, especially on the part of young Americans. Civil discourse reached such a low level that the president of the United States could not appear in public without provoking violent demonstrations. When President Johnson came to New York for the funeral of Cardinal Spellman in December 1967, he had to be spirited in and out of St. Patrick's Cathedral by a rear door.

The radicalism of the 1960s spawned a revival of Greenwich Village's reputation as the bohemia of America, at least east of California. Unlike the radicals who first gave Greenwich Village its bohemian reputation in the first two decades of the twentieth century, however, their latter-day counterparts were short on talent but awash in narcissism and adept at self-advertisement. The radicals of the 1960s were more likely to be known as hippies or beatniks than as bohemians. Many were weekend visitors to Greenwich Village who combined a taste for radical politics with long hair, faded denim clothes, motorcycles, bad manners, alcohol, drugs, and loud music. Their behavior made them thoroughly obnoxious to many residents of the Village, who voiced the same complaints that their parents and grandparents had a half-century earlier.

In the summer of 1964, Edward I. Koch, the future mayor of New York City, was a promising young politician who had just wrested control of the local Democratic organization from Carmine De Sapio. That summer he was instrumental in founding a community organization, the MacDougal Street Area Neighborhood Association, in an effort to redress the complaints of many residents. At a raucous public meeting that lasted three hours, the participants hooted down Allen Ginsberg, an icon of the hippie generation, who asked in mock innocence, "Do you think that we should not read poetry here?" Koch tried to calm the angry crowd in his own inimitable way with a variation of Barry Goldwater's famous campaign slogan. "Extremism in the pursuit of sleep is no virtue," Koch proclaimed.[17]

Koch later admitted, "The people who live on [MacDougal] Street haven't been able to get a decent night's sleep for years." His complaints were echoed by the local assemblyman, William F. Passannante, who called attention to "the enormous influx of perverts, derelicts, street pedlars and motorcycle gangs." In the fall of 1965, the *New York Times* reported that Greenwich Village had become as notorious as Times Square as a gathering place for bizarre individuals. One shopkeeper on MacDougal Street offered his own blunt assessment of the difference between the old bohemians and their successors. "These bums don't care about art the way Villagers did when Sinclair Lewis and Crane Hart lived here," he opined. "They're just slobs."[18]

The deterioration of the Village reached the point where even the easygoing Lindsay administration decided it was time to act. In the spring of 1966, the chief inspector of the New York City Police Department, Sanford D. Garelik, announced a crackdown on illegal activities in Times Square and Greenwich Village. He declared that the two areas "have become magnets for some of the more disreputable elements in our society and require our immediate and urgent attention." Garelik's campaign included an increased police presence and a short-lived experiment in closing fourteen blocks of the Village to outside vehicular traffic. The crackdown brought an immediate protest from the New York branch of the American Civil Liberties Union, whose executive director, Aryeh Neier, accused the police of equating deviant social behavior with criminal activity. "It is not a crime to be a degenerate, derelict or alcoholic," the ACLU contended.[19]

Mayor John Lindsay responded by holding a meeting with repre-

17. *New York Times,* July 29, 1964.
18. *New York Times,* October 4, 1964; November 21, September 9, 1965.
19. *New York Times,* March 16, 18, 19, 1966.

sentatives of the ACLU and local coffee house and cabaret owners at a restaurant on Bleecker Street owned by one of the critics of the police crackdown. Sipping a bloody mary, the Mayor assured the assemblage that there would be no entrapment of homosexuals and no harassment of avant-garde artists in the Village. “It was a great civil liberties happening,” crowed Aryeh Neier. “I’ve never seen anything like it.” The proprietor of the restaurant told the press that Mayor Lindsay said he had had as much fun at the meeting as in his sessions with Mike Quill during the transit strike. Commissioner Garelik was also present at the meeting. His reactions were not recorded, but it was the end of his attempt to clean up Times Square and Greenwich Village.[20]

A year later conditions in the Village were no better. This time the judiciary intervened in the person of State Supreme Court Justice Charles A. Tierney, in response to a suit brought by six resident owners of property on MacDougal Street. Justice Tierney found in their favor and described the deplorable social conditions on a four-block stretch of MacDougal Street in almost the same language that Justice William Caffrey had used in 1922. “The illicit activities,” Tierney wrote in his decision, “are contributing factors to the madness and unhealthy situation which is rapidly enveloping not only the petitioners’ street, but the entire Greenwich Village, affecting thousands of its respectable inhabitants and visitors.” He ordered the mayor and city officials to take immediate action. Once again, however, Mayor Lindsay objected and blamed the situation on the lenient sentences handed down by the judges.[21]

In the summer of 1968, Homer Bigart, a prize-winning journalist, interviewed several of the Catholic clergy in the Village. They were unanimous in deploring the deterioration in the quality of life. Monsignor James Searson, the Catholic chaplain at New York University, said that Holy Trinity Chapel had been vandalized so many times that he had developed a siege mentality. “We’ve lost paschal

20. *New York Times,* May 3, 1966.
21. *New York Times,* December 27, 29, 1967.

candles, acolyte benches and tabernacle candles made in Spain and costing $500. They've stolen everything but the cross." Crossing Washington Square, said Searson, was "like walking through an open ward of a mental institution." At Our Lady of Pompei Church, the pastor, Father Guido Caverzan, echoed many of the same complaints. He had discovered people using the confessionals for sleeping and as bathrooms. "I have found dope addicts lying in the sanctuary screaming and crying," he said. "During Sunday Masses we have to station someone at the door to throw them out."

A few blocks farther north on Sixth Avenue, at St. Joseph's Church, Monsignor Timothy Herlihy had similar horror stories. Thieves were constantly rifling the poor boxes and, only a few weeks earlier, had stolen the collection at the 7:00 A.M. Mass. Herlihy showed Homer Bigart the front steps of the church littered with broken bottles and discarded beer cans. "This is the filthiest place I've ever seen in my life," he said, mentioning that he was thinking of erecting a fence to prevent derelicts from blocking the entrance to the church. Like many Villagers, he blamed lax law enforcement for failing to correct these appalling conditions. "People feel they can do whatever they like here," he said, "that they have absolute license and to hell with the community."[22]

A number of local political leaders, including Assemblyman William Passannante and Councilwoman Carol Greitzer, shared Monsignor Herlihy's conviction that city officials were taking advantage of the Village's tolerant reputation to use it as a dumping ground for homeless men, many of them former convicts. Edward Koch, never bashful about expressing his opinions and now a member of Congress, charged in 1970 that "there was a conscious decision by the [Lindsay] administration in 1965 to make Greenwich Village wide open for every circus program imaginable." The result, warned Koch, was that city policies were "turning a liberal community into a reactionary community."[23]

22. *New York Times,* August 9, 1968.
23. *New York Times,* September 28, 1970.

The outspoken Monsignor Herlihy, a former Navy chaplain who spent four years aboard the U.S.S. *Intrepid* in World War II, had become pastor of St. Joseph's Church only the previous fall. A native of All Saints parish in East Harlem, he had been pastor of St. Stanislaus Church in Pleasant Valley before succeeding Monsignor John McCaffrey at St. Joseph's in September 1967. Unfortunately his tenure lasted only three years. He died of lung cancer in St. Vincent's Hospital on September 9, 1970, at the relatively young age of sixty-two. Monsignor Herlihy's successor, Monsignor John P. A. Sullivan, appointed in October 1970, was pastor of St. Joseph's for only six months. Baptized in St. Veronica's parish, Monsignor Sullivan was proud of his local roots. In a letter to the Landmarks Preservation Commission, he boasted, "I am a Villager born and raised," and he assured the commission, "I have a stake in keeping what is left of the Village intact." Monsignor Sullivan died of a massive heart attack in March 1971 at the age of sixty-nine, before he had the opportunity to put his own stamp on the parish.[24]

Vatican II in Greenwich Village

The 1960s and 1970s were particularly turbulent decades for American Catholics. Not only did they have to contend with the same conflicts in American society as the rest of their fellow citizens, but they also had to face a period of unprecedented turmoil in the Catholic Church in the aftermath of Vatican Council II. The Council met in Rome for three-month sessions every fall from 1962 to 1965, inaugurating a series of far-reaching changes in the Church. Although the changes were often equated with *aggiornamento* or "modernization," the Council in fact mandated both *aggiornamento* and *ressourcement,* that is, a modernization of Catholic life that was to be rooted in the recovery and revitalization of the authentic Catholic tradition in such areas as scripture, liturgy, ecclesiology, and ecumenism. The finer points of the bishops' deliberations at the

24. New York *Catholic News,* September 17, 1970; March 18, 1971. Ryan, "St. Joseph's Church," 120.

Council may have gone over the heads of many lay people, but the practical impact of the Council became evident to every Catholic once the liturgical changes were implemented on the parish level. Depending on local circumstances, and on such variable factors as the receptivity of the laity to the changes and the pastoral sensitivity of the clergy in implementing them, the liturgical innovations met with varying degrees of acceptance or resistance. In St. Joseph's Church, the crucial period was to be the early 1970s.

Three new priests came to St. Joseph's Church in 1971. The first was Father Robert Wilde, who succeeded Monsignor Sullivan as pastor in May 1971. Father Wilde had earned a doctorate in the classics from the Catholic University of America and had spent some twenty years as a teacher of Greek at Cathedral College, the minor seminary of the archdiocese. He had combined his teaching career at Cathedral College with an intensive pastoral ministry at St. Elizabeth's Church in Washington Heights, where he resided. This combination of scholarly and pastoral work had earned him the respect of many priests, especially his former students, and made him an ideal candidate, or so it seemed, to implement the reforms of Vatican II in the challenging atmosphere of Greenwich Village.

Two young priests joined Father Wilde at St. Joseph's as his assistants. Within a few weeks of Father Wilde's arrival, Father Paul Dinter, a newly ordained priest, was appointed to St. Joseph's as his first parochial assignment. In October, Father Robert Lott, who had been ordained six years earlier and had served in two Westchester parishes, joined them. All three priests came to the parish of their own volition and they seemed well suited for Greenwich Village. They had strong intellectual interests and progressive political and theological views. Moreover, they liked one another, and were eager to put into practice the decrees of Vatican II, especially those pertaining to the liturgy.

Although Wilde was canonically the pastor and had the primary responsibility for the administration of the parish, the three priests agreed that they would act collegially in making all major decisions and that they would also consult with the laity. Among other innovations, they decided to pray together every day, a practice that was the norm in many religious communities but was rarely to be found among the more individualistic diocesan clergy. The experiment in shared leadership, and more specifically their attempt to bring *aggiornamento* to Greenwich Village, lasted little more than two years, but it caused deep divisions among the parishioners that took many years to heal. Not since the bitter battles over lay trusteeism in the 1830s and 1840s was St. Joseph's Church the center of such heated controversy and internal division.

Aside from ideological issues, Father Wilde's pastorate coincided with major changes in the neighborhood. Until the late 1960s, St. Joseph's Church had been more or less impervious to the social and economic changes that had severely affected the other Catholic churches in Greenwich Village. By the time Father Wilde assumed the position of pastor, however, the full impact of these changes was becoming evident. Estimates of the total number of parishioners in 1971 varied from 1,200 to 1,700. Sunday Mass attendance hovered around 1,100, half of what it had been only a decade earlier. There were 270 children in St Joseph's School, but 129 of them lived outside the parish. The chairman of the parish council, George J. Lyons, pointed out that high rents were forcing many parishioners to leave, and that many of the new residents were Jewish. Young families with children were especially likely to move, even if they could afford the rents, because of crime and the permissive atmosphere. Although the parish was free of debt and had $30,000 in the bank, the church needed repairs that were estimated to cost as much as $80,000. The decline in the number of parishioners meant that it was increasingly difficult to maintain the parish societies or to find volunteer workers for parish projects. "There are few new members and fewer young people," Mr. Lyons reported somberly. Another problem was the large number of Catholic churches in the area, all of them competing for a dwindling number of local Catholics. The Episcopalians were facing some of the same problems. Two of their well-endowed parishes, Grace Church and the Church of the Ascension, were even said to be considering the possibility of a merger.[25]

The new team at St. Joseph's Church, consisting of Fathers Wilde, Lott, and Dinter, was not beginning with a tabula rasa in introducing the results of Vatican II to St. Joseph's parish. Monsignor Herlihy had already organized an elected parish council with five committees, one of them an active liturgy committee. Some modest liturgical changes had already been introduced at Mass, such as an offertory procession, the exchange of a sign of peace, and the reception of Holy Communion at the center aisle rather than at the Communion rail. With the approval of Monsignor Sullivan, the parish liturgical committee had invited Monsignor Charles McManus, the chairman of the Archdiocesan Liturgical Commission, to speak at the parish in November 1970. The initial liturgical innovations had already raised the hackles of some of the more conservative parishioners. One member of the parish liturgical committee sent up a warning flare early in 1971 when she expressed concern that the priests of the parish had not done an adequate job of explaining the liturgical changes to the people.[26]

Transition and Resistance

Over the next two years, as the pace of liturgical change in the parish quickened, so did the number of complaints from dissatisfied parishioners. Robert Moses had once commented that Greenwich Village had more ideas per person than any other area of New York City. That observation seemed to be verified in the early 1970s as St. Joseph's Church embarked upon its local version of *aggiornamento.* The focus of many complaints was the renovation of the interior of the church in 1972. At that time every parish had to make some architectural changes to accommodate the new liturgical norms. Some parishes did no more than place a free-standing wooden altar

25. AANY, James P. Mahoney, Memorandum for His Eminence, Terence Cardinal Cooke, September 25, 1970; George J. Lyons, Report on St. Joseph's Church, April 1971; Mrs. Madeleine Edwards, Report on St. Joseph's School, April 1971.

26. AANY, Lydia Haggerty to John Duffell, March 30, 1971.

in the sanctuary. Other parishes, like St. Joseph's, used the opportunity to embark upon more ambitious remodeling projects. Upon the advice of the liturgical committee of the parish council, it was decided not only to renovate the sanctuary for the new liturgy, but also to restore the original character of the interior of the building.

This decision added immeasurably to the problem of winning general acceptance of the architectural changes. Unlike almost every other Catholic church in New York City, St. Joseph's Church had been constructed in the Greek Revival style, with a plain Georgian interior that reflected the restrained piety of eighteenth-century English and Irish Catholics. However, over the course of the following century, the interior had been transformed (or deformed) by the addition of numerous statues, pictures, and other Victorian and pseudo-Gothic embellishments, culminating in 1937 with the addition of two marble columns flanking the main altar. Many of the additions had little intrinsic artistic value and clashed with the original design of the church, but they had nurtured the piety of generations of parishioners. The sudden removal of this eclectic assemblage of statues and other devotional objects, however justified esthetically, was bound to offend the religious sensibilities of many parishioners. John de Latour, an American art specialist who was the coordinator of the restoration, did little to soothe hurt feelings when he commented publicly: "Over the years the original had been covered with so much gimcrackery that it began to look like a spoof of itself."[27]

Some parishioners complained about the transfer of the Blessed Sacrament from the main altar to a side area of the church. Others objected to covering the picture of the Crucifixion behind the main altar after it was declared "liturgically unacceptable [since] our present emphasis is on the resurrected Christ."[28] Still others protested the removal of statues and pictures of the Blessed Mother and the saints, especially a statue of St. Joseph that had stood above the main

27. *New York Times,* December 4, 1972.

28. ASJC, Master Plan for the Renovation and Restoration of St. Joseph's Church, May 15, 1972.

door of the church for many years. "They are slowly making our once beautiful church into a Protestant church," was the reaction of some disgruntled parishioners.[29] The complaint was not as far-fetched as it may seem, for the eighteenth-century English Catholic chapels that were the model for St. Joseph's Church did resemble contemporary Anglican churches.

Some of the complaints reflected the paranoia that surfaced in certain right-wing circles after Vatican II. It was alleged that the parish priests were promoting a communist agenda by discouraging the recitation of the rosary, featuring Protestant hymns at Mass, and dissuading people from joining traditional Catholic organizations like the Knights of Columbus. Some irate Irish American parishioners even saw a sinister significance in a banner that was displayed behind the main altar. "The dark blue and orange colors are those of William of Orange," they claimed, "whose banner is still flaunted by Paisleyite Protestants as they parade past Catholic cathedrals and play their insulting songs exulting over the slaughter of 100,000 Irish Catholics at the battle of the Boyne in 1690." "Unless we are lucky enough to get rid of [Father Wilde] by July 12," they predicted, "he will probably include 'Croppie Lie Down' in the liturgy." Father Dinter's homilies criticizing American involvement in the Vietnam War provoked criticism also, leading one parishioner to speculate that he was a "fellow traveler."[30]

Other complaints were more substantive, however, such as the claim that the removal of the confessionals from the church had deprived people of privacy in the sacrament of penance. What seemed to irk at least one longtime parishioner most was what she perceived to be a lack of genuine consultation and the assumption that St. Joseph's Church had been languishing in the Dark Ages before 1972. This person gave eloquent expression to these concerns when she told Terence Cardinal Cooke in December 1972: "There is nothing wrong with change and certainly every group needs new blood to

29. AANY, Parishioners of St. Joseph's Church to Msgr. Lawrence J. Kenny, January 19, 1972.

30. AANY, Parishioners to Kenny, n.d.

carry on, but when a new minority can ignore all views but their own, and all tradition, and people are pushed aside as though they never had an intelligent thought about anything concerning their Church, this is not a healthy change—this is simply 'my way or else.'" This same person called the Cardinal's attention to "the fine hard-working priests of the past who were dedicated to the sacramental life of the parish. Their time and energies too," she said, "were expended in community affairs, ecumenical involvement, adult education, the school and the center for our youth. Our new ministers would have you believe that all this and liturgy too were unheard of before they arrived."[31]

One of the priests she undoubtedly had in mind was Monsignor John J. Casserly, who spent all of his thirty-four years as a priest as an assistant at St. Joseph's, earning the respect of both liberals and conservatives. His continued presence in the parish might have provided a much-needed element of continuity and unity during this difficult period of transition. No one appreciated Casserly's services more than Wilde. He described him to Cardinal Cooke as "one who in himself bears the past both of the Village community and of our parish life into the present and into the future." Casserly was grievously ill by the time Wilde became pastor. He graciously insisted that Casserly should not go to a nursing home but remain at St. Joseph's with the title of first assistant. He died after a long illness on January 9, 1972.[32]

On Sunday, December 3, 1972, Cardinal Cooke celebrated a Mass of Thanksgiving marking the formal reopening of the church. A compulsive optimist who shied away from confrontation, the Cardinal referred obliquely to the conflicts that had shaken the parish, but

31. AANY, Letter of parishioner to Cooke, December 11, 1972.

32. AANY, Wilde to Cooke, October 8, 1971. Cardinal Cooke made Casserly a monsignor three months before his death. In writing to thank Cooke, one parishioner said: "For many, many different pastoral regimes, Father Casserly has served the people of God at St. Joseph's Church. He has been to many of us the single and continuing sign of a renewing Church. Long before Vatican II and certainly after Vatican II, he incarnated that spirit of the renewing Church." AANY, Robert E. Rambusch to Cooke, October 18, 1971.

he likened them to family quarrels that often had a healthy outcome. On display that morning on the rear wall of the church was a fresco of the Transfiguration that dated from the 1830s. For decades it had been hidden under six coats of paint and was only discovered accidentally in the course of the restoration. After the Mass, Cardinal Cooke proceeded to the basement of the church, which he dedicated in honor of Monsignor Casserly. Always a gracious public figure and a master of small talk, he spent an hour shaking hands and conversing with the parishioners.[33]

Father Wilde managed to defray some of the cost of the renovation of the church with the help of some seventy-five volunteers who donated their services. However, financial management was not Wilde's forte, and he found himself involved in a running battle with the Chancery Office over the parish's assessment by the Commission for Inter-Parish Financing. This was a body established by Cardinal Cooke to levy a fixed tax on the income of every parish. The commission used the funds to subsidize poor parishes. Father Wilde balked at paying his assessment on the grounds that he was already subsidizing other parishes by admitting their children to his parochial school. In making an issue of this matter, he chose his ground poorly and won little sympathy from his fellow pastors.[34]

Father Donald Johnston, the pastor of St. Theresa's Church, a poor parish on the Lower East Side of Manhattan, pointed out to Father Wilde and his two associates that many parishes educated children who lived outside the parish boundaries. "If parishes could designate their own favorites charities," he said pointedly, "no organized method of sharing resources would be possible." The priests of St. Joseph then said that they could not meet their assessment be-

33. ASJC, A Record of Services and Events: St. Joseph's Church, Greenwich Village, New York, December 3, 1972.

34. Some of Wilde's financial problems stemmed from the expenses he incurred during the renovation of the church in 1972. In reviewing the plans, Monsignor William J. McCormack, the secretary of the Board of Diocesan Consultors, noted dryly that "unhappily it appears that the Finance Committee of the parish is less creative than the art and liturgy groups." AANY, McCormack, Memorandum for the Meeting of the Diocesan Consultors on May 25, 1972, May 23, 1972.

cause of the declining Mass attendance and income. When Father Johnston mentioned that they could at least pay part of their assessment, Father Wilde said that it was the first time he had heard that it would be possible to satisfy his obligations in this fashion.[35]

In the protracted disagreements that unsettled many parishes in the wake of Vatican II, parishioners sometimes became so fixated on their own concerns that they overlooked the stress and strain that these conflicts imposed on their priests. Father Wilde came under fire from both conservatives who thought he was too liberal and liberals who thought he was too conservative. He incurred the ire of the latter when he refused to disregard the diocesan guidelines in the appointment of extraordinary ministers of the Eucharist. At a general meeting of the parish council in April 1973, one participant said that "the feeling permeating the air bordered almost on hatred."[36]

By that time the accumulated pressures of being the pastor of St. Joseph's Church had taken their toll on Father Wilde. He experienced a severe personal crisis during that spring and summer, not a crisis of faith, but a crisis of vocation. On August 28, he resigned from the parish and from the active ministry, married a short time later, and lived thereafter as an exemplary Catholic husband and father. Worldwide there were many casualties connected with Vatican II. Not the least of them in New York was the resignation from the priesthood of Robert Wilde after almost thirty years of service to the archdiocese. He attempted, not always with tact or success, but always with sincerity and conviction, to bring the benefits of Vatican II to the people of St. Joseph's Church.

35. AANY, Donald Johnston to Cooke, February 3, 1973. Wilde also failed to take up the annual collection for Cathedral Preparatory Seminary until he was prompted to do so by the diocesan authorities. He finally took up the collection three months late, announcing it in the parish bulletin with the following explanation: "This collection was scheduled for October, but the United States Mails did not deliver the letter from the Cardinal wherein he mandated it." *Bulletin of St. Joseph's Church,* December 10, 1972.

36. ASJC, Minutes of the Meeting of the Parish Council, May 7, 1973; Parishioner to Natalie Darcy, May 2, 1973.

Searching for a Shepherd

After Wilde's resignation, Father Lott and Father Dinter jointly pleaded with Cardinal Cooke not to appoint an interim administrator, on the grounds that it would polarize the parish. When they learned that the Cardinal had already decided to do so, they asked him to reconsider his decision, since they felt that it would indicate a lack of confidence in them. However, Cooke declined to reverse himself and named Father John M. McCarthy the temporary administrator of the parish. Almost immediately Father Lott submitted his bid to be the next pastor. He had the enthusiastic support of Father Dinter, who intended to reside in the parish while he pursued a doctoral degree at Columbia University.[37]

Dinter used the occasion of Father Wilde's resignation to reflect on the events of the previous two years, particularly those involving the liturgy. He admitted that the changes had come too quickly and too radically for some parishioners, but he insisted that they had been formulated on a collaborative basis. He had a low opinion of the liturgical expertise of his fellow diocesan clergy, many of whom, he thought, needed "a real re-education." In fact he attributed some of the difficulties at St. Joseph's to neighboring churches where the clergy resisted liturgical change and gave tacit endorsement to accusations of heterodoxy at St. Joseph's. "What was being developed was a certain style at St. Joseph's," he explained, "not in any superficial sense, but in the conviction that the highly pluralistic and sophisticated portions of the population of Greenwich Village needed and were entitled to an articulate, modern approach to the Church and to theology."[38]

Like a crucial parliamentary by-election in Great Britain, the appointment of the new pastor of St. Joseph's Church in the fall of 1973 was closely watched by the diocesan clergy as a sign of the prevailing ideological winds in the archdiocese. Rarely in diocesan history had

37. AANY, Lott and Dinter to Cooke, September 1, 1973; Lott to Thomas Leonard, September 17, 1973.

38. AANY, Dinter to Leonard, September 19, 1973.

the appointment of a pastor been the object of such intense scrutiny or such widespread consultation. The dramatic exit of the previous pastor and the well-known internal conflicts in the parish heightened interest in the outcome far beyond the confines of Greenwich Village. However, the more thoroughly the parish was picked over by various evaluators and prognosticators, the less appeal the office of pastor had to the diminishing number of candidates who were interested in the post.

The parishioners who supported Father Lott ranged from a feisty eighty-four-year-old woman who railed against the possible appointment of a reactionary pastor to a young man who said that the liturgy and social activism of St. Joseph's Church had led him to return to the practice of the faith. Other parishioners demurred. They pointed to the friction that had already surfaced between Father Lott and the more conservative Father McCarthy, and they feared that Father Lott would react badly to the appointment of anyone who did not share his own sometimes idiosyncratic views.

Three members of an Ad Hoc Evaluation Committee of the Lower West Clergy Conference Committee—Father James Abbarno, C.S., Monsignor Gustav J. Schultheiss, and Father John Duffell (the chairman of the Area Clergy Conference)—visited the parish on September 18, the day after Father Lott submitted his application for pastor. Monsignor Schultheiss drew up a preliminary report listing the qualities that would be needed in the next pastor. They included such characteristics as a willingness to work closely with the parish council, an openness to the creation of a "pastoral team" with shared authority, and an interest in community involvement, social service, and outreach to the growing gay community. Most, if not all, of the qualities listed seemed ready at hand in the person of Robert Lott, which was a thought that would not have escaped his attention.[39]

The Ad Hoc Committee returned to St Joseph's Church twice again in October, first to meet with the parish council, and then to

39. AANY, Gustav J. Schultheiss, Preliminary Draft of Lower West Side Clergy Conference Committee to Report on Vacancy at St. Joseph's [Church], September 20, 1973.

be present at an open meeting of the parishioners. As a result of these further deliberations, Monsignor Schultheiss submitted his own recommendations to the chairman of the Ad Hoc Committee. Schultheiss was one of the senior priests of the diocese and had been a close confidant of Cardinal Spellman. His recommendations would presumably carry considerable weight with Cardinal Cooke. Observing that it was useless to try to assess blame for the division in St. Joseph's Church, Schultheiss declared that the parish needed new leadership. For that reason, he recommended that Father Dinter should sever his ties with St. Joseph's and that Father Lott should be invited to do the same prior to the appointment of a new pastor. He pointed out that "there were no guidelines for the three who became a team with Father Wilde as pastor. Hence, there was no blueprint for the administrator and the two associates. With two camps it will be difficult to obtain unity and the common good."[40]

Unfortunately, when Cardinal Cooke failed to follow his recommendations, Schultheiss' predictions proved to be all too accurate. Always a leader who preferred conciliation to conflict, Cooke tried to find a peaceful compromise for the troubled situation at St. Joseph's Church. He refused to appoint Robert Lott the pastor, but he did not force him to leave the parish. Instead he allowed him to remain as the associate pastor when he gave the parish to Father John P. O'Leary. When O'Leary was installed as the new pastor on January 20, 1974, he must have felt a certain kinship with John McCloskey, who had been dispatched to St. Joseph's Church on a similar mission of pacification 130 years earlier.

40. AANY, Schultheiss to Kenneth F. O'Connell, November 12, 1973. Father O'Connell was the chairman of the Ad Hoc Evaluation Committee. He was not present at the meeting on September 18, 1973.

9 Nova et Vetera

DURING THE LAST QUARTER of the twentieth century, St. Joseph's Church had only two pastors, Father John D. O'Leary (1973–1985) and Father Aldo J. Tos (1986–2003). Their combined tenure, which lasted thirty years, gave the parish stability and continuity of leadership during a period of unprecedented stress and strain in American Catholicism and in American society as a whole. By any objective standard, St. Joseph's remained a progressive parish throughout these three decades, committed to implementing the reforms of Vatican II. However, the internal dissension that contributed to Father Wilde's resignation as pastor did not disappear with his departure. As might be expected in a parish with a high percentage of articulate, college-educated parishioners, many of whom were excited by the new possibilities opened to them by Vatican II, there were many different opinions about the scope and pace of *aggiornamento.* Similar differences appeared among the parish clergy, leaving both pastors with the unenviable task of trying to respect diversity of opinion while preserving the unity and peace of the parish.

Father John D. O'Leary

Father O'Leary, who was ordained in 1954, brought to his new assignment wide experience as a high school teacher and prison chaplain as well as many years of service in the pastoral ministry. One of the most nettlesome problems that he had to face was the role of the parish council in the administration of the parish. Parish councils were a prime facet of the effort inspired by Vatican II to accord the laity a substantive role in the governance of their local faith communities. The precise nature of that role was left largely undefined and varied from parish to parish. Unlike many other parishes, however, St. Joseph's Church had in place a comprehensive constitution for its parish council, which specified the respective roles of the clergy and laity in considerable detail. The Founding Fathers of the American Republic would have admired the ingenious system of checks and balances that the parish council established for itself and the pastor.[1]

St. Joseph's Parish Council

Throughout the 1970s and 1980s, the members of the parish council analyzed the constitution with talmudic diligence, often invoked it in disputes, and amended it several times. Some parishioners regarded it as their Magna Carta and zealously resisted any amendments that threatened to diminish their role in the administration of the parish. Whether they realized it or not, their attitude recalled that of the board of lay trustees in the 1830s and 1840s, who vigorously asserted the prerogatives of the laity as specified in the parish bylaws of 1833. Needless to say, like the trustees in the early nineteenth century, the members of the parish council in the 1970s and 1980s were committed Catholics, who saw their role as integral to the life of a post-Vatican II parish.

It should be remembered that parish councils were a new phenomenon in American Catholic life in the 1970s. There was no living American Catholic tradition of lay participation in parish administration, and friction developed in many parishes as clergy and laity

1. Consider the following example of the separation of powers as practiced at St. Joseph's Church: "The work of the Council shall be advisory in nature and shall be accomplished within a framework that acknowledges the pastor's right to veto power as the spiritual and temporal representative of the authority of the Church. However, the Council may, in the event of a veto, by a ⅔ vote of its voting members, request that the issue be re-discussed with the pastor. If the issue is again vetoed, the Council may by a ⅔ vote of its voting members have recourse to the Bishop or to his representative." ASJC, The Constitution of the Parish Council, Article III, Section 1, Revised July 15, 1974.

tried to demarcate their respective rights and duties. After some initial difficulties, they usually settled down to an amicable modus vivendi. In St. Joseph's parish, the process took longer than in many other places, leading to an ongoing polarization that lasted for more than a decade. In the mid-1970s it looked as if St. Joseph's Church was about to experience once again the wrenching internal conflicts that had disrupted the life of the parish during its first dozen years.

Since the parish council considered itself the watchdog of the parish constitution, the council members resisted any effort on the part of the clergy to modify it in their favor. Thus, in the fall of 1971, when Father Wilde suggested that the ex officio members of the parish council (including the pastor) should have the right to vote, the council rejected the request. In the spring of 1973, Father Wilde asked one gentleman to withdraw his candidacy for the parish council on the grounds that it would be divisive. "It is an effort to defuse the campaign," he explained to him politely, "so that the election will be issue-centered, not person-centered." However, when the individual refused to withdraw his candidacy, Father Wilde vetoed it.

The would-be candidate then appealed to the Archdiocesan Director of Parish Councils, Monsignor Henry J. Mansell, who persuaded Father Wilde to drop his veto. All these procedures took place in strict accordance with both the parish constitution and the archdiocesan guidelines for parish councils. However, while such carefully scripted parliamentary maneuverings were well suited to the rough and tumble world of secular politics, they worked less well in the context of a parish, where a broad consensus rather than a slender ballot-box victory was essential for peace and harmony.[2]

The laity could be at least as assertive as the clergy in pushing the envelope of their perceived prerogatives. In the fall of 1974, when the parish council considered proposals for reducing the school deficit, it was suggested that perhaps St. Joseph's School could merge with

2. ASJC, Minutes of the Meeting of the Constitutional Committee of the Parish Council of St. Joseph's Church, October 21, 1971; Wilde to Parishioner, n.d. [May 1973]; Henry J. Mansell to Participants in the Meeting of May 7, 1973, May 8, 1973.

other local Catholic schools. Sensing a developing crisis, Father O'Leary intervened and forbade the parish council to pursue the matter further. He made it clear that he was open to suggestions, but insisted that he alone would make the final decision about any merger of the school. In most parishes the pastor would need to say no more than that. In the litigious atmosphere that had developed at St. Joseph's, however, O'Leary felt it necessary to justify his stance by appealing to "Section 1 of Article III of the Constitution."[3]

Another solution for the school materialized the following year when Cathedral High School closed its St. Joseph's Annex, which was housed in the former parochial school building on Washington Place. O'Leary moved St. Joseph's School back to that building (which had been erected in 1897 as the new parish school) from its quarters on Christopher Street, and then rented the former school building on Christopher Street to St. Vincent's Hospital School of Nursing. It was at this time also that the Franciscan Sisters of Peekskill, who had been staffing the school, announced that they could no longer continue to do so. A Sister of Charity served as principal for one year, but after 1977, St. Joseph's School had an entirely lay staff.[4]

After attending a dozen or so meetings of the parish council, O'Leary put his thoughts on paper and shared them with the members of the council during Holy Week of 1975. While recognizing the many good things that the council had accomplished, O'Leary also confessed that "when I attend our meetings, I sense a charged field of emotions that puts a strain on all of us." The Holy Father had designated 1975 as a Year of Reconciliation, and O'Leary attempted to foster that spirit in the parish council. "What grieves me the most," he admitted, "is that varying opinions are seen as an adversary relationship, instead of as a difference of opinion." These personal differences seemed especially unfortunate to O'Leary because there was fairly consistent agreement about general goals. "What I

3. ASJC, Minutes of the Meeting of the Parish Council, October 14, 1974.
4. Ryan, "St. Joseph's Church," 131.

am asking for your consideration," said O'Leary, "is that we try and see the other person's opinion as just that, an opinion, without all sorts of moral, subjective judgments about it. . . . I assure you that, for my part, I shall strain to achieve the objectivity that I look for in you."[5]

The Parish and the Community

In such areas as liturgy, social activism, adult education, community involvement, and ecumenism, the parish under John O'Leary continued to move in the direction that had been mapped out by the new team that came to St. Joseph's in 1971. The parish continued its tradition of a communal celebration of the sacrament of penance during Advent and Lent, the Liturgy of the Hours was introduced as a regular liturgical practice, and St. Joseph's Church took part in the Palm Sunday Christian Unity Service in Washington Square Park. The church was a beehive of activity seven days a week in an area of New York City that never seemed to sleep. On weekends, St. Joseph's Church still had seven Masses, probably too many for an average attendance of only 800 people. The early morning Masses on Sunday rarely attracted more than fifty people. The Sunday collection averaged a disappointing total of $1,700, little more than $2 per person. At St. Joseph's Church, weekdays were as busy as Sundays. There were three Masses every day, at morning, noon, and early evening. Casserly Hall was in use almost continuously from early afternoon to late at night, with a variety of parish and outside activities that ranged from the Senior Citizens to the Boy Scouts to the Rosary Society to the School of Ballet and Tap.[6]

St. Joseph's was also a parish with an aging Catholic population, as it had been for some time. Attendance was increasing at the "Senior Socials" that were held every Tuesday afternoon in Casserly Hall. More and more parishioners were also taking advantage of Meals-on-Wheels, a program administered by the Caring Community of

5. ASJC, O'Leary to Dear Council Member, Tuesday of Holy Week, 1975.
6. *St. Joseph's Parish Bulletin*, January 6, 13, 20, 1974.

Greenwich Village, a coalition of Village churches, synagogues, and hospitals. Father Lott had been instrumental in establishing the Caring Community and served as a director. For many years he also served as president of the Village Nursing Home.[7]

Beyond the confines of the church and Casserly Hall, Greenwich Village remained a unique combination of quiet tree-lined streets and noisy avenues filled with every species of humanity. Father Robert F. Griffin, a Holy Cross priest from the cornfields of northern Indiana, spent the summer of 1974 in residence at St. Joseph's Church. He described his chance encounters with four local residents early one morning. One of them was an elderly bag lady wandering up and down Sixth Avenue searching for a place to sleep. Another was an eighteen-year-old boy on Christopher Street who gulped down a pint of whiskey and then went looking for a fight. In Sheridan Square another young man with a painted face cavorted about in a woman's dress; one of the habitués of the Square explained, "John has destroyed his mind with drugs." The fourth person was an attractive young woman "with great sadness in her face" who was begging for cigarettes and money.

Even after twenty years as a priest, Father Griffin found that his summer at St. Joseph's gave him a new appreciation of his vocation. "St. Joseph's is not just a neighborhood of discalced winos and sad-eyed children on a misadventure," he insisted. "It is a believing community of men and women redeemed to victory, whom sin cannot defeat and suffering can never discourage. It is a place of worship where a cleric may come on a summer holiday and learn again that faith is more than an affair of pieties preached in college chapels on Sunday afternoons." As he took leave of St. Joseph's Church after an eventful summer in the Village, he offered the priests and parishioners a gracious compliment. "I shall go back to Notre Dame," he said, "loving all of you for the renewal of grace you have given to the sacrament of my ordination."[8]

7. *Parish Bulletin,* January 13, 1974; Ryan, "St. Joseph's Church," 130.
8. *Parish Bulletin,* August 4, 11, 1974.

The range of programs and activities reflected the diversity of both the parish and the neighborhood. This was especially true of the liturgy, where old and new observances often existed side by side, although, no doubt, appealing to different constituencies. Traditional devotions like the monthly Mass and Communion breakfast of the Holy Name Society and the Monday evening novena continued to attract a following among older parishioners, even as morning prayer from the Liturgy of the Hours was being introduced. Private confession was available on Saturday afternoon, but communal penance services in Advent and Lent drew much larger numbers of penitents. The communal celebration of baptism and of the anointing of the sick also became the norm. There were few parishes in New York City, or anywhere else in the country for that matter, that could rival the diversity of St. Joseph's congregation. On one Sunday in November 1979, the West Meath Men's Association attended 11:00 A.M. Mass as a group for their deceased members, while at 5:00 P.M. Congresswoman Elizabeth Holtzman spoke at a special Interfaith Vesper Service. It is not likely that there was a heavy representation from West Meath at Vespers.

The Parish and the Wider World

The general liberal tenor of the parish showed itself in the attention given to such issues as the morality of nuclear war, immigration legislation, American involvement in Vietnam and Latin America, and gay rights. In 1983, when the Archdiocese of New York expressed opposition to pending gay rights legislation in the City Council, the *Parish Bulletin* commented tartly: "This week's unhappy implication of the local church's rejection of a whole class of human beings, many of them sisters and brothers in faith, is regrettable."[9] The guest preacher at one Advent Vespers in 1972 was Paul Moore, the liberal Episcopal Bishop of New York, whose presence never graced the pulpit of St. Patrick's Cathedral. Speakers on other occasions included Edward Schillebeeckx and Hans Küng, Peter Steinfels, the execu-

9. *Parish Bulletin,* February 27, 1983.

tive editor of *Commonweal,* and Ramsay Clark, the former attorney general, who spoke at St. Joseph's on October 19, 1975, on the topic of unconditional amnesty for those opponents of the Vietnam War who fled the country rather than serve in the military.

John Cardinal Krol, the conservative Archbishop of Philadelphia, was an unlikely candidate for attention in the *Parish Bulletin,* but he was pressed into service when he criticized the nuclear arms race in testimony before a congressional committee. A more likely hero was Archbishop Oscar Romero, who was often praised for his defense of civil rights in war-torn El Salvador. He died a martyr's death when he was gunned down by assassins while celebrating Mass in his own cathedral. Even Romero's severest critics could hardly take offense at the balanced way that his death was commemorated at St. Joseph's. "Almost alone among moderates," the *Parish Bulletin* reported, "Archbishop Romero retained the trust of the despairing poor. He preached against violence, but he did not equate that with submissiveness by the poor. He stood for an honest effort to build a more just society. Even the bold new redistribution of land, he warned, would end in disaster if it was coupled with oppression."[10]

Community involvement and commitment to social justice remained strong at St. Joseph's. That was evident in the annual Thanksgiving food collection, Christmas baskets for the poor, donations to support the work of Mother Theresa in Calcutta, and the promotion of the U. S. Bishops' Campaign for Human Development. In 1981, when Mayor Koch issued a plea for churches and synagogues to provide overnight shelters for the homeless during the winter months, St. Joseph's was one of the first churches to respond. Cots for ten men were set up in Casserly Hall, parishioners provided food and coffee, and 150 volunteers from the parish offered to staff the shelter seven nights a week. "We saw homeless people in our own parish," said James Sullivan, the coordinator of the shelter. "Instead of theorizing, we said we have to do something."[11] Two of the

10. *Parish Bulletin,* March 30, 1980.
11. *New York Times,* January 29, 1982.

early directors of the shelter, Peter Smith and Charles Green, were also instrumental in founding Partnership for the Homeless, a city-wide advocacy organization for the homeless.

The *New York Times* commented in an editorial that St. Joseph's Church "is reinforcing the ancient image of the Church as sanctuary . . . and providing what the Bible calls 'a place of light, refreshment and peace.'" "It can do so," the *Times* noted, "not only out of a sense of mission, but because the parish has a long history of neighborhood involvement, the right physical setup and a long list of volunteers—a powerful, practical base. Without that kind of base, such a scheme talks beautifully and walks badly." More than twenty years later, St. Joseph's Shelter was still making a significant contribution to the community, as was the Saturday afternoon soup kitchen, directed by Patricia Dempsey, and later by Miriam Lee, and staffed by a dedicated core of volunteers, including Tom Goodrich, Connie Fitzgerald, Jonathan Ross, Joseph Calto, and many others.[12]

Gains and Losses

In the course of the 1970s and the early 1980s, the Sunday Mass attendance declined by a quarter, to around 600 people, but the parish income increased to about $2,000 per week. However, the additional income was far from adequate to meet the needs of the parish. Finances reached such a precarious condition that in 1978 Father O'Leary even threatened to discontinue the coffee hour after Sunday Mass. The Christmas collection the following year was a hefty $9,000, but in the spring of 1980 O'Leary revealed that he had unpaid bills of $15,000, due mainly to increased fuel costs, and he appealed for a family contribution of $25 in the Easter collection. Three years later the Easter collection netted $10,871.95, nearly $3,000 more than the previous year.

However, just as the financial picture began to improve, O'Leary had to face another and more serious problem. Disagreements between him and Father Lott, which had been simmering for years,

12. *New York Times*, January 30, 1982; *Parish Bulletin*, December 23, 1984.

came to a head late in 1983. At O'Leary's request, Lott resigned as an associate pastor and announced his resignation at all the Sunday Masses. O'Leary's decision to ask for Lott's resignation had the approval of the other members of the parish staff, including Father Robert Hovda, the well-known liturgist, Father Karl Laird, S.J., and Sister Mary Danagher, S.C. However, after eleven years of service at St. Joseph's, Father Lott enjoyed considerable support among the parishioners. No fewer than three hundred people, many of them parishioners, attended a reception in his honor at St. Vincent's Hospital the following February.[13]

Father Lott remained a priest in good standing after resigning as associate pastor of St. Joseph's. But instead of going to another parish, which would have been the normal sequence of events, he chose to remain in Greenwich Village and devote himself to the management of the Village Nursing Home in his capacity as president of the institution. The Masses that he celebrated there for the residents also attracted a number of sympathetic parishioners who felt that he had been ill used by the archdiocese. The inevitable result was a continuation of the divisions that had plagued the parish for the previous decade.

Less than two years later, in October 1985, as his term of office was drawing to a close, Father O'Leary announced that he would soon be leaving St. Joseph's Church. There was an almost tangible sigh of relief in his otherwise matter-of-fact announcement. He added a carefully worded postscript which must have conveyed the intended meaning to those to whom it was addressed. "I am overwhelmingly grateful to the people of St. Joseph's Parish, its staff," he said, "and all who have allowed me to work with them in an open manner for the good of the Kingdom."[14]

Father Aldo J. Tos

One day in the late fall of 1985, after Father O'Leary had announced his intention to leave St. Joseph's Church, two New York

13. Ryan, "St. Joseph's Church," 134–35.

14. *Parish Bulletin*, October 13, 1985.

priests who were classmates and friends, Aldo Tos and Vincent Taglienti, visited St. Joseph's Church while passing through Greenwich Village on their day off. By chance they met an apprehensive Father Hovda, who expressed concern about who the next pastor might be. "Do you think that any good men are applying for this place?" he asked. Tos did not have the heart to tell him that, only the day before, he had applied for the parish. By the end of the week he received notice that he had been selected; he was officially appointed the pastor of St. Joseph's Church by Cardinal John O'Connor in December 1985.

Father Tos was the son of immigrants from northern Italy and a native of Holy Cross parish on West 42nd Street in Manhattan. Ordained in 1953, he was sent to the Catholic University of America, where he earned a doctorate in the philosophy of education. Thereafter he spent most of the following twenty-five years as a teacher, at one point combining a full-time assignment as a curate at Our Lady of Mount Carmel Church in Poughkeepsie with teaching religious studies at both Marist College and Our Lady of Lourdes High School. Subsequently he served as the spiritual director and the chairman of the religion department at Cardinal Spellman High School in the Bronx and at Monsignor Farrell High School on Staten Island. He also pursued postdoctoral studies in Scripture and liturgy at Union Theological Seminary and General Theological Seminary. Later he became the pastor of St. Patrick's Church, a rapidly growing suburban parish on Staten Island.

For a veteran priest, St. Joseph's Church in Greenwich Village had once been a highly sought-after assignment, a prestigious "city" parish where he could end his days in comfort with a large congregation and few financial worries. By 1985, however, those days were long gone. The well-publicized dissension that had afflicted the parish for over a dozen years made most priests hesitate to go there. The precarious financial condition of the church and school was an additional liability. However, there were compensating factors that induced Father Tos to accept the parish. The unique character of the neighborhood, and St. Joseph's reputation as an avant-garde parish, represented a challenge that appealed to his own progressive views and creative sensibilities. For a loyal native son of the West Side of Manhattan, being the pastor of St. Joseph's also offered a unique opportunity to continue the work of reshaping a historic parish according to the model envisioned by Vatican II. He was only the second Italian American (and the second non-Irish) pastor in the parish's history, the other exception being the unfortunate Father Constantine Pise, whose stormy pastorate lasted from 1836 to 1837.

In the general ethos of St. Joseph's Church with regard to such matters as liturgical renewal, ecumenism, social justice, and community involvement, little changed with Father Tos' arrival. If anything, the parish's commitment in those areas grew even stronger. A less welcome aspect of continuity in parish life, however, was the perennial divisiveness at St. Joseph's, which did not disappear with the advent of a new pastor. At least self-doubt among the more outspoken parishioners was not a pressing pastoral concern for the new pastor. For Father Tos, a welcome addition to St. Joseph's was the arrival in the summer of 1987 of Father Robert Norris, a young diocesan priest who had been his associate pastor at St. Patrick's Church on Staten Island. Father Norris remained at St. Joseph's for the next six years, making an important contribution to the parish, especially in such areas as liturgy and religious education.

The Church and the Gay Community

One of the first tests of Father Tos' leadership at St. Joseph's Church centered around the Catholic Church's teaching on homosexuality. As the pastor of a parish in one of the largest gay communities in the United States, he could not ignore the issue without abdicating his pastoral responsibility. The situation was complicated in October 1986 when the Congregation for the Doctrine of the Faith issued an instruction to the bishops, *The Pastoral Care of Homosexual Persons,* that offended many gay people with its description of homosexuality as an intrinsically disordered condition.

Father Tos responded with a tactic that he would use many other times in similar situations, a combination of disseminating information to his parishioners and inviting discussion among them. Suspecting that many people, even many Catholics, had never read the controversial document in its entirety, he had six hundred copies printed and distributed at Sunday Mass. He followed that initiative with plans for an open parish forum to discuss the Vatican document. The result was a gathering on March 23, 1987, which featured an opening presentation by Margaret O'Brien Steinfels, the editor of *Church,* eight short commentaries by parishioners, a heated discussion period, and some general conclusions.[15]

A few months later, on July 26, some three hundred gay activists staged a noisy demonstration outside St. Patrick's Cathedral during Sunday Mass, protesting President Ronald Reagan's appointment of Cardinal O'Connor to a national commission on AIDS. Tos reacted with a restrained but forcefully written two-page "statement of pastoral concern" in the *Parish Newsletter.* He expressed his sympathy for all the victims of AIDS, but he also castigated the intolerance and hypocrisy of demonstrators who could feel no pain but their own. "My concern," he explained, "at this time of strong feelings about the teachings of the Church concerning human sexuality, is not with theoretical or theological foundations for the teachings or for the dissent and protest. It is rather with the tactics that are used in expressing dissent and protest." Getting to the heart of the matter, he declared: "Protests and demonstrations of dissent which offend charity, justice, truth or the sacredness of religious worship are irresponsible. They do not deserve support."[16]

Father Tos invited reactions to his statement. They were not slow

15. *Parish Bulletin,* January 25, 1987; *Parish Newsletter,* March 15, 22, 1987.

16. *New York Times,* July 27, 1987. Tos, Statement of Pastoral Concern, July 31, 1987, in *Parish Newsletter,* August 2, 1987. For O'Connor's own reaction to this appointment, see his weekly column in *Catholic New York,* July 30, 1987, which Tos reprinted in the *Parish Newsletter* of August 2, 1987. Four months earlier, on March 15, 1987, some sixty people staged a silent protest at Sunday Mass in the cathedral by standing during the Cardinal's homily. They were unhappy with his decision to order the discontinuation of the Mass that had been celebrated since 1979 at St. Francis Xavier Church for members of Dignity, an organization of Catholic homosexuals that did not have church approval. *New York Times,* March 9, 16, 1987.

in coming. Two gay parishioners, while admitting "some discomfort" at the disruption of the Mass in the cathedral, questioned the pastor's right to use the *Parish Newsletter* to air "a personal opinion." "Neither of us can understand what your intent was," they claimed, and accused Tos of issuing his statement in order to curry favor with the Cardinal. This letter, highly critical of the pastor, was published anonymously in the *Parish Newsletter*, and in turn provoked other letters in support of Father Tos.

The author of one of these letters explained the reasons for his distress at the criticism of the pastor. "St. Joseph's was the first Catholic church in Greenwich Village that, without reservations, opened its doors to the gay community," he declared. "It encouraged, even nurtured gay people and extended every opportunity for them to express themselves and be a vital part of this parish." Addressing himself directly to Father Tos, he said: "As with former pastors, you continued to follow in the same footsteps and provide an equal and continuing area for self-expression on all levels. It is because of this generosity of spirit and sense of fairness that I find this attack so distressful." Needless to say, this brouhaha did not promote parish unity, but it was not an issue of Tos' making, and it is hard to see how he could have responded otherwise.[17]

Liturgy, Lectures, and Catholic Education

The liturgy was a happier story. A committee of dedicated parishioners, especially Michael Elmore and Benedict McCaffree, prepared the liturgical celebrations and the ministries associated with them. By the spring of 1987, the parish could boast of thirty-seven lectors, thirty-eight Eucharistic ministers, and twenty-six acolytes, nine of them teenagers. A series of workshops provided them with a better understanding of the theological foundations of their ministries. The liturgical renewal in the Church had been closely connected with the biblical renewal, and parishioners were offered a deeper understanding of the Bible through scripturally grounded homilies,

17. *Parish Newsletter*, August 2, 16, 23, 1987.

workshops, and lectures. Recognizing the value of the *Parish Bulletin* as a teaching tool and as a means of communication, Tos redesigned it, expanded it, and renamed it the *Parish Newsletter.* Beginning with the first Sunday of March in 1987, the *Parish Newsletter* appeared in an attractive four-page format with advertisements that helped to defray the cost. Almost every Sunday, the parishioners found the *Parish Newsletter* filled with other items as well, sometimes reprints of articles from Catholic periodicals, sometimes original essays written by the pastor himself.

St. Joseph's was one of the few Catholic churches in New York City that still had a tradition of sponsoring lectures. That tradition was continued and expanded. To commemorate the birthday of Dr. Martin Luther King, Jr., in 1987, Father Edward K. Braxton, an African American priest (and future bishop) who was then in residence at St. Joseph's Church, gave a talk entitled "Black Catholics in America: Where Do We Go from Here?" That fall St. Joseph's hosted a series of five lectures entitled "Beyond Anger: On Being a Feminist in the Church." The speakers included Father Joseph O'Hare, S.J., the president of Fordham University, and Professor Sidney Callahan of Mercy College. During Advent, another tradition of more recent vintage was continued when four local Protestant ministers (two of them women) were invited to preach at Evening Prayer. The following Lent the speakers at a series of Wednesday evening talks included Monsignor Myles M. Bourke, the nationally known Scripture scholar, who spoke on the New Testament concept of reconciliation.

Two other initiatives reflected the background and tastes of the new pastor. The first was a renewed interest in music, not only in the context of the liturgy, but also in the form of parish concerts and recitals. This development was in fact a recovery of a tradition that went back to the earliest years of the parish and had already been revived in the 1970s. In the mid-1980s the parish sponsored a series of concerts featuring vocal and piano recitals and chamber music that eventually developed into annual spring concerts.

St. Joseph's School

The second innovation was a more intensive promotion of St. Joseph's School. This was an initiative that became especially important after the departure of the last sisters. By the 1980s, many pastors in the Archdiocese of New York were eager to close their parochial schools because they were such a heavy financial drain on the parish. At St. Joseph's, however, an opportunity was rarely let slip to tout the high quality of the education offered in the school and to publicize the achievements of the students. "It is part of our parish's commitment to serving people and thus putting the Gospel into action," the *Parish Bulletin* explained at the beginning of 1987. "In it 235 girls and boys spend their school-day in an environment that is multi-racial and ecumenical where teachers help them to grow toward maturity."[18]

By 1990, the enrollment was 50 percent Hispanic, 20 percent black, 20 percent white, and 10 percent Asian; many of the students lived outside the boundaries of the parish. "Our school is a mosaic formed by children of all races, ethnic traditions and religious experiences," the pastor boasted. "It is rooted in the best Catholic tradition and ecumenical in the fullest sense." He was especially proud of the fact that the students at St. Joseph's School generally scored higher on standardized tests than many other schoolchildren in Manhattan. In an effort to provide even more professionalism, St. Joseph's School applied for accreditation from the Middle States Association of Schools and Colleges, and eventually received it, at a time when only two other Catholic elementary schools in Manhattan possessed such accreditation.[19]

Many of the children of the parish did not attend Catholic schools. Their religious needs were not neglected either. A catechetical program was developed for them on Sunday morning and tied in with the liturgy. During the 9:00 A.M. Mass, the children leave the church for their own Liturgy of the Word and then rejoin the con-

18. *Parish Bulletin,* February 8, 1987.

19. *Parish Newsletter,* June 3, 1990.

gregation at the presentation of the gifts for the Eucharist. After Mass they receive more formal religious instruction in the parish school, in classes taught by volunteer catechists. The whole program is coordinated by Patricia Flanagan, the director of catechetics, who is herself an experienced public school teacher.

Parish Finances

The parish finance council and the parish manager, especially Carol Reina and Alvin Donius, played important roles in helping to keep the parish in the black. By the 1990s almost every parish in the archdiocese with a parochial school found it necessary to subsidize the school from the general funds of the parish. St. Joseph's was no exception. The basic yearly tuition of $1,340 per child ($1,520 for non-parishioners) did not come close to financing the school. For example, during the first six months of the fiscal year beginning in September 1988, the parish provided a subsidy of $25,000. Total parish expenses for that period amounted to $273,000, while the income was only $101,041. Some parishioners were extraordinarily generous to St. Joseph's Church. Eighteen of them contributed over $1,000 per year, while others made donations of several thousand dollars. Cardinal O'Connor sent a personal gift of $7,100 to the school in 1989. However, one-quarter of the 411 parishioners who regularly used the Sunday envelopes still gave no more than $1 per week.[20]

The pastor was actually understating the gravity of the situation when he told his parishioners in the spring of 1989 that "St. Joseph's has not had a history of financial stability for some years." Even though repairs and improvements had been delayed, the annual deficit was around $250,000. "Each month," he said, "we must withdraw substantial amounts from our investments to pay salaries, insurance and utility expenses, taxes, and many other essential bills. At the present rate, within the next two years or so, there will be no more money to help make up our monthly deficits."[21]

20. *Parish Newsletter,* June 4, 1989.
21. Tos to Dear Parishioners, May 30, 1989, in ibid.

More bad news was still to come. Cardinal O'Connor had ordered a structural evaluation of all diocesan property. The investigators who visited St. Joseph's School concluded that the building needed new windows and a new roof, which together would cost $122,000. Just before Christmas of 1989 the Archdiocesan Building Commission also informed the pastor that he would have to replace the two oil burners that heated the church, school, and rectory, at a cost of another $117,000. In addition, the 156-year-old church building needed extensive repairs. The interior had been renovated in the early 1970s and had been repainted again in 1984, but what was now required was a thorough overhaul of both the interior and exterior of the building. Back in 1983, a master plan for restoring the church had been formulated, and preliminary sketches had been made and discussed at parish meetings. However, only piecemeal repairs had been made due to lack of funds. By 1990 the situation had become critical.

"During the past two weeks," Father Tos told the parishioners in February 1990, "four major contractors have examined every foot of our church. I accompanied them as they looked carefully at the ceiling, walls, and flooring. What a revelation! Ceiling and walls are coated with soot, cracked in many places, and peeling. The floor is in poor condition, aisles and carpeting need serious attention. The side doors and those on the left and the right of the main entrance require replacement. Electrical system probably needs rewiring. Sound system is close to complete failure. Radiators need replacement. Most kneelers are in bad shape or missing. The windows facing Sixth Avenue require repair and glass replacement. That is only a summary of what the examiners pointed out."[22]

Making "No Small Plans"

A fund-raising campaign was launched on Sunday, October 7, 1990, with the goal of collecting $750,000. Ten weeks later $500,000 had already been pledged. However, not all of the money was ear-

22. Tos, Church Interior Update, *Parish Newsletter,* February 11, 1990.

St. Joseph's Church, interior restoration and renovation, 1991.

marked for St. Joseph's. The archdiocese had suspended the annual Cardinal's Appeal for 1991 with the understanding that 20 percent of the money raised in parish campaigns like that conducted by St. Joseph's Church would go to the archdiocese. Although the campaign in St. Joseph's fell short of its goal, it eventually netted over $600,000, a generous sum from only three hundred donors and enough money to begin the long-delayed renovations. As so often happens under such circumstances, however, the contractors soon discovered additional structural problems in the balcony and the floor of the church, necessitating the expenditure of another $125,000.[23]

The church was closed after the last Mass on Sunday, July 7, 1991. Thereafter the Sunday and weekday Masses were celebrated in Farrell Hall, the auditorium of the school building on Washington Place. Father Maurice Carroll, the pastor of St. Vincent de Paul Church on West 23rd Street and a close friend of Father Tos, graciously made his church available for funerals. Originally it had been expected that the renovations would take four months, but they dragged on for six months. The church reopened for Midnight Mass on Christmas Eve, and the formal liturgical rededication took place on March 19, 1992, the Feast of St. Joseph. Auxiliary Bishop William J. McCormack celebrated Mass, consecrated the new altar, and blessed the new baptismal font of immersion. Once completed, the church was a stunning example of both the old and the new, a restoration as well as a renovation. Thanks to years of research and planning by the fabric committee—which oversees the environment, maintenance, and art of the church and has included longtime parishioners like Natalie Darcy, Michael Mongiello, James Kreydt, Fred Schult, Sheila Houlihan, and Marie Dunn—the parishioners of St. Joseph's now had a sparkling new interior that was also a faithful replica of the original chaste Georgian design of the church as it had appeared in 1834.

The pastor of St. Joseph's believed in making "no small plans." To

23. *Parish Newsletter,* December 16, 1990; November 24, 1991.

celebrate the successful completion of the project, he organized the Restoration Series—concerts, lectures, and dramatic presentations, sixteen events in all, extending from January to May 1992. Subscriptions to the series ranged from a princely contribution of $2,500 to a mere $100. The musical offerings included presentations by the choir of St. Thomas Episcopal Church, the Greenwich Village Singers, the New York Baroque Ensemble, and the New York Debut Orchestra. The speakers ran the gamut from Father Richard John Neuhaus, the editor of *First Things,* to Margaret O'Brien Steinfels, now the editor of *Commonweal,* to the actor Leonardo Defillipi, who presented a one-man dramatization, "The Passion According to Luke." Other lecturers included Father Richard Dillon of Fordham University, the Reverend John Andrew of St. Thomas Episcopal Church, Lutheran Bishop William H. Lazareth, Episcopal Bishop Richard Grein, Francis Cardinal Arinze, the African-born president of the Pontifical Council for Inter-Religious Dialogue, and Auxiliary Bishop Patrick V. Ahern, who spoke on his favorite topic, St. Thérèse of Lisieux.

In the midst of all this fanfare, it is pleasant to record that there was another celebration to welcome back to St. Joseph's a group of people who were not likely to subscribe to the Restoration Series. In fact it was a group that could easily have been completely forgotten. They were the homeless men who made use of St. Joseph's Shelter at night during the winter months. The parishioners organized a "Welcome Home the Homeless Party" for them on January 6, 1992, to inaugurate the opening of another year of the shelter. Parishioners were urged to bring food, drink, balloons, and presents to the party. "Bring anything at all," they were advised. "It's the thought that counts, *and the wrapping paper.* That's right, whatever you bring, even if it is a little teeny weeny present, wrap it really nice with a BIG BIG BIG bow! And of course if you can't bring anything, then just make sure that you bring yourself. And a BIG BIG smile. Your just being there will mean more than you will ever know to your homeless brothers."[24]

24. *Parish Newsletter,* January 5, 1992.

The Church in the Secular City

There were few, if any, Catholic churches in New York City that took note of the fact that the week of June 21, 1993, was Gay Pride Week. The reluctance was understandable, since the annual Gay Pride Parade was often the occasion for crude demonstrations of anti-Catholic bigotry. Recognizing the diversity within the gay community, however, St. Joseph's tried to establish contact with those individuals who were amenable to dialogue and were likely to respond to some positive initiative from the Catholic Church. It was announced at the conclusion of the Saturday evening Mass on June 26, 1993, that there would be a memorial service for all those who had died of AIDS. The parish extended an invitation to everyone in Greenwich Village, especially to homosexual men and women, and their friends, to participate in the service. The Mass would be offered, it was explained, "with prayer for mutual understanding, appreciation and love among all persons without any form of discrimination because of differences of sex, age, religion or sexual orientation."[25]

This was not the first overture that St. Joseph's had made to Catholics in the gay community. In 1989, as the AIDS crisis intensified, there was a twenty-four-hour "event" that included lectures by counselors and medical personnel, and all-night exposition of the Blessed Sacrament. A practical pastoral result of these and other gestures was the formation of a group of gay and lesbian Catholics who met every Sunday morning in the rectory. As others joined, the group grew and became a regular feature of parish life. "There are no requirements or conditions for participating," the *Parish Newsletter* announced every week, "other than interest and sincerity in exploring together what it means to be Catholic and gay in the Church today."[26]

The welcome extended to gay and lesbian Catholics at St. Joseph's

25. *Parish Newsletter,* June 20, 1993.
26. *Parish Newsletter,* May 21, 1989.

Church no doubt offended those who regarded any recognition of their existence as an implicit criticism of Church teaching on homosexuality. However, if Tos made few friends in that camp with his outreach to gays and lesbians, he incurred the wrath of those at the other end of the ideological spectrum with the stance that he adopted with regard to two controversial papal encyclicals, *Humanae Vitae* and *Veritatis Splendor.* The first was Pope Paul VI's encyclical of 1968 reaffirming the prohibition of contraception, the twenty-fifth anniversary of which occurred in 1993; the second encyclical was Pope John Paul II's defense of objective moral norms, released in 1993.

In both cases, Tos adopted the same tactic that he had used several years earlier with the Vatican document *The Pastoral Care of Homosexual Persons.* He distributed free copies of both encyclicals to his parishioners at Sunday Mass and urged them to read them in their entirety rather than rely on summaries in the secular media. With regard to *Humanae Vitae,* he noted that its publication twenty-five years earlier had provoked much dissent and a great crisis of authority in the Church, a crisis "which continues to our own time." He also pointed out that many Catholics who debated and criticized the encyclical had never actually read it. "This, I think, is not the way to engage in intelligent and informed discussion about this document," he said. Announcing that he would make free copies of the encyclical available the following week, he added: "I hope that everyone will take the time to read it carefully, and then continue the discussion and reflection which, with prayer, will lead to an informed Catholic conscience."[27]

After the appearance of *Veritatis Splendor* in 1993, Tos remarked that reactions to it had ranged from careful studies of its text to caricatures of its contents. For that reason, he also made the full text of this encyclical available to his parishioners and urged them to read it as a timely critique of the moral relativism that had become endemic in much of Western society. There was no doubt where Tos stood on the issue. "The cumulative result of such thinking," he said, "is

27. *Parish Newsletter,* June 27, 1993.

the rejection of objective norms and their replacement with subjective ones which, although not always evil-intentioned, tend to contribute to individualism and relativism that can contradict many of the moral dimensions of the Gospel of Jesus Christ and the teachings of the Church."[28]

The positions that Tos took on gays and lesbians, on *Humanae Vitae* and *Veritatis Splendor,* defy facile categorization. Some of Tos' clerical confreres may have dismissed his statements and actions as evidence of wooly-minded thinking on the part of a publicity-seeking priest. However, other observers of St. Joseph's Church may have come to the opposite conclusion and viewed the positions that he took as not only intellectually honest but pastorally sound. As Tos was well aware, he was not the first pastor of St. Joseph's to become the center of controversy. By his public statements he was connecting St. Joseph's with its own history in the era of Thomas Farrell.

Father Tos also represented a creative intellectual tradition in the New York presbyterate that had long sought to engage the contemporary culture in fruitful dialogue. While that tradition had never been widespread among the generally conservative New York clergy, it had deep roots. It counted among its achievements the formation of the New York Accademia in the nineteenth century (at St. Joseph's Church, no less), and the publication of the *New York Review* in the early years of the twentieth century at St. Joseph's Seminary at Dunwoodie. That famous but short-lived theological journal, founded in 1905, was the creation of Father Francis J. Duffy and other New York priests who sought to meet the intellectual challenges of their day. They declared their purpose on the masthead of each issue, which described the *New York Review* as "A Journal of the Ancient Faith and Modern Thought." The priest-editors who adopted that motto would have understood what the pastor of St. Joseph's Church in Greenwich Village was trying to do a century later, even if they did not always agree with him.

28. *Parish Newsletter,* November 7, 1993.

Eat at Joe's

NO
SMOKING

Welcome

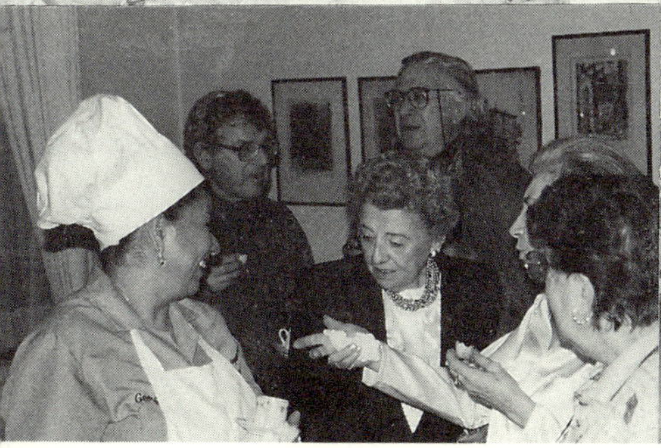

10 *The Millennium and Beyond*

The Fin-de-Siècle *Village*

IN THE 1990s Greenwich Village continued to evolve as it had been doing for three hundred years. One of the most notable changes was the shift in the center of Manhattan's gay population from the Village to Chelsea, the adjacent West Side neighborhood north of West 14th Street. Nothing dramatized this change more than the decline of Christopher Street as the gay mecca of America. Christopher Street's iconic status in the American gay community seemed secure after the riot at the Stonewall Inn at 53 Christopher Street on June 27, 1969, when a group of gay men unexpectedly fought back during a police raid. The event marked a turning point in the treatment of homosexuals by the police and came to be regarded as the beginning of the gay civil rights movement. In the 1970s and 1980s, the six-block stretch of Christopher Street was lined with gay bars and shops. Tourist buses made it a stop on their itinerary. One merchant boasted: "Sooner or later every gay man in America will pass in front of my store."[1]

By the 1990s the scene had changed. The bars on Christopher Street, especially those near the Hudson River, still attracted large numbers of gay men on weekends. However, many of the patrons were African American and Hispanic teenage males from outside Manhattan who were seeking a freedom and anonymity that were not available to them in

1. *New York Times,* June 21, 1993.

their own neighborhoods. Many others who crowded Christopher Street on the weekends were not gay at all, but young people who were looking for a good time. Their loud and boisterous behavior, often fueled by drugs and alcohol, irritated many Village residents, gay as well as straight. By this time the resident gay population was in decline for a variety of reasons. Some had died from AIDS, others had been forced to move because of escalating rents and increased property values. Ironically, by giving them wider housing opportunities throughout the city, the increased social acceptance of homosexuality also contributed to a decline in the gay population of the Village. For many young gay men in Manhattan in the 1990s, even the more affluent who could afford to settle wherever they pleased, Chelsea seemed a more attractive place to live than the Village.[2]

Real estate values in the Village rose to new levels in the 1980s and 1990s, thanks to the booming economy and the bullish stock market. As a result, developers cast covetous eyes on the relatively neglected area of the Village near the Hudson River, and dubbed it the Far West Village. This neighborhood, tucked away between Hudson Street and the river, was dotted with old but solidly built factories and commercial buildings, many of which were now transformed into expensive co-ops and rental apartments. The "new" residential buildings included a former police station on Charles Street and the former Federal Archives Building on Christopher Street. The median price of a one-bedroom co-op apartment in 1996 was $185,000, while the price of lofts ranged from $400,000 to $600,000. Some of the new residents were young couples with children, reversing a longtime decline in the number of children in the Village.[3]

As the Far West Village filled up (the population numbered almost eleven thousand by 1990), the developers moved farther north into the old meatpacking district, a grimy, odiferous six-block area of cobblestone streets west of Ninth Avenue between Gansevoort

2. *New York Times*, June 19, 1994; Jesse Green, "Where The Boys Went," *New York Times Magazine*, October 19, 1997.

3. *New York Times*, January 14, 1996.

Street and West 14th Street. It had long been known as a gathering place for transvestites. Every day for decades, the High Line of the New York Central Railroad had deposited strings of refrigerator cars loaded with frozen carcasses on the upper floors of the meatpacking plants, while all night long trucks idled below at the loading docks waiting to bring the finished product to restaurants and butcher shops throughout the city. As the meatpacking industry declined, many of the old warehouses and processing plants were converted into expensive condominiums and galleries, as well as trendy shops, bars, and night clubs. "This is the last neighborhood. It's the last frontier," said the manager of one of the chic bars, capitalizing on the sinister underworld aura that clung to the area at night.[4]

Greenwich Village remained one of the few areas of New York City where visitors could step into a different world as they turned a corner. Christopher Gray, the architectural critic of the *New York Times,* noted that some regarded West 10th Street between Fifth and Sixth Avenues as the most beautiful block in New York City. He described the lush tree-shaded street as embodying "the peculiar quality of New York living." He wrote: "It is as if an entire town were compressed into a single block, a messy stew of disparate ingredients that, when combined, produce a rewarding dish." Many of the other narrow leafy side streets of the Village retained their own distinctive character and charm. Real estate prices confirmed the impression. The mid-range rent for a one-bedroom apartment in 1999 was $2,300, while the median price of a town house more than doubled from $1 million in 1994 to $2,075,000 in 1999.[5]

West 8th Street presented a less attractive face of the *fin-de-siècle* Village. Once famous for its good little restaurants and fine bookstores, it had degenerated into a noisy strip of fast-food outlets, sleazy shops, and chain drugstores, all protected at night with ugly metal grills. Mimi Sheraton counted twenty-nine shoe stores on the block, an infallible sign of a neighborhood in decline, as she had

4. *New York Times,* October 2, 1997; October 29, 1999.
5. *New York Times,* July 6, 1997; October 10, 1999.

once been told by an old newspaperman. Sixth Avenue from West 8th Street to Bleecker Street was another depressing thoroughfare, the street crowded with taxicabs and trucks at all hours of the day and night, and the sidewalks lined with tourist traps and greasy eateries. Amid the noise and visual pollution of Sixth Avenue, the stately façade of St. Joseph's Church stood out incongruously and reassuringly as a beacon of hope to harried Villagers that there was more to life than the human rat race that passed before the front doors of the church every day.[6]

Shepherding the Flock

One index of the success of St. Joseph's Church in appealing to the diverse constituencies who composed the Catholic community in Greenwich Village in the 1990s was the background of the people who stood for election to the pastoral council every year. Some were longtime residents of the Village whose parents had been baptized in St. Joseph's Church. Others were relative newcomers, many of whom had been actively involved in other parishes before moving to Greenwich Village. Once settled in the Village, they found themselves within walking distance of a half-dozen Catholic churches. Affiliating with St. Joseph's was obviously a carefully considered decision. They offered a variety of reasons why they did so.

One person said she decided to become a parishioner because of St. Joseph's commitment to the reforms of Vatican II; another pointed to the parish's understanding of the diverse larger community of which it was a part. A lawyer revealed that he was attracted to St. Joseph's because of its "strong sense of community commitment, extraordinary liturgies, a comfortable and warm atmosphere, [and] homilies that were inspirational." A young man with an M.B.A. degree cited "the extraordinary level of participation during Mass and the sophistication of the people." An administrator at New York University, who boasted of his affection for New York City, admitted: "Much as I enjoy my life here, it is only since discovering St.

6. *New York Times,* January 10, 1997.

Joseph's that I really feel that this is my home. The parish community and pastoral staff are like my second family."

Still others found a home at St. Joseph's through teaching children in the religious education program on Sunday morning, or through the music during Sunday Mass, or the adult education courses, or the "humbling experience of volunteering at the homeless shelter." A convert to the Catholic faith attributed her association with St. Joseph's to "grace" and the guidance she received in the Rite of Christian Initiation of Adults program from Sister Anne Tahaney, a Dominican sister of Sparkill, who became a pastoral associate at St. Joseph's in 1988. An Irish-born lapsed Catholic who returned to the practice of the faith at St. Joseph's said, "A long-lost love and neglect of my faith were rekindled, nourished and restored here."[7]

In the late 1990s the parish council was renamed the parish pastoral council. The change in nomenclature was more than a matter of semantics. It reflected the evolving nature of the parish council from a model inspired by secular representative bodies to one that was more closely linked with the pastoral staff in formulating and executing policies affecting the spiritual life of the parish.

Sacramental Life and Social Justice

Since Vatican Council II, there has been no aspect of Catholic parish life in which the combination of continuity and change is more apparent than in the celebration of the liturgy. The Council called for both *aggiornamento* and *ressourcement,* which one might translate as going forward by looking backward, that is, equipping the Church to meet the needs of the modern world by recovering

7. St. Joseph *Parish Newsletter,* May 22, 1994; May 5, 1996; May 4, 1997; May 10, 1998; June 4, 2000; May 27, 2001; April 28, 2002. In 1998 the Archdiocesan Office of Pastoral Research and Planning estimated that the total population of St. Joseph's parish was 51,017. The affluence of the neighborhood was evident from other statistics. The per capita income was $57,140; only 263 families were classified as living in poverty; more than 25,000 individuals had a college or graduate degree. Of course there is no way of correlating these statistics for the whole neighborhood with the parishioners of St. Joseph's Church. *Parish Newsletter,* April 25, 1999.

and revitalizing her authentic tradition. In the case of the liturgy, that meant the return to a vernacular liturgy in which the laity, by virtue of their baptism, played their proper role as active participants, not passive observers. This active participation of the laity, enhanced by good music and good preaching, has been a notable feature of the life of St. Joseph's Church since the early 1970s.

Another part of the Catholic liturgical heritage that was recovered as a result of Vatican II is the communal nature of the sacramental life of the Church. At St. Joseph's Church in the early twenty-first century that aspect of *ressourcement* is reflected in the communal celebration of the sacraments of baptism, confirmation, penance, and the anointing of the sick. Baptisms are celebrated once a month, always during Sunday Mass, so that they take place in the presence of the community into which the baptized person is being received. During the renovation of the church in 1991, an immersion pool was installed, one of the first in the archdiocese, making baptism by immersion for both children and adults the norm at St. Joseph's Church.

The baptism of adults is usually celebrated during the Easter Vigil for the candidates who have successfully completed the R.C.I.A. program. As was the practice in the ancient Church, the catechumens step into the immersion pool and are covered with water. They are then led to a changing room from which they emerge dressed in white robes to receive the sacrament of confirmation. Later, during the Easter Vigil Mass, they receive their First Communion, thus participating in the ancient custom of receiving together the three sacraments of Christian initiation. Children receive confirmation during the Sunday Mass at which they also receive their First Communion.

There are also communal celebrations of the sacrament of penance during Advent and Lent. At these services, which have proved to be extremely popular, provision is made for individual confession for those who wish to avail themselves of it. Confession is also available on an individual basis throughout the year. Finally, the sacrament of the anointing of the sick is celebrated during the noon Mass on the first Saturday of the month. In keeping with the tradition of Marian devotions on that day, Mass is celebrated in honor of Mary under one of her many titles, and some twenty to thirty people usually receive the anointing of the sick.

During the early days of the liturgical revival of the 1920s and 1930s, pioneer liturgical reformers in the United States like Virgil Michel emphasized the intimate connection between liturgy and social justice, as did Monsignor John P. Monaghan a decade later at St. Margaret Mary Church in Midland Beach, Staten Island.[8] That connection still exists at St. Joseph's Church, where the pastor is fond of saying that "everything flows from the liturgy, especially the Eucharist, and flows to it." The social action committee of the pastoral council, under the leadership of Judy Kelly-Magida, remains active on many levels, sponsoring discussions of the death penalty and environmental issues, and conducting an annual clothing drive for poor and homeless men and women. Mention has already been made of two of the most notable efforts of the parish to serve the needs of the community, St. Joseph's shelter for homeless men and St. Joseph's soup kitchen, both of which have been in operation for more than twenty years. Under the direction of John van Rens and other volunteers, the shelter continues to provide a safe, clean haven where ten men sleep each evening, while the soup kitchen regularly feeds between four hundred and five hundred people every Saturday afternoon.

Keeping the Flock Informed

Like the New York discount clothing store that proclaimed in its ads, "an informed consumer is our best customer," Father Tos seemed to believe that well-informed Catholics were likely to be the best parishioners. St. Joseph's was one of the first Catholic churches in New York City to have its own web site (www.stjoseph-village.com). The parish also sponsored an extensive adult education pro-

8. On Monaghan, see Thomas A. Lynch, "'Above All Things the Truth': John P. Monaghan and the Church in New York," *Dunwoodie Review* 16 (1992–1993): 109–65.

gram, with classes taught by the pastor, Sister Anne Tahaney, Father William White (who replaced Father Norris in 1993), and more recently by Father Michael Holleran, a former Carthusian monk, and Father Owen Lafferty, both of whom joined the staff as associate pastors in the 1990s.

However, the primary means of communication and catechesis remained the *Parish Newsletter*, which seemed to grow progressively thicker during the 1990s, with inserts on a wide range of subjects. Many of the inserts were comments and observations by the pastor himself on topics that were of particular interest to his parishioners. They were never dull and they never shied away from controversial issues. Father Tos also assured his readers that none of his pronouncements were of an infallible nature. For the historian, the newsletters of the 1990s are an invaluable record of how one parish offered guidance and direction to its people as they confronted critical religious, moral, and even political issues during that decade. Tip O'Neill, the Massachusetts congressman and Speaker of the House of Representatives, said famously that "all politics is local." In the same vein one might say that all religion is local—not in the sense that religious truth comes from the local community, but in the sense that the vitality of religious belief and practice can best be measured in the local faith community.

Shepherding the Catholics of Greenwich Village continues to be both a delight and a challenge—a delight because the members of the Catholic community are conversant with the cutting-edge issues in the Church, but a challenge because they are not likely to be satisfied with simplistic appeals to ecclesiastical authority. Two examples among many were the ordination of women and the reception of Holy Communion by divorced and remarried Catholics. Rarely, if ever, was either issue raised publicly in most of the 412 parishes of the Archdiocese of New York, but in Greenwich Village neither issue could be ignored. Father Tos tackled them in a way that by the 1990s had become characteristic of his style of pastoral leadership: he published the pertinent Vatican documents in the *Parish Newsletter* and invited responses from his parishioners.

To be fair, Tos did more than that. He did not hide behind official Church documents, but offered his own interpretation of them in a thoughtful and provocative way, while insisting on respect for legitimate Church authority. In the case of *Ordinatio Sacerdotalis,* Pope John Paul's apostolic letter of May 22, 1994, banning the ordination of women, Tos cautioned his parishioners that the pope's decision must be accepted seriously and faithfully. "However," he was quick to add, "because the document does not use the word *infallibly* also means that the reception and discussion of the Pope's teaching must balance fidelity with careful theological understanding of the level of authority with which this document, and every other papal/church document, is issued." The ordination of women was a theoretical question of interest to a few, but the reception of Holy Communion by divorced and remarried Catholics was a pressing pastoral problem for many Catholics. When the Congregation for the Doctrine of the Faith issued a declaration in September 1994 reaffirming the exclusion of divorced and remarried Catholics from the Eucharist, Tos published the full text of the Vatican declaration. He also explained that he had made the complete text available, not to stifle discussion, but "so that everyone can read it, think about it, then engage in dialogue that will help to develop an informed personal conscience."[9]

The Annual Mass with Gay and Lesbian Catholics

The Gay Pride Parade in June 1994 had particular relevance in Greenwich Village, since it was the twenty-fifth anniversary of the Stonewall Inn riot. It threatened to be an ugly occasion for Catholics because a breakaway group of gay activists refused to accept the city's decision that they should march up First Avenue to their rally in Central Park. Instead, this dissident group insisted on marching up Fifth Avenue in front of St. Patrick's Cathedral, where in years past gay activists had vented their spleen against the Catholic Church and Cardinal O'Connor. In a notorious incident on the

9. *Parish Newsletter,* June 26, November 13, 1994.

morning of December 10, 1989, some 4,500 protestors demonstrated outside St. Patrick's Cathedral while several dozen of them disrupted the 10:15 A.M. Mass celebrated by Cardinal O'Connor by chaining themselves to pews and heckling the Cardinal during his homily. Several demonstrators even received Holy Communion for the sole purpose of desecrating the Eucharist.[10]

New York Catholics had good reason, therefore, to fear that the Gay Pride Parade in 1994 might degenerate into similar outrages against their religion. Despite such well-justified apprehensions, however, St. Joseph's reiterated its longstanding practice of welcoming everyone, and called for dialogue and mutual understanding rather than angry confrontation between Catholics and gays and lesbians. "Maintaining commitment to essential Church teaching," the *Parish Newsletter* announced, "we must meet the 'other'—whoever he/she is—with a welcome and expression of love that are signs of our witness to the Gospel of Jesus Christ in today's world."[11]

On the Saturday before the Gay Pride Parade, following the evening Mass, there was a prayer service in St. Joseph's Church in remembrance of all those who had died of AIDS. Almost one thousand names were read from a list that was preserved in St. Joseph's

10. *New York Times,* December 11, 1989. The *New York Times,* hardly an admirer of Cardinal O'Connor, referred to the demonstration in an editorial as "the Storming of St. Pat's" and declared: "To deny clergy and laity alike the peaceful practice of religion grossly violates a decent regard for the rights of others, let alone the law. Far from inspiring sympathy, such a violation mainly offers another reason to reject both the offensive protestors and their ideas." *New York Times,* December 12, 1989. The day after the incident Tos wrote to O'Connor to assure him of his support. "Although you and I might differ in the manner or style of preaching and teaching the one Catholic faith," he told the Cardinal, "I assure you that I stand united with you in that faith which at times, even here at St. Joseph's, requires particular proclamation and witness." O'Connor thanked Tos for his support, adding, "When one literally comes face to face with so much anger and hatred, it certainly has an effect." ASJC, Tos to O'Connor, December 11, 1989; O'Connor to Tos, December 19, 1989. Former Mayor Edward Koch was present in the cathedral on December 10 to lend moral support to O'Connor, a close friend. The irrepressible Koch, who was Jewish, had little sympathy for the demonstrators. "If you do not like the church, go out and find one you like—or start your own," he commented to a reporter. *New York Times,* December 11, 1989.

11. *New York Times,* June 24, 27, 1994; *Parish Newsletter,* June 5, 1994.

AIDS Memorial Book. Participants were invited to add additional names of relatives and friends. At the end of the service, the congregation formed a procession to the Eucharistic side chapel and placed lighted candles before the Blessed Sacrament in remembrance of loved ones who had died of AIDS. That weekend many pulpits in New York City rang with denunciations of the Gay Pride Parade, but few Catholic parishes did as much as St. Joseph's to offer tangible solace to the families and friends of victims of AIDS.[12]

This Mass for gay and lesbian Catholics and the candlelight service became an annual event at St. Joseph's Church. In announcing the Mass in June 1998, the pastoral staff said: "St. Joseph's Church in the Village is pastorally committed to the inclusiveness evident in the life and ministry of Jesus portrayed in the Gospels. Therefore, with open hearts and outstretched hands, we invite Catholics who are straight, gay, and lesbian, and everyone else who is searching for a spiritual home, to become a member and to help this parish community to continue its tradition of being one body, one spirit in Christ, rich in diversity and united in faith, hope and love."[13]

Preserving Living Tradition

Although St. Joseph's had a long-established reputation for progressive liturgy, it also fostered an inclusive spirituality that sometimes involved revitalizing venerable practices that had fallen by the wayside in other parishes. On the Feast of Corpus Christi in 1993, for example, there was an outdoor procession of the Blessed Sacrament through the neighborhood. "Faith on pilgrimage in Greenwich Village," the pastor called it. After the 11:30 Mass, several hundred people marched through the streets of Greenwich Village, followed by the clergy carrying the Blessed Sacrament. They proceeded out the front door of the church, down Washington Place,

12. *Parish Newsletter,* June 12, 1994. On October 1, 1997, the U.S. bishops issued "Always Our Children: A Pastoral Message to Parents of Homosexual Children and Suggestions for Pastoral Ministers." The full text was published in the *Parish Newsletter* of June 28, 1998.

13. *Parish Newsletter,* June 21, 1998.

around to Waverly Place, and then back down Sixth Avenue to the church. No one was more impressed with the results than the pastor. "To see people blessing themselves as the procession passed, one man even knelt in the street," said Father Tos, "helped to make us more appreciative of the wonder of the great mystery of the Real Presence of Christ in the Holy Eucharist."[14]

Those who attended the 11:30 Mass at St. Joseph's Church on the Feast of Christ the King in 1997 witnessed an unusual event—a Mass celebrated entirely in Latin. Father Tos explained why. "It is not because we are antiquarians who wish to preserve ancient artifacts," he said. "Then, why the Mass in Latin today?" He answered his own question by saying: "Simply because we are part of the Catholic Church, which is *catholic,* universal in space and time. Latin is one of its many languages, including English and other vernaculars." In some parishes Latin Masses came to be identified with people who were nostalgic for the pre-Vatican II Church, which they tended to view through rose-colored lenses. "Nostalgia and romanticism can be comforting," Father Tos observed. "They might offer solace and security temporarily. However, they are not firm foundations for authentic and adult Catholic faith in today's Church and society, particularly in New York—and, yes, in Greenwich Village."[15]

A Consistent Ethic of Life

No American Catholic could ignore the moral dimension of abortion as the number of abortions rose sharply in the wake of the U.S. Supreme Court's *Roe v. Wade* decision in 1973. At St. Joseph's Church, opposition to abortion and related right-to-life activities manifested themselves in various ways. Joseph Cardinal Bernardin's concept of a "seamless garment" of life, that is, a consistent ethic of life, struck a responsive chord at St. Joseph's. This ethic of life included opposition not only to abortion, but also to euthanasia, the death penalty, the arms race, and nuclear war. As an illustration of

14. *Parish Newsletter,* June 12, 1994.
15. *Parish Newsletter,* November 23, 1997.

the commitment to this inclusive ethic of life on the part of the bishops of New York State, the parishioners received copies of the Legislative Agenda of the New York State Catholic Conference, the bishops' watchdog and lobbying organization in Albany. Likewise, the pastor called their attention to *Evangelium Vitae,* Pope John Paul II's encyclical of March 30, 1995, with its criticism of a "culture of death." "*Evangelium Vitae* is a profoundly moral and religious document," he concluded in his briefing to his parishioners, "that urges us to reflect intelligently and seriously about the meaning and value of all human life and threats to it."[16]

January 25, 1998, marked the twenty-fifth anniversary of the *Roe v. Wade* decision. In those twenty-five years it is estimated that as many as forty million abortions were performed in the United States. At St. Joseph's, the anniversary was the occasion for a reaffirmation of the consistent ethic of life. Explicitly and cleverly repudiating the insinuation that such an approach was intended to play down the heinousness of abortion, Father Tos stated unambiguously in an open letter to the parishioners: "We must affirm, respect, and protect human life throughout its continuum from origin in mothers to the moment of natural death. Only then do we prove our belief that every human being is created in the image and likeness of God and has an equal right to life, liberty and the pursuit of happiness with all other persons, regardless of race, religion, ethnicity, age, orientation, sexual or other."[17]

Paying the Bills

Shepherding the flock also included the mundane task of keeping a roof over the flock's heads so that they could have a place to worship. It was not an easy job in a 160-year-old church that seemed to be in chronic need of repairs. Just before Christmas in 1995, when it was discovered that the roof was so badly deteriorated that it would have to be replaced, the parishioners came very close to worshipping

16. *Parish Newsletter,* August 28, 1994; March 10, May 5, 1996.
17. *Parish Newsletter,* January 11, 1998.

under umbrellas. "St. Nicholas and Reindeer, Please Stay Off Our Roof," Father Tos pleaded in the *Parish Newsletter* for Christmas of that year. The cost of replacing the roof, and additional repairs to the windows, doors, and façade of the church, amounted to $40,000.[18]

No sooner was the roof fixed than the old ship sprang another leak elsewhere. This time it was the creaky balcony of the church, which was found to be in imminent danger of collapse. It required $50,000 to make the necessary repairs. Hard on the heels of that unexpected expense came the discovery of another structural problem in the century-old school building. The steel beams in the basement area under the sidewalk had rusted so badly that they had to be replaced, at a cost of over $102,000. The archdiocese provided a loan of $67,000, but the parish had to find the remaining $35,000.[19]

Despite these extraordinary and unforeseen expenses, the Church remained solvent, but only barely so. For the six-month period between September 1994 and February 1995, the total income was $301,884.00 and the total expenses were $291,250.18, leaving a modest surplus of $10,633.82. However, more than half of the income came from special donations and bequests rather than from the Sunday collection. It was questionable how long the church could continue to pay its bills by depending on special donations of over $150,000 per year. In addition St. Joseph's Church owed the archdiocese $40,000 in unpaid bills and had yet to repay the archdiocese loans of $200,000, some dating back to 1977. Some parishioners were extraordinarily generous; others much less so. An analysis of the collection for one Sunday in the fall of 1995 revealed that 112 envelope users contributed $4,211.00, an average of $37.50 each, an unusually large per capita contribution for a Catholic congregation. On the other hand, 156 people still put no more than a dollar bill in the collection basket, less than the fare for a bus or subway ride.[20]

18. *Parish Newsletter,* December 24, 1995.
19. *Parish Newsletter,* June 9, 1996; April 13, 1997.
20. *Parish Newsletter,* March 12, October 1, 1995.

An article in *America* magazine in the fall of 1996 documented a fact that many Catholic pastors had long suspected. American Catholics contributed far less to the support of their Church than Protestants contributed to theirs. Such a discrepancy was understandable in the nineteenth century, when the Catholic community was composed largely of poor immigrants with low-paying jobs. That was no longer the case in the 1990s, however, certainly not at St. Joseph's Church. Consequently Father Tos followed the example of many other pastors throughout the country and introduced tithing into his parish. "It's simple," he explained. He urged his parishioners to calculate their weekly or monthly income, and then to say: "90% for me; 10% for you, God."[21]

Thanks to this and other efforts, most notably a program called "Sponsoring Our Parish's Future," by the end of 1998, the weekly collection had increased by 40 percent.[22] On Sunday, October 3, 1999, the collection was $8,700, the highest it had ever been on a Sunday. However, St, Joseph's was still not home free. The projected budget for the following year was $547,000, which meant that even the increased Sunday collection would fall short of the needed income by almost $2,000 per week. As Father Tos struggled hard to close the gap, a notice appeared in the real estate section of the *New York Times* that brought the pastor to the brink of apoplexy and threatened to undo his diligent fund-raising efforts. It was a short article revealing that St. Joseph's convent on Waverly Place had been sold for a cool $3 million. There was a trace of panic in the next issue of the *Parish Newsletter* explaining that the convent had been owned by the archdiocese, not the parish. "Unfortunately the sale has NOTHING to do with St. Joseph's Church. . . . Only the name 'ST. JOSEPH' is the same. . . . We gain NOTHING from the sale." Judging by the continued increase in the Sunday collection, the parish-

21. *Parish Newsletter,* September 29, 1996.

22. Among the more than 160 people who committed themselves to the Sponsorship Program were Father Tos, Father Holleran, Father Lafferty, and Sister Anne Tahaney. *Parish Newsletter,* December 6, 1998.

ioners read the block letters, got the message, and allowed the pastor to breathe easier.[23]

One last rebuilding project undertaken by Father Tos was the renovation of Casserly Hall, the large basement meeting room beneath the church. Like the church itself, Casserly Hall dated from 1834. It had served many purposes over the years, including that of being the first site of St. Joseph's School. By the 1990s, as a result of frequent use by various parish and community groups, the Saturday soup kitchen, and the men's shelter, it was badly in need of a major overhaul. Thanks to personal gifts of well over $100,000 from friends, Father Tos had to ask the parishioners for very little money to complete the work. When the renovations were finished, Casserly Hall was a sparkling new meeting place with new lighting, flooring, plumbing, sound system, and brightly painted walls adorned with a variety of pictures and posters. A thoughtful touch was the decision to leave one small section of the stone basement wall as it had been in 1834.

The Pastor and the Cardinal

The ministry to gay and lesbian Catholics at St. Joseph's Church was not the only effort of its kind in the Archdiocese of New York. Early in 1994, at the suggestion of Bishop Patrick J. Sheridan, the vicar general, a group of priests who were engaged in this ministry formed a consultative committee with the intention of meeting on a regular basis. The group aired a wide variety of opinions on the volatile issue of the pastoral care of homosexual Catholics, but failed to reach any agreement on how to proceed.

Shortly thereafter, Father Tos received a query from the Chancery Office, requesting a written description of the approach he used in this ministry at St. Joseph's Church. Accompanying the request from the Chancery Office was a memorandum from Father John Harvey, O.S.F.S., a member of the consultative committee who had long been active in promoting Courage, an organization for Catholic ho-

23. *Parish Newsletter,* November 1, December 6, 1998; October 10, 1999.

mosexuals that enjoyed the public approbation of the archdiocese. Harvey objected to some of the views expressed at the meetings by those who called for a more nuanced approach to this issue. He feared that such statements were muddling the clear teaching of the Church on homosexuality and fostering a "pseudo-good faith" attitude on the part of Catholic homosexuals.

Tos took exception to Harvey's memorandum, contrasting its suspicious tone with the confidence that Cardinal O'Connor had repeatedly expressed in the good pastoral judgment of his priests. Without questioning the teaching of the Church on homosexuality, Tos also pointed to the need for more factual information on homosexuality and on the variety of individuals to be found in the homosexual community. Unless those involved in this ministry were well informed on these matters, Tos doubted that their efforts would be effective. "The experience of pastors, and other priests engaged in pastoral ministry on a daily basis, must also be understood and appreciated," he insisted, "as a valuable source of pastoral experience for the development of any ministry to homosexuals."

Tos favored a continuation of the meetings of the consultative committee in the hope that the pooled resources of the participants would help them find an effective way to present the teaching of the Church to the homosexual community and to listen to their lived experience. "Do we not agree," he asked, "that sometimes it is not a teaching or a message in itself that is the primary reason for its rejection, but rather the manner or method used by the messenger who is the medium of its delivery?" With regard to his own ministry at St. Joseph's, Tos mentioned his weekly meetings with gays and lesbians for prayer and discussion. He defended such initiatives on the grounds that effective outreach to homosexuals "has to originate within the local parish where those for whom this ministry is developed are involved as parishioners and interact with the members of its pastoral staff."[24]

A few years later, Bishop Sheridan accepted an invitation from

24. ASJC, Tos to Sheridan et al., May 16, 1994.

gay and lesbian Catholics at St. Joseph's Church to celebrate Mass with them on June 28, 1997, and to take part in a dialogue and dinner afterwards. He remained for three hours, fielding questions with his well-known self-deprecating Irish charm. Tos was delighted with his performance. He told him: "You were a hit. It was the first time that those present had the opportunity to meet with a member of the hierarchy, particularly one who holds the office of Vicar General. Your presentation and answers certainly were faithful to the teachings of the Church. You were also a listener who was understanding and compassionate." Tos had previously discussed the arrangements for the Mass with Cardinal O'Connor and told him afterwards: "St. Joseph's Church [was] filled with worshipping, grateful and faithful men and women. Everything was both pastorally sensitive and faithful to the teachings of the Church. Many thanks."[25]

In the fall of 1998, Tos invited Thomas J. Gumbleton, the Auxiliary Bishop of Detroit and one of the most liberal members of the American hierarchy, to speak at St. Joseph's Church on the topic of homosexuality and the Church. Press reports stated that Gumbleton told a questioner that sex between homosexuals could be moral. The press report set off alarm bells at the New York Chancery Office and brought a request from Bishop Sheridan for a clarification of Gumbleton's remarks. Tos explained that Gumbleton's answer to the question had been misunderstood by those who did not grasp the distinction that Gumbleton made between objective and subjective morality.

Father Tos also used his exchange with Bishop Sheridan to unburden himself concerning the toll that St. Joseph's Church was taking on him personally. "I must confess," he told Sheridan, "that my ministry as pastor is very challenging, demanding and also tiring. I affirm my fidelity to all that our Church teaches, and I respect the leadership and authority of my Bishop, Cardinal O'Connor." At the same time, Tos felt enough confidence in Cardinal O'Connor to give him a gentle nudge through Bishop Sheridan to improve his own re-

25. ASJC, Tos to Sheridan, February 4, 1999; Tos to O'Connor, July 21, 1997.

lationship with the gay community by moderating his language.[26]

O'Connor himself never interfered with Tos' ministry to the gays and lesbians in his parish. The Cardinal was invariably friendly and politely acknowledged Tos' suggestions over the years, not only about gay ministry, but also various other matters. For example, when the rectorship of St. Joseph's Seminary fell vacant in the summer of 1993, Tos told the Cardinal that his seminary was in "very sad condition." He explained that "the atmosphere of the seminary is perceived as intellectually stultifying and more conducive to a narrow vision of the Gospel than what the Church is called to be in the modern world—especially in our archdiocese." Earlier that year, Tos did not mince words either when the archdiocese announced that it would cooperate with the Christian Coalition of the Reverend Pat Robertson, the conservative Protestant evangelist, in the school board elections of that May. Tos complained to O'Connor that he had failed to consult his priests about this decision and offered him his own reaction. "I am of the opinion," he said, "that the present alliance between the archdiocese and the Christian Coalition is, at the very least misguided, if not erroneous, and will have severe ecclesial and social consequences in the long run."[27]

Despite the public perception of O'Connor as a stern authoritarian figure, he mellowed during his years in New York. One measure of that mellowing was the fact that he and Tos maintained a cordial relationship that was marked by candor and mutual respect. "You have admitted your own limitations and mistakes often," Tos reminded O'Connor. "These are things we have in common as humans and also as priests in the service of the Lord and his Church." Far from taking umbrage at such plain speaking, O'Connor told Tos on one occasion: "I am happy that you *do* believe that you can approach me on any issue. That's the highest compliment you could

26. ASJC, Tos to Sheridan, February 4, 1999.

27. ASJC, Tos to O'Connor, September 16, April 20, 1993. A young friend of John Tracy Ellis who entered St. Joseph's Seminary in the early 1980s reported to Ellis that he found three kinds of seminarians at Dunwoodie, "conservatives, arch-conservatives and reactionaries." ACUA, John Tracy Ellis Papers, student to Ellis, June 18, 1983.

pay me, and I am grateful." On another occasion, however, when Tos sent the Cardinal an anguished protest about a sharp increase in his parish's financial assessment, O'Connor sidestepped the issue (leaving it for his successor to settle), but he did assure Tos: "I have never thought of you for a moment as less than loyal, respectful and always willing to tell me what you believe I should know."[28]

Nonetheless, despite the good-humored banter between the two of them, the Cardinal kept the pastor of St. Joseph's Church at arm's length. Except for the monthly meetings of the Priests' Council, during the years when Tos was an elected member of that body and they faced one another across the conference table, most of their communications took place in writing. Somehow or other the Cardinal always managed to find excuses for refusing repeated invitations to speak at St. Joseph's Church, although four other present and future cardinals did do so. After his ordeal in the cathedral on December 10, 1989, O'Connor even declined an invitation to attend an informal gathering of priests at the rectory. Nor was it an oversight that O'Connor failed to make Tos a monsignor, a widely distributed papal honor in New York, which would have been welcome as a public rather than another private statement of approbation and appreciation for his work at St. Joseph's Church.[29]

Early in 2000, however, when the Cardinal was dying and putting his affairs in order, he sent Tos a personal note in which he expressed his appreciation for him personally and as a pastor. "I have great regard for you," O'Connor told him, "which stems mostly from the integrity which has been your guide in everything you attempt." Paying tribute to both Tos' orthodoxy and his pastoral sensitivity, he told him: "I am both impressed by and grateful for your concern that you accord with what you know would be my personal guidance in conducting all the affairs of the Church. At the same time, you have the courage to adapt to the needs of the people that

28. ASJC, Tos to O'Connor, December 11, 1989; O'Connor to Tos, March 3, 1992; Tos to O'Connor, February 26, 1999; O'Connor to Tos, March 5, 1999.

29. ASJC, O'Connor to Tos, July 8, 9, 1993; September 16, 21, 1993; Tos to O'Connor, July 21, 1997; December 11, 1989.

God has placed in your hands. . . . I am most proud to be your bishop." At the time that the Cardinal wrote the letter, he was waging a losing battle with cancer, but, nonetheless, at the bottom of the page, he added in his own hand, "One day when I'm fully up to par, I'll be able to express what I mean." Four months later he was dead.[30]

The Millennium Lecture Series

Few institutions ever have the occasion to celebrate a life span of two thousand years. A rare exception is the Catholic Church, which observed the beginning of the third millennium of the Christian era on January 1, 2000. Purists pointed out that the new millennium would really not begin until the following year, and that estimates of the exact year of Jesus' birth ranged from 6 B.C. to 4 B.C. Nevertheless, everyone, including unbelievers for whom it was merely a secular milestone, agreed to celebrate the beginning of the new millennium on New Year's Day 2000. In many parishes the occasion came and went with little fanfare. In St. Joseph's, however, the unique character of the event appealed to the showman in Father Tos, who was determined to usher in the new millennium in an original and creative way.

On New Year's Eve, the church remained open after the 5:30 P.M. Mass for private prayer before the Blessed Sacrament and for a series of services that included the recitation of the Rosary and the litany of the saints. At 11:00, Benediction of the Blessed Sacrament was followed by an Act of Dedication of the parish community to the "New Advent and the New Evangelization" called for by Pope John Paul II. At midnight the congregation had the opportunity to watch the revelers in Times Square on television monitors set up in the church, thus combining the secular and spiritual celebrations. At 12:15 the first Mass of the new millennium was celebrated in St. Joseph's Church, followed afterwards by a champagne toast in the narthex of the church.

Well before New Year's Day, the parish had decided to observe the

30. ASJC, O'Connor to Tos, January 10, 2001.

advent of the new millennium in a more formal and extensive way through a series of lectures that eventually extended to two dozen spread over six years, from September 1996 to June 2002. Although St. Joseph's Church had a long tradition of sponsoring public lectures, it had never attempted anything on this scale before. In fact, no other church or institution in the archdiocese organized anything comparable to this lecture series in observance of the new millennium. The lecturers included some of the most distinguished Catholic scholars in the United States and abroad, who spoke on a wide variety of topics, some of them quite controversial. What was noteworthy was not only the scholarly credentials of the speakers, but also the fact that they represented a broad spectrum of Catholic thinking on both the left and the right. The first speaker in the series was Raymond E. Brown, the Sulpician Scripture scholar, now deceased, who spoke on the beginnings of the Church. Father Brown was followed a month later by Sara Butler, who entitled her lecture "Women's Ordination and the Development of Doctrine." Early in 1997 another Scripture scholar, Father Eugene Laverdière, S.S.S., gave a talk titled "Proclaiming the Death of the Lord," while Father Gerald O'Collins, S.J., the well-known Australian theologian and professor at the Gregorian University in Rome, devoted his talk to the Resurrection. In March, Father Avery Dulles, S.J., the future cardinal, addressed the question of Jesus and faith. A month later another Jesuit, Father Richard McCormick, the premier American Catholic moral theologian, discussed the highly sensitive issue of dissent in the Church. The final speaker that spring was Father David Tracy, a diocesan priest and distinguished member of the Divinity School of the University of Chicago, whose lecture was entitled "The Surprising Rediscovery of God in Contemporary Culture."

The Millennium Lecture Series continued in the fall and winter of 1997 with talks on four widely divergent topics. The lecture by Professor Luke Timothy Johnson of Emory University was on a topic about which he had written extensively: "The Real Jesus: Challenge of Current Scholarship and the Truth of the Gospels." Michael

Novak, the well-known neoconservative religious writer, offered a presentation that combined theology and economics: "How Jesus Changed Political Economy." Father Robert Imbelli, a New York diocesan priest in the theology department of Boston College, spoke on the Holy Spirit, while Father Enda McDonagh, the Irish moral theologian, directed his listeners to the subject of ecumenism with his lecture, "Inter-Church Christians: A Vocation to the Third Millennium."

The series resumed in the new year with a lecture by Monsignor Myles M. Bourke, who drew upon many years of experience in supervising the translation of biblical texts in his talk, "The New Lectionary: A Response to an Urgent Need." Dr. Elizabeth Johnson, a Sister of St. Joseph and one of the leading Catholic feminist theologians in the country, devoted her talk not to Christian feminism but to another topic of deep interest to her, Christianity and ecology, with a lecture entitled "Reclaiming the Cosmos as a Spiritual Issue." Father John P. Meier, then at the Catholic University of America and in the process of completing his magisterial four-volume study of the historical Jesus, lectured on the Gospel miracles. The last speaker was Father Thomas J. Shelley, a New York diocesan priest. His talk, "Whatever Happened to Church History?" was a plea for a renewed interest in that neglected discipline.

In addition to these speakers, in February 1998 Father Tos also persuaded a personal friend, Cardinal Carlo Maria Martini, S.J., the Archbishop of Milan and a distinguished Scripture scholar in his own right, to participate in the Millennium Lecture Series. Cardinal Martini came to the United States specifically to speak at St. Joseph's Church and referred to St. Joseph's as "a parish for the new millennium." His lecture, "A Christian Community Towards the Third Millennium," was clearly the outstanding event of the first part of this impressive lecture series.

After a lapse of two years, the Millennium Lecture Series was resumed in November 2000 with a lecture by Professor Lisa Sowle Cahill of Boston College, "The Moral Challenges Facing Women Today." A month later Andrew Sullivan, the English-born former editor of *The New Republic*, took as his topic the pastoral challenge presented by the presence of gays and lesbians in the Catholic community. Sullivan identified himself as a gay Catholic, and with characteristic bravado he called his talk "We're Here: Homosexuals and the Catholic Church."

In the fall of 2001, Enda McDonagh made a return appearance with a lecture entitled "The Risk of God." In November Godfried Cardinal Danneels, the Archbishop of Malines-Brussels and the Primate of Belgium, attracted a capacity crowd for his talk, "Where Do I Find Hope in the Church?" an optimistic reflection on the state of the Church, which was published in *Origins*, the documentary news service of the U.S. Conference of Catholic Bishops.[31] A week later, at the beginning of December, Dr. Farid Esack, a Muslim scholar and theologian, gave an address entitled "Islam and Christianity: Conflict or Dialogue?" a much debated topic in the aftermath of September 11, 2001.

The final four speakers in the Millennium Lecture Series were scheduled for the spring and summer of 2002. Mary Gordon, the feminist author and novelist, offered a feminist perspective on the Rosary. Jacques Dupuis, a Belgian Jesuit, professor at the Gregorian University in Rome, and a leading expert on the relationship of Catholicism to non-Christian religions, took the evolving nature of this relationship as the subject of his lecture, "Sharing and Communion in Interreligious Dialogue." James Alison, the young English Catholic theologian, gave a talk called "Being Wrong and Telling the Truth: A Gay Perspective." The final speaker was Father Donald B. Cozzens, a priest of the Diocese of Cleveland and a former seminary rector, whose book *The Changing Face of the Priesthood*, a candid assessment of the subject, became an instant best seller among American Catholics when it appeared in 2000. In the aftermath of the clerical abuse scandal, two weeks after the U.S. bishops met in Dallas to

31. Godfried Cardinal Danneels, "Where Do I Find Hope?" *Origins* 31:27 (December 13, 2001): 446–52.

address the issue, Father Cozzens' talk was timely: "Dying and Rising: The Priesthood in Peril."

September 11, 2001

For years, whenever visitors to Greenwich Village became confused in the maze of narrow, winding streets, they could look up at the twin towers of the World Trade Center, only a mile or so to the south, to regain their sense of direction. On the morning of September 11, 2001, therefore, horrified Villagers could clearly witness the terrorist attack on those towers from their windows and rooftops. Standing on the roof of St. Joseph's rectory, Father Tos photographed the terrible sequence of events as first the south tower and then the north tower collapsed, with the loss of some 2,819 lives. It was the worst terrorist attack in American history and left both the city and the nation profoundly shaken.

Mayor Rudolph Giuliani was having breakfast at a midtown hotel when he first received news that a plane had crashed into the north tower of the World Trade Center. It was not yet clear whether it was an accident or an act of terrorism. As the mayor's car raced down Seventh Avenue through Greenwich Village to the scene of the attack, he passed by St. Vincent's Hospital. As he later described the scene in front of the hospital, he said: "I see on the street half a dozen stretchers and doctors and nurses in operating gowns. It registers that they must know something—that this is really bad. And then the second plane hits."[32]

In the days after the terrorist attack, Houston Street, the southern boundary of Greenwich Village, became the dividing line between Ground Zero (as the site of the attack came to be called) and the rest of the city. No one except residents was allowed south of the line. West Street became an emergency thoroughfare through Greenwich Village for fire engines, police cars, ambulances, and emergence vehicles of every description. Crowds as many as five deep lined West Street, waving American flags and homemade signs as they cheered the rescue workers on their way to Ground Zero. Three months lat-

32. *Time,* December 31, 2001–January 7, 2002.

er, even on Christmas Eve, a handful of people still kept vigil at the intersection of West Street and Christopher Street, where a small Christmas tree, flags, and tattered "Thank You" signs adorned the traffic island.[33]

Adam Gopnik, writing in *The New Yorker*, described the scene in Greenwich Village immediately after September 11. "Near Washington Square, the streets empty out," he wrote, "and the square itself is beautiful again. 'I saw it coming,' a bicycle messenger says. 'I thought it was going to take off the top of that building.' He points to the little Venetian-style campanile [of the Judson Memorial Church] on Washington Square South." In the aftermath of the tragedy, as vehicular traffic was banned from most of lower Manhattan and many bewildered people stayed indoors, an unusual silence descended upon the area. "The Village is a village again," thought Adam Gopnik. For weeks afterwards, depending on the direction of the wind, a rancid, acrid odor filled the air.[34]

The cover of the *Parish Newsletter* the following Sunday was a reproduction of one of the photographs that Father Tos had taken from the roof of the rectory on the morning of September 11. It showed lower Manhattan shrouded in smoke from the burning wreckage of the twin towers before they collapsed. The same issue of the *Parish Newsletter* reproduced in toto the words of Pope John Paul II at his audience on September 12. "Yesterday was a dark day in the history of humanity, a terrible affront to human dignity," said the pope. "Today my heartfelt sympathy is with the American people," he added, "subjected yesterday to inhuman terrorist attacks which have taken the lives of thousands of innocent human beings and caused unspeakable sorrow in the hearts of all men and women of good will."[35]

Two parishioners of St. Joseph's Church narrowly escaped death. Bob Kaminski worked on the 94th floor of the north tower. On September 11, he arrived at 8:30, a half-hour before his starting time. He

33. *New York Times*, December 26, 2001.
34. Adam Gopnik, "The City and the Pillars," *The New Yorker*, September 24, 2001, 34.
35. *Parish Newsletter*, September 16, 2001.

had stopped for a cup of tea in a fast food deli when the first plane struck. As he hurried away from the scene, he related, "people started to jump or were blown out by the gas and the fire." Kaminski kept walking north until he reached Greenwich Village and got to St. Joseph's Church in time for the noon Mass. Another parishioner, John Dowdell, delayed a trip to Staten Island that would have taken him past the World Trade Center at the time of the attack. He was still at home when the planes hit the two towers. "It was the worst sight of my life," he said. "I trembled, cried and became disoriented." Writing the next day, he added, "Manhattan is like a war zone. No traffic. People walking silently with stunned gazes. The sounds of sirens are continuous. Chelsea Piers, where I kayak, is set up as medical triage. Fighter jets roaring overhead. My eyes are stinging with the acrid smoke in my apartment even with the windows sealed. The worst, I trust, is over. I awoke on September 12 to see a new skyline from my window."[36]

In the aftermath of the terrorist attack on September 11, the heroes of the hour were the rescue workers, especially the police officers and firefighters, who rushed into the two burning towers in spite of the danger to themselves. In little more than an hour, 343 members of the New York Fire Department perished in the line of duty. The dead included the department's two highest-ranking officers, seventeen lieutenants, forty-seven battalion chiefs, and Father Mychal Judge, a Franciscan friar who was a Fire Department chaplain. The firefighters carried Father Judge's limp body away from the north tower and placed it reverently in the sanctuary of St. Peter's Church, the closest Catholic church to the scene of the disaster. All over the city local firehouses became instant shrines, as New Yorkers spontaneously placed flowers and personal tributes outside of them. The three firehouses in Greenwich Village all lost personnel in the terrorist attack, as did many others throughout the five boroughs. At St. Joseph's there were special memorial Masses for the deceased firefighters from each of the three firehouses located in the neighborhood.

36. *Parish Newsletter*, September 23, 2001.

"New York City took a hit for America on September 11," one New York City official commented. The attack left all Americans, especially New Yorkers, aware of their vulnerability. In a country challenged and devastated as never before by a foreign foe, Americans sought strength and solace from their religion, symbolized by the National Day of Prayer that was observed on September 14. For a brief period, at least, churches and synagogues were crowded with worshippers who came to pray for the dead and to ask divine guidance for the future. Houses of worship took on a reassuring stability and permanence in a city where everything seemed to be in flux. Even some secular-minded New Yorkers unexpectedly saw their religious institutions as outposts of the transcendent in a throwaway society.

The Clerical Sexual Scandal

Just as the city and the nation began to recover slowly and painfully from the shock of September 11, American Catholics had to face one of the worst crises in the history of their church. Early in the year 2002, stories began to appear in the press and on television with increasing frequency about the sexual abuse of children by Catholic priests and even bishops. Some of the reports were recycled news, involving incidents that had already been made public, but many of the revelations were new. As the trickle of stories from across the country became a flood, exposing the full dimensions of the scandal, the cumulative effect was devastating. It became headline news for weeks, not only in the sensationalist tabloids, but even in the *New York Times.* Although only a small fraction of the clergy was implicated (about 1.8 percent of the priests ordained from 1950 to 2001, including 30 priests in the Archdiocese of New York), a cloud of suspicion descended upon all American Catholic priests, who suddenly found themselves the butt of jokes on late-night television talk shows.[37] The laity directed their anger especially at bishops who had reassigned serial sexual offenders from one parish to another, where they continued to prey upon vulnerable young people.

37. *New York Times,* January 12, 2003.

The scandal horrified both liberal and conservative Catholics, who offered different explanations for it, but were united in their indignation over the crimes committed against children and the bishops' handling of the situation. The firestorm, fueled but not created by the media, began to subside only after the meeting of the U.S. bishops in Dallas in June, when they voted to remove from ministry any priest who had ever been guilty of the abuse of a minor. It did not go unnoticed that the assembled U.S. hierarchy took no action against fellow bishops whose ineptitude and malfeasance especially outraged the laity. Nor did priests derive much encouragement from the bishops' panicky decision to turn over to the secular authorities even the flimsiest allegations of misconduct made against them.

Despite their hurt and indignation, very few American Catholics left the Church. On the contrary, one beneficial side effect of the scandal was the loyalty demonstrated by lay Catholics, who took the occasion to assert their rightful role in their Church and to demand accountability from their ecclesiastical leaders. Even in Boston, one of the major centers of the scandal, where dissatisfaction with Cardinal Bernard Law was so intense that he was eventually forced to resign as archbishop, the laity made discerning distinctions in assigning responsibility and remained remarkably supportive of their own parish priests, as long as those priests offered them honest and caring leadership.

That was the situation that prevailed at St. Joseph's Church. In the *Parish Newsletter* of March 17, the parishioners received a four-page fact sheet, placing the crisis in historical perspective and offering them suggestions for further reading on the subject. They were also cautioned not to blame the crisis on either homosexuality or clerical celibacy, which were the simplistic explanations put forward respectively by some conservative and liberal commentators. In the course of the following weeks, Father Tos kept his parishioners informed about the results of the meeting of the clergy at St. Joseph's Seminary on April 29 with Edward Cardinal Egan, who had become the new Archbishop of New York on May 11, 2000. Virtually everywhere, parish priests discovered that people wanted some opportunity to express their views and concerns. To accommodate this desire at St. Joseph's, there were two public meetings, which were open to all the parishioners.[38]

The pastor's own concerns were focused on the effects of the scandal on young adult Catholics. "I wonder about the fact that it was members of their age group who were victims when they were young children and adolescents," said Father Tos. "Many of those victims carry memories, psychological and spiritual scars, as young adults." He was also unafraid to put in print what many priests and lay people were saying privately. "The crisis is due also to the lack of responsible leadership by members of the hierarchy who have been inadequate respondents to indefensible actions and their consequences," he wrote in the *Parish Newsletter.* "They appear to have lacked the wisdom and/or courage to take more direct action to protect young children and adolescents from clergy predators."[39]

The result of the deliberations among the parishioners of St. Joseph's Church was an open letter from the eighteen members of the parish pastoral council to each member of the U.S. Conference of Catholic Bishops, the national organization of the American bishops. A carefully crafted document that avoided both polemics and recrimination, it was timed to reach them just before their meeting in Dallas in June. The parish pastoral council expressed gratitude for the support that they had received from their own parish clergy and gave credit to those bishops who had tried to address the problem in the mid-1980s. They also urged the hierarchy not to equate pedophilia with homosexuality, and called upon the civil authorities to accord due process to accused priests. Getting to the heart of the matter, they told the bishops candidly: "[W]e are dismayed at the reports of sexual misconduct, including criminal abuse of minors, by Catholic priests and bishops. We are further dismayed at your failure to respond effectively to reports of abuse, pro-

38. *Parish Newsletter,* March 17, 2002.
39. *Parish Newsletter,* June 16, April 28, 2002.

tect endangered children in your reassignment of accused priests, confess wrongdoing and seek forgiveness, and reach out to victims." Ending on a positive note, the parish pastoral council asked the bishops to exercise genuine leadership, observe civil law, and establish permanent structures for ongoing dialogue among themselves and with the laity.[40]

Plus Ça Change

The Catholic Church in New York entered the new millennium doubly wounded, battered from without by the terrorist attack on the city and bruised from within by the revelations of sexual misconduct by the clergy. Perhaps never before in the 350-year history of the American Catholic Church had the laity been angrier or the clergy more dispirited. Those sentiments were very much in evidence among the clergy and parishioners of St. Joseph's Church, but they could both gather strength from the recognition that, throughout its 175 years, their parish had been no stranger to danger from without or crisis from within.

St. Joseph's Church opened its doors in 1834, only twenty years after the end of our first foreign conflict, the War of 1812. During its first two decades it experienced the disruptive impact of trusteeism, as clergy and laity alike struggled to adapt Catholicism to the American scene. Throughout the Civil War, St. Joseph's Church proudly displayed the Stars and Stripes high above Sixth Avenue, in a city where Southern sympathies ran strong. A Catholic outpost in the strongly Protestant "American Ward" for most of the nineteenth century, its immigrant congregation bore the brunt of Nativist bigotry. Toward the end of that century, it was the cradle of an intellectual revival among the New York diocesan clergy thanks to Father Thomas Farrell, who was also the key figure in the establishment of New York's first African American parish. As the Catholic population continued to grow, by the turn of the twentieth century St.

40. "An Open Letter to the United States Conference of Catholic Bishops, May 26, 2002," *Parish Newsletter*, May 26, 2002.

Joseph's had become the mother church of a dozen other churches in the Village proper or the vicinity.

A century later, however, the wheel had come full circle. Most of the daughter churches had either disappeared or been reduced to mission chapels of other churches, leaving St. Joseph's once again the center of Catholic life in Greenwich Village. The first of the daughter churches to go was St. Benedict the Moor, New York's earliest African American church, which followed its congregation uptown as far back as 1898. The little French chapel of Our Lady of Mercy disappeared in 1947, to be replaced by the Catholic chapel of New York University. St. Alphonsus Church, its German congregation long since gone, closed its doors in 1980 and was demolished shortly thereafter to make room for a parking lot. St. Ann's, once the thriving bon ton parish of the vicar general, was given to the Armenian Catholics for their cathedral in 1982. St. Veronica's, whose establishment Father Salter resisted so tenaciously in 1887, became a mission of St. Bernard's in the 1980s. Our Lady of Guadalupe, New York's first Spanish parish in 1902, was consolidated with St. Bernard's by Cardinal Egan exactly one hundred years later. Our Lady of Vilna, renamed Our Lady of Vilnius, New York's only Lithuanian church, preserves a precarious existence amid the noise and fumes from the endless stream of vehicular traffic entering the Holland Tunnel at its doorstep.

Of the dozen daughter churches of St. Joseph's, the only four that remained as independent parishes at the beginning of the new millennium were Our Lady of Guadalupe–St. Bernard's on West 14th Street, St. Francis Xavier on West 16th Street, and the two Italian churches of St. Anthony of Padua and Our Lady of Pompei. Either for reasons of geography or ethnicity, none of them could fill the role played by St. Joseph's Church in the life of Greenwich Village's Catholics.

As a consequence, in 2002 St. Joseph's was once again what it had been in 1829 and for most of its long history, the focal point of Catholic life in Greenwich Village. Although the congregation was much reduced in size from the salad years of a century earlier, it remained a thriving Christian community in the midst of one of the most secular neighborhoods in New York City. Few parishes anywhere in the Archdiocese of New York could match its record of good liturgy and music, inspirational homilies, community involvement, Christian education, and commitment to realizing both the *aggiornamento* and *ressourcement* envisioned by Vatican II.

Like St. Paul, the people and pastoral staff of St. Joseph's Church have reason to be proud that, in season and out of season, they have handed on to others what was handed on to them. They leave a rich and enviable legacy to all those who come after them.

The day that changed our world and parish forever: September 11, 2001
(Photo taken from the roof of the rectory)

"Through him
with him,
in the unity
of the
Holy Spirit,
all glory and honor
is yours,
almighty Father,
for ever and ever.
Amen."

Appendix I: The Pastoral Staff of St. Joseph's Church. 1829–2003

	Pastor	Associate Pastors		
1829	?			
1830	?			
1831	Patrick Duffy			
1832	Patrick Duffy			
1833	Patrick Duffy			
	James Cummiskey			
1834	James Cummiskey	Constantine Pise		
1835	James Cummiskey	Constantine Pise		
1836	James Cummiskey			
	Constantine Pise	James Cummiskey		
1837	Constantine Pise	James Cummiskey	James Quinn	Richard Hardey
	John McCloskey			
1838	John McCloskey	Bernard Carraher		
1839	John McCloskey	Bernard Carraher		
1840	John McCloskey	Bernard Carraher		
1841	John McCloskey	Bernard Carraher	David Bacon	
1842	John McCloskey	Bernard Carraher	David Bacon	
1843	John McCloskey	Bernard Carraher	Joseph P. Burke	
1844	John McCloskey	Joseph Stokes	Joseph P. Burke	
	Ambrose Manahan			

	Pastor	*Associate Pastors*		
1845	Ambrose Manahan	Joseph Stokes	John Smith	
1846	Michael McCarron	John Maginnis	William Quinn	
1847	Michael McCarron		William Quinn	
1848	Michael McCarron		William Quinn	
1849	Michael McCarron	Jerome Nobriga	William Quinn	
1850	Michael McCarron	Jerome Nobriga	Bernard O'Hara	
1851	Michael McCarron	Jerome Nobriga	Thomas McLoughlin	
1852	Michael McCarron	Jerome Nobriga	Thomas McLoughlin	
1853	Michael McCarron	Jerome Nobriga	Thomas McLoughlin	William Everett
1854	Michael McCarron	Jerome Nobriga	P. McCarron	William Everett
1855	Michael McCarron	Jerome Nobriga	P. McCarron	Patrick Egan
1856	Michael McCarron	Jerome Nobriga	Eugene Maguire	Patrick Egan
1857	Michael McCarron	Jerome Nobriga	Eugene Maguire	
	Thomas Farrell			
1858	Thomas Farrell	Jerome Nobriga	Eugene Maguire	Hugh Brady
1859	Thomas Farrell	Jerome Nobriga		Hugh Brady
1860	Thomas Farrell	Jerome Nobriga		
1861	Thomas Farrell	Jerome Nobriga		
1862	Thomas Farrell	Jerome Nobriga	Patrick McSweeny	

PASTORS OF ST. JOSEPH'S CHURCH

John McCloskey 1837-1844
Archbishop of New York 1864-1885
First American Cardinal 1875

1857-1880

1880-1882

Dennis P. O'Flynn
1892-1906

John Edwards
1906-1922

John J Hickey
1922-1944

John P. McCaffrey
1944-1967

Timothy F. Herlihy
1967-1970

Robert Wilde
1971-1973

John D. O'Leary
1973-1985

Aldo J. Tos
1985-2003

	Pastor	Associate Pastors			
1863	Thomas Farrell	Jerome Nobriga	Patrick McSweeny		
1864	Thomas Farrell	Jerome Nobriga			
1865	Thomas Farrell	Jerome Nobriga	Reuben Parsons		
1866	Thomas Farrell	Jerome Nobriga	Reuben Parsons		
1867	Thomas Farrell	Jerome Nobriga	Reuben Parsons	James O'Leary	
1868	Thomas Farrell	Jerome Nobriga	Reuben Parsons		
1869	Thomas Farrell	Jerome Nobriga	Reuben Parsons	Edward A. Dunphy	John P. McClancy
1870	Thomas Farrell	Jerome Nobriga	Edward A. Dunphy	John P. McClancy	
1871	Thomas Farrell	Jerome Nobriga	Edward A. Dunphy	John P. McClancy	
1873	Thomas Farrell	Jerome Nobriga	Edward A. Dunphy	John P. McClancy	John J. Duffy
1874	Thomas Farrell	Jerome Nobriga	Edward A. Dunphy	John Fitzharris	John J. Duffy
1875	Thomas Farrell	Jerome Nobriga	Edward A. Dunphy	John Fitzharris	John J. Duffy
1876	Thomas Farrell	Jerome Nobriga	John B. Salter	John Fitzharris	John J. Duffy
1877	Thomas Farrell	Jerome Nobriga	John B. Salter	John Fitzharris	J.J. McCauley
1878	Thomas Farrell	Jerome Nobriga	John B. Salter	John Fitzharris	J.J. McCauley
1879	Thomas Farrell	Jerome Nobriga	John B. Salter	John Fitzharris	J.J. McCauley
1880	Thomas Farrell Felix H. Farrelly	Jerome Nobriga	John B. Salter	John Fitzharris	Joseph P. Brennan
1881	Felix H. Farrelly	Jerome Nobriga Charles O'Keefe	John B. Salter	John Fitzharris	Joseph P. Brennan Eugene Smyth

	Pastor	*Associate Pastors*			
1882	Felix H. Farrelly John B. Salter	Charles O'Keefe		John Fitzharris	Eugene Smyth
1883	John B. Salter	Charles O'Keefe		John Fitzharris	Eugene Smyth
1884	John B. Salter	Cornelius G. O'Keefe	John F. Weir	John Fitzharris	Eugene Smyth
1885	John B. Salter	Cornelius G. O'Keefe	John F. Weir	John Fitzharris	Thomas F. Galligan
1886	John B. Salter	Cornelius G. O'Keefe Francis C. Lenes	John F. Weir	John Fitzharris	Thomas F. Galligan
1887	John B. Salter	Francis C. Lenes	John F. Weir	John Fitzharris	Thomas F. Galligan
1888	John B. Salter	Francis C. Lenes	John F. Weir	John T. Downes	Thomas F. Galligan
1889	John B. Salter	Leo C. Beaudet	John F. Weir		Thomas F. Galligan
1890	John B. Salter	P.R. Hickey Michael J. Murray	John F. Weir	Michael J. Mulhearn John J. Morris	Thomas F. Galligan
1891	John B. Salter		John J. Hughes	John J. Morris	James F. McLaughlin
1892	John B. Salter Denis P. O'Flynn	David J. O'Keefe	Nicholas Ferreti	John J. Morris	James F. McLaughlin
1893	Denis P. O'Flynn	David J. O'Keefe	Nicholas Ferreti	John J. Morris	James F. McLaughlin
1894	Denis P. O'Flynn	David J. O'Keefe	Nicholas Ferreti	John J. Morris	James F. McLaughlin
1895	Denis P. O'Flynn	David J. O'Keefe	Thomas F. McManus	John J. Morris	Jeremiah F. Keane
1896	Denis P. O'Flynn	David J. O'Keefe	Thomas F. McManus	John J. Morris	
1897	Denis P. O'Flynn	Thomas F. McManus	John J. Morris	Wiliam J. Mulcahy	

	Pastor	*Associate Pastors*			
1898	Denis P. O'Flynn	Thomas F. McManus	John J. Morris	Wiliam J. Mulcahy	
1899	Denis P. O'Flynn	Thomas J. Doyle	Thomas F. McManus	John J. Morris	Wiliam J. Mulcahy
1900	Denis P. O'Flynn	Thomas J. Doyle	Thomas F. McManus James A. Moloney	William J. Donovan Martin O'Gara	Wiliam J. Mulcahy
1901	Denis P. O'Flynn		Thomas J. Doyle	James A. Moloney	Wiliam J. Mulcahy
1902	Denis P. O'Flynn	Thomas J. Doyle	Peter W. Spellman	Martin J. Burke	William J. Mulcahy James Corridan
1903	Denis P. O'Flynn	Thomas J. Doyle	Peter W. Spellman	Martin J. Burke	James Corridan
1904	Denis P. O'Flynn	Thomas J. Doyle	Peter W. Spellman		James Corridan
1905	Denis P. O'Flynn	Thomas J. Doyle	Peter W. Spellman	William P. Egan David A. Murray	James Corridan
1906	Denis P. O'Flynn John Edwards	Thomas J. Doyle	Peter W. Spellman	David A. Murray	James Corridan
1907	John Edwards	Thomas J. Doyle	Peter W. Spellman William J.B. Daly	David A. Murray	James Corridan\
1908	John Edwards	Thomas J. Doyle Joseph B. Scully	William C. Humphrey	David A. Murray	James Corridan\
1909	John Edwards	Joseph B. Scully	William C. Humphrey	David A. Murray	Arthur J. Avard
1910	John Edwards	Joseph B. Scully	William C. Humphrey	David A. Murray	Arthur J. Avard
1911	John Edwards	Joseph B. Scully	William C. Humphrey	David A. Murray	Arthur J. Avard

	Pastor	Associate Pastors			
1912	John Edwards	John A. Grogan	William C. Humphrey	David A. Murray	Arthur J. Avard
1913	John Edwards	John A. Grogan	William C. Humphrey	David A. Murray	Arthur J. Avard
1914	John Edwards	John A. Grogan	William C. Humphrey	David A. Murray	Arthur J. Avard
1915	John Edwards	John A. Grogan	William C. Humphrey	David A. Murray	Arthur J. Avard
1916	John Edwards	John A. Grogan	William C. Humphrey	David A. Murray	Arthur J. Avard
1917	John Edwards	John A. Grogan	William C. Humphrey	David A. Murray	Joseph A. Breslin
1918	John Edwards	John A. Grogan	William C. Humphrey	David A. Murray	Joseph A. Breslin
1919	John Edwards	John A. Grogan	William C. Humphrey	Charles E. Fitzgerald	Joseph A. Breslin
1920	John Edwards	John A. Grogan	William C. Humphrey	Charles E. Fitzgerald	Joseph A. Breslin
1921	John Edwards	John A. Grogan	William C. Humphrey	Charles E. Fitzgerald	Joseph A. Breslin
1922	John Edwards	John A. Grogan John J. Hickey	Justin A. Lyons	Charles E. Fitzgerald	Joseph A. Breslin
1923	John J. Hickey	John A. Grogan	Justin A. Lyons George B. Fagan	Charles E. Fitzgerald	Joseph A. Breslin
1924	John J. Hickey	John A. Grogan	George B. Fagan	Charles E. Fitzgerald	Joseph A. Breslin
1925	John J. Hickey	John A. Grogan	George B. Fagan	Charles E. Fitzgerald	Joseph A. Breslin
1926	John J. Hickey	John A. Grogan	George B. Fagan	Charles E. Fitzgerald	Joseph A. Breslin
1927	John J. Hickey	Albert J. McGovern	George B. Fagan	Charles E. Fitzgerald	James J. Davitt
1928	John J. Hickey	Albert J. McGovern John J. Croke	George B. Fagan	Charles E. Fitzgerald	James J. Davitt

	Pastor	*Associate Pastors*			
1929	John J. Hickey	John J. Croke	George B. Fagan	Charles E. Fitzgerald	
1930	John J. Hickey	John J. Croke	George B. Fagan	Charles E. Fitzgerald	
1931	John J. Hickey	John J. Croke	George B. Fagan	Charles E. Fitzgerald	
1932	John J. Hickey	John J. Croke	George B. Fagan	Charles E. Fitzgerald	
1933	John J. Hickey	John J. Croke	George B. Fagan	Charles E. Fitzgerald	
1934	John J. Hickey	John J. Croke	George B. Fagan	Charles E. Fitzgerald	
1935	John J. Hickey	John J. Croke	George B. Fagan	Charles E. Fitzgerald	
1936	John J. Hickey	John J. Croke	George B. Fagan	Charles E. Fitzgerald	Joseph A. Dunn
1937	John J. Hickey	John J. Croke	George B. Fagan		Joseph A. Dunn
1938	John J. Hickey	John J. Croke	George B. Fagan	John J. Casserly	Joseph A. Dunn
1939	John J. Hickey		George B. Fagan	John J. Casserly	Joseph A. Dunn
1940	John J. Hickey		George B. Fagan	John J. Casserly	Joseph A. Dunn
1941	John J. Hickey	A. William Meyers	George B. Fagan	John J. Casserly	Joseph A. Dunn
1942	John J. Hickey	Philip J. Potter	George B. Fagan	John J. Casserly	John F. White
1943	John J. Hickey	Philip J. Potter	George B. Fagan	John J. Casserly	John J. Lennon
1944	John J. Hickey	Philip J. Potter	George B. Fagan	John J. Casserly	John J. Lennon
	John P. McCaffrey				
1945	John P. McCaffrey	Philip J. Potter	John P. Fitzgerald	John J. Casserly	John J. Lennon
1946	John P. McCaffrey	Philip J. Potter	John P. Fitzgerald	John J. Casserly	John J. Lennon

	Pastor	*Associate Pastors*			
1947	John P. McCaffrey	Philip J. Potter	John P. Fitzgerald	John J. Casserly	John J. Lennon
1948	John P. McCaffrey	Philip J. Potter	John P. Fitzgerald	John J. Casserly	John J. Lennon
1949	John P. McCaffrey	Philip J. Potter	John P. Fitzgerald	John J. Casserly	John J. Lennon
1950	John P. McCaffrey	Philip J. Potter	John P. Fitzgerald	John J. Casserly	John J. Lennon
1951	John P. McCaffrey	Aloysius A. Weber	John P. Fitzgerald	John J. Casserly	John J. Lennon
1952	John P. McCaffrey	Aloysius A. Weber	John P. Fitzgerald	John J. Casserly	John J. Lennon
1953	John P. McCaffrey	Aloysius A. Weber	John P. Fitzgerald	John J. Casserly	John J. Lennon
1954	John P. McCaffrey	Aloysius A. Weber	John P. Fitzgerald	John J. Casserly	John J. Lennon
1955	John P. McCaffrey	Aloysius A. Weber	John P. Fitzgerald	John J. Casserly	John J. Lennon
1956	John P. McCaffrey	Aloysius A. Weber	John P. Fitzgerald	John J. Casserly	John J. Lennon
1957	John P. McCaffrey	Aloysius A. Weber	John P. Fitzgerald	John J. Casserly	John J. Lennon
1958	John P. McCaffrey	Aloysius A. Weber	John P. Fitzgerald	John J. Casserly	Kenneth J. O'Donnell
1959	John P. McCaffrey	Aloysius A. Weber	John P. Fitzgerald	John J. Casserly	Kenneth J. O'Donnell
1960	John P. McCaffrey	Aloysius A. Weber	John P. Fitzgerald	John J. Casserly	Kenneth J. O'Donnell
1961	John P. McCaffrey	Aloysius A. Weber	John P. Fitzgerald	John J. Casserly	Thomas A. Neilson
1962	John P. McCaffrey	Aloysius A. Weber	John P. Fitzgerald	John J. Casserly	Thomas A. Neilson
					*Laurence J. Gibney
1963	John P. McCaffrey	Aloysius A. Weber	John P. Fitzgerald	John J. Casserly	Thomas A. Neilson
					*Laurence J. Gibney

*In Residence

	Pastor	*Associate Pastors*			
1964	John P. McCaffrey	Aloysius A. Weber	John P. Fitzgerald	John J. Casserly	Thomas A. Neilson *Laurence J. Gibney
1965	John P. McCaffrey	Aloysius A. Weber	John P. Fitzgerald	John J. Casserly	Thomas A. Neilson *Laurence J. Gibney
1966	John P. McCaffrey		Thomas A. Neilson	John J. Casserly	*Laurence J. Gibney
1967	John P. McCaffrey Timothy F. Herlihy	Philip P. Shannon	Thomas A. Neilson	John J. Casserly	*Laurence J. Gibney
1968	Timothy F. Herlihy	Daniel P. Donovan	Victor Ratigan	John J. Casserly	*Laurence J. Gibney
1969	Timothy F. Herlihy	Daniel P. Donovan	Victor Ratigan	John J. Casserly	*Laurence J. Gibney *Walter Niebrzdowski
1970	Timothy F. Herlihy John P.A. Sullivan	Daniel P. Donovan	John J. Drew, MM	John J. Casserly	*Laurence J. Gibney
1971	John P.A. Sullivan Robert Wilde	Daniel P. Donovan Robert V. Lott	John J. Drew, MM Paul Dinter	John J. Casserly	*Laurence J. Gibney
1972	Robert Wilde	Robert V. Lott	Paul Dinter	John J. Casserly	
1973	Robert Wilde **John M. McCarthy John O'Leary	Robert V. Lott	Paul Dinter	 *John M. McCarthy	
1974	John O' Leary	Robert V. Lott	*Paul Dinter	*John M. McCarthy	
1975	John O' Leary	Robert V. Lott	Michael J. Crimmins	*George Byrne	***Mary Danagher, SC

*In Residence **Administrator ***Pastoral Associate

	Pastor	*Associate Pastors*			
1976	John O' Leary	Robert V. Lott		*George Byrne	***Mary Danagher, SC
1977	John O' Leary	Robert V. Lott		*George Byrne	***Mary Danagher, SC
1978	John O' Leary	Robert V. Lott		*George Byrne	***Mary Danagher, SC
1979	John O' Leary	Robert V. Lott		*Noel Meehan	***Mary Danagher, SC
1980	John O' Leary	Robert V. Lott		*Noel Meehan *Francis J. Principe	***Mary Danagher, SC
1981	John O' Leary	Robert V. Lott	Robert Hovda	*Francis J. Principe	***Mary Danagher, SC
1982	John O' Leary	Robert V. Lott	Robert Hovda	Karl Laird, SJ	***Mary Danagher, SC
1983	John O' Leary	Robert V. Lott	Robert Hovda	Karl Laird, SJ	***Mary Danagher, SC
1984	John O' Leary		Robert Hovda	Karl Laird, SJ	***Mary Danagher, SC
1985	John O' Leary Aldo J. Tos		Robert Hovda James Gardiner, SA	Karl Laird, SJ	***Mary Danagher, SC ***Anne Abbot, OSU
1986	Aldo J. Tos		James Gardiner, SA	Karl Laird, SJ	***Anne Abbot, OSU
1987	Aldo J. Tos	Robert J. Norris	James Gardiner, SA	Karl Laird, SJ	***Anne Abbot, OSU
1988	Aldo J. Tos	Robert J. Norris	*Robert J. Robbins	*Edward K. Braxton	***Anne Abbot, OSU ***Anne Tahaney, OP
1989	Aldo J. Tos	Robert J. Norris	*Robert J. Robbins	*Edward K. Braxton	***Anne Tahaney, OP
1990	Aldo J. Tos	Robert J. Norris	Thomas Pivinski	John Gilvey, OSFS	***Anne Tahaney, OP
1991	Aldo J. Tos	Robert J. Norris	Thomas Pivinski	John Gilvey, OSFS	***Anne Tahaney, OP

*In Residence **Administrator ***Pastoral Associate

	Pastor	*Associate Pastors*			
1992	Aldo J. Tos	Robert J. Norris		John Gilvey, OSFS	***Anne Tahaney, OP
1993	Aldo J. Tos	Robert J. Norris	George H. Hill	John Gilvey, OSFS	***Anne Tahaney, OP
1994	Aldo J. Tos		George H. Hill	John Gilvey, OSFS	***Anne Tahaney, OP
1995	Aldo J. Tos			John Gilvey, OSFS	***Anne Tahaney, OP
1996	Aldo J. Tos	William A. White	Michael K. Holleran	John Gilvey, OSFS	***Anne Tahaney, OP
1997	Aldo J. Tos	William A. White	Michael K. Holleran		***Anne Tahaney, OP
1998	Aldo J. Tos	Owen J. Lafferty	Michael K. Holleran		***Anne Tahaney, OP
1999	Aldo J. Tos	Owen J. Lafferty	Michael K. Holleran		***Anne Tahaney, OP
2000	Aldo J. Tos	Owen J. Lafferty	Michael K. Holleran		***Anne Tahaney, OP
2001	Aldo J. Tos	Owen J. Lafferty	Michael K. Holleran		***Anne Tahaney, OP
2002	Aldo J. Tos	Owen J. Lafferty	Michael K. Holleran	*Michael J. Crimmins	***Anne Tahaney, OP
2003	Aldo J. Tos	Owen J. Lafferty		*Michael J. Crimmins	***Anne Tahaney, OP

*In Residence **Administrator ***Pastoral Associate

Appendix II: The Millennium Lecture Series: 1996–2002

September 26, 1996
Raymond E. Brown, S.S., Ph.D., S.S.L.
"The Beginnings of the Church"

November 21, 1996
Sara Butler, M.S.B.T., Ph.D.
"Women's Ordination and the Development of Doctrine"

January 23, 1997
Eugene LaVerdière, S.S.S., Ph.D., S.S.L.
"Proclaiming the Death of the Lord"

February 6, 1997
Gerald O'Collins, S.J., Ph.D.
"The Resurrection of Jesus"

March 20, 1997
Avery Dulles, S.J., Ph.D., S.T.D.
"Jesus and Faith"

April 24, 1997
Richard McCormick, S.J., S.T.D.
"Dissent in the Church: Loyalty or Liability?"

May 8, 1997
David Tracy, S.T.D.
"The Surprising Rediscovery of God in Contemporary Culture"

September 25, 1997
Luke Timothy Johnson, Ph.D.
"The Real Jesus: Challenge of Current Scholarship and the Truth of the Gospels"

October 16, 1997
Michael Novak, Ph.D.
"How Jesus Changed Political Economy"

November 20, 1997
Robert P. Imbelli, Ph.D.
"The Holy Spirit: The New Creation and the Call to Transformation in Christ"

December 11, 1997
Enda McDonagh, D.D., D.C.L.
"Inter-Church Christians: A Vocation to the Third Millennium"

February 12, 1998
Myles M. Bourke, S.S.L., S.T.D.
"The New Lectionary: A Response to an Urgent Need"

February 24, 1998
Cardinal Carlo Maria Martini
"A Christian Community Towards the Third Millennium"

April 2, 1998
Elizabeth Ann Johnson, C.S.J., Ph.D.
"Reclaiming the Cosmos as a Spiritual Issue"

April 24, 1998
John P. Meier, S.S.D., S.T.L.
"Gospel Miracles: The Historical Jesus and the Modern Mind"

May 7, 1998
Thomas J. Shelley, Ph.D.
"Whatever Happened to Church History?"

November 8, 2000
Lisa Sowle Cahill, Ph.D.
"The Moral Challenges Facing Women Today"

December 8, 2000
Andrew Sullivan, Ph.D.
"We're Here: Homosexuals and the Catholic Church"

October 25, 2001
Enda McDonagh, D.D., D.C.L.
"The Risk of God"

November 29, 2001
Cardinal Godfried Danneels
"Where Do I Find Hope in the Church?"

December 5, 2001
Farid Esack, Ph.D.
"Islam and Christianity: Conflict or Dialogue?"

February 28, 2002
Mary Gordon, M.A.
"A Feminist Re-Reading of the Rosary"

April 18, 2002
Jacques Dupuis, S.J., S.T.D.
"Sharing and Communion in Interreligious Dialogue"

May 30, 2002
James Alison, S.T.D.
"Being Wrong and Telling the Truth: A Gay Perspective"

June 27, 2002
Donald B. Cozzens, Ph.D.
"Dying and Rising: The Priesthood in Peril"

Appendix III: Maps

Map 1: Greenwich Village and Manhattan

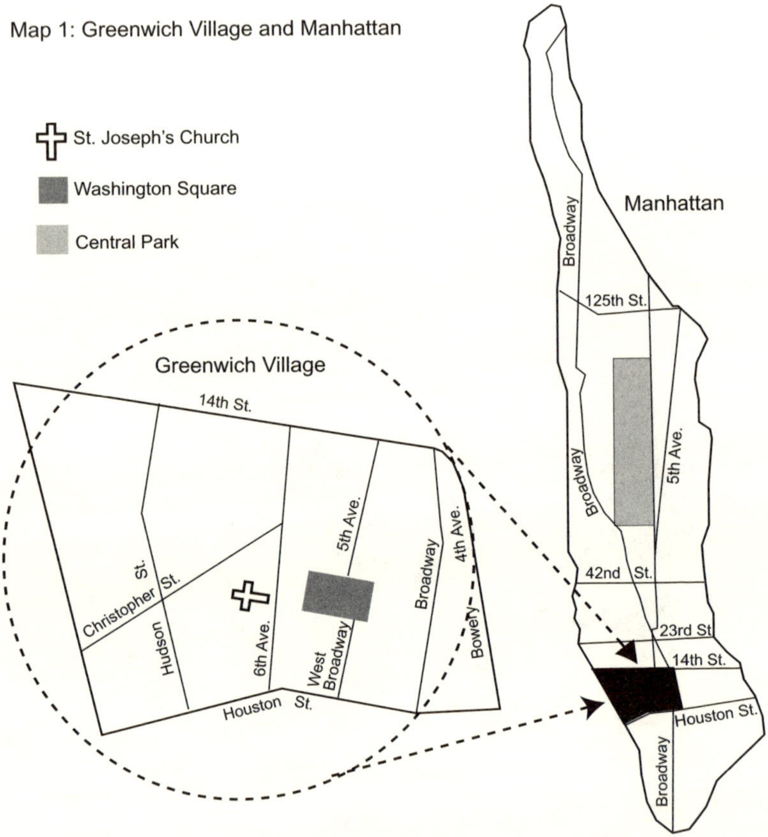

Map 2: Catholic New York in 1834

The Location of the Catholic Churches

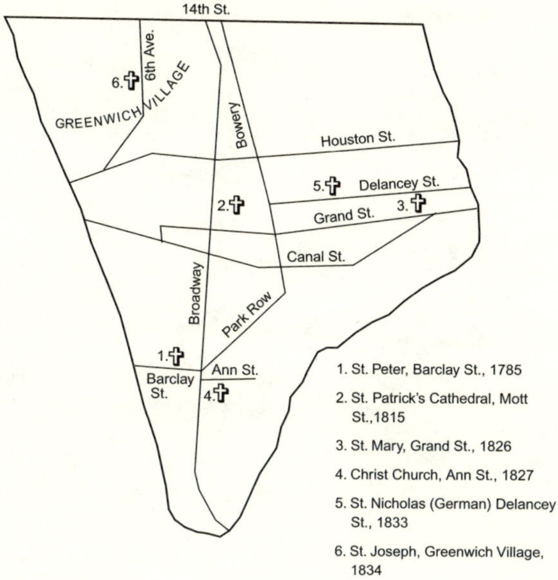

Map 3: St. Joseph's Parish, 1829 –1887

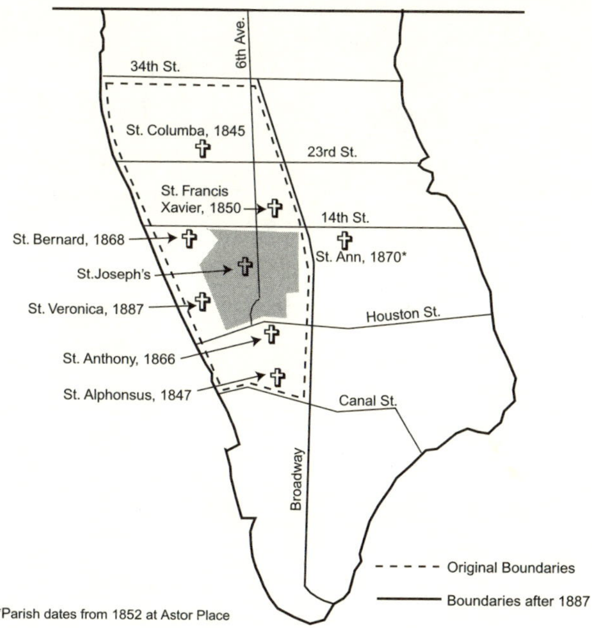

Map 4: St. Joseph's Parish in 1896

Source: St. Joseph's Church. Note that Seventh Avenue ends at West 11th Street and that Sixth Avenue ends at Carmine Street.

Map 5: Catholic Greenwich Village in 1905
The Location of the Catholic Churches

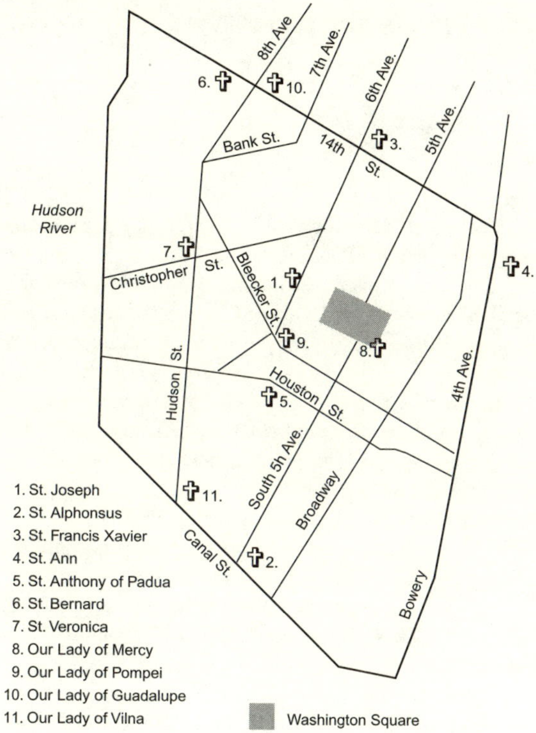

Appendix IV: Comments on the Photo Illustrations

To the Reader:

The center of our parish's life is the celebration of the Eucharist, our primary and most important action as people of God. It is the summit toward which all our activities, ministries, councils, committees, and social outreach to people in need are directed. The Body of Christ of which we are members worships and praises God, and serves people while practicing the inclusion evident in the ministry of Jesus Christ. The Eucharist, particularly on Sundays, and the other sacraments are the fount from which flows our strength. This vision and commitment are the embodiment of what was affirmed during Vatican II in the Constitution on the Liturgy (December 4, 1963, paragraph 10): "The liturgy is the summit toward which the activity of the Church is directed; it is also the fount from which all her power flows."

The photos in this book attempt to portray the preceding truth and commitment. They present the Church not as buildings and institutions (as significant as they might be) but as people reborn in baptism and celebrating life in all its manifestations. Children, young adults, and older members—laity, religious, and priests—are St. Joseph's Church in Greenwich Village.

A leading American theologian, Joseph A. Komonchak, reminds us of an important ecclesiological truth when he says: "Do we respect the fact that 99 percent of the Church are lay people? And what do we mean by 'Church'? There is not some universal Church, in the singular, apart from the local churches." The great Catholic and Anglican scholar-theologian, Cardinal John Henry Newman (1801–1890), said: "The Church would look foolish without them."

A few of the photos are from the yesterdays of our parish. Most of them show today's living Church. They show many parishioners engaged in varieties of activities and represent all others who, together with the religious and priests, are the Church. St. Joseph's Church in Greenwich Village would indeed look foolish without the laity.

Together with this carefully researched history of our parish written by Monsignor Thomas J. Shelley, and thanks to the assistance of Marie Dunn, the photos and commentary are my tribute to the great people who were and are participants in the continuing evolution of this local faith community.

Reverend Aldo J. Tos, Pastor

Photos, page 223

The Easter Triduum is the center of the liturgical year. These photos present the Holy Thursday *Mandatum,* washing of feet in fulfillment of the command of Jesus at the Last Supper; carrying the Eucharist to the repository in Farrell Hall; the rite with the Cross on Good Friday; and the beginning of the Easter Vigil. The new fire lit on the portico of our church announces to everyone on Sixth Avenue that Christ is risen. We celebrate the rest of the Vigil with the culmination of the Rite of Christian Initiation of Adults: baptism, confirmation, and celebration of the Eucharist.

Photos, page 224

This page records some significant persons and events in the life of St. Joseph's Church: Cardinal Carlo Maria Martini (Milan), who spoke during our Millennium Lecture Series (February 24, 1998) is seen here during Mass and with Rabbi Jack Bemporad (on the left), international scholar and proponent of Christian-Jewish understanding and interreligious affairs, and Brother William Martyn, S.A., ecumenist. Photos include Cardinal Godfried Danneels (Brussels) during our lecture series (November 29, 2001) and Cardinal Edward Cassidy, president of the Pontifical Council for Promoting Christian Unity (May 6, 2001). Included are children during the celebration of the Mass, the principal and students of St. Joseph's School, and others.

Photos, page 225

Photos are of the celebration of the Eucharist, center of our life. An infant baptized by immersion during a Sunday Mass expresses the life-and-death power of this sacrament for the whole community. Scenes include celebrations of other sacraments, including Mass with Cardinal Edward Cassidy, social and educational events with children, adult parishioners, and others.

Photos, page 226

The Church as people of God—laity, religious, and clergy—are united from the moment of baptism. Here again that unity is seen in the celebration of the Eucharist and participation in many other happy times. Feasts of the Church are celebrated with special services and social gatherings, including the arrival of St. Nicholas (a parishioner), who greets our director of religious education and the children in our Sunday morning catechesis program, which includes the Liturgy of the Word for children.

Photos, page 227

The parish community grows with new members being welcomed into the Church. Our long tradition of the soup kitchen every Saturday depends on many volunteers from our parish and other friends who serve those who "Eat at

St. Joe's." Photos show children during their Christmas enactment of the Nativity, young adults, and older parishioners who meet to enjoy their lives of faith and community. Without the generous service of parishioners, we could not welcome homeless men to our shelter during the cold winter months.

Photos, page 228

Serious discussions, friendly gatherings of families, parishioners, playful children are all part of life at St. Joseph's, which extends from prayer and worship to our social center, Casserly Hall, renovated and made beautiful thanks to the generosity of several parishioners and friends of the parish (December 2000). It is in Casserly Hall that we have our soup kitchen on Saturdays and shelter for the homeless during winter. It was here that many members of the Police Department and others were welcomed for rest, food, and refreshments during their long hours of service throughout the day and night of September 11, 2001, when history and our parish were changed forever. Everything in our parish happens because of the generosity and compassionate service of parishioners and friends.

Photos, page 229

Parishioners and students in St. Joseph's School enjoy being part of a parish that welcomes everyone with love. It is the dedication of parish workers that provides the careful maintenance of our church, Casserly Hall, the school, and other facilities in which we gather for so many meetings and other activities.

Photos, page 230

The Church is the people of God and the Body of Christ, the totality of laity, religious, and clergy. These photos show the Church present in St. Joseph's, with people relating to one another and contributing to growth and joy.

Photos, page 231

This exemplifies what has been said: all members of the parish form one body and contribute to each other's well-being. Here we are reminded of our special dedication to St. Joseph, devoted husband of Mary, protector and teacher of Jesus, patron of the universal Church, and ours also since our parish was founded in 1829. The picture shows the stained glass window in the church. The crystal chandeliers are from the last century and add particular beauty thanks to the attention given to them by parish volunteers. One of the photos shows a youngster drinking from the Cup in fulfillment of what Jesus said to his disciples: "Take and eat" and "Take and drink." Everyone is invited to experience the fullest sacramental sign of the presence of the Body and Blood of the Risen Christ during every Mass celebrated in our church.

Bibliography

Archival Sources

AAB Archives of the Archdiocese of Baltimore
AANY Archives of the Archdiocese of New York
ACUA Archives of the Catholic University of America
APF Archives of the Paulist Fathers
ARML Archives of the Ryan Memorial Library and Historical Collection, St. Charles Borromeo Seminary, Philadelphia
ASJC Archives of St. Joseph's Church, Greenwich Village
ASJSD Archives of St. Joseph's Seminary, Dunwoodie
ASJPH Archives of St. Joseph's Provincial House, Emmitsburg, Maryland
AUND Archives of the University of Notre Dame
GHP Greenwich House Papers, Tamiment Library, New York University

Newspapers

Catholic New York
New York Catholic American
New York *Catholic News*
New York Catholic Register and Freeman's Journal
New York Catholic Review
New York Commercial Advertiser
New York Daily Tribune
New York Evening Post
New York Herald
New York Sun
New York Times
New York Weekly Register and Catholic Diary
The Truth Teller

Doctoral Dissertations and Unpublished Paper

Brown, Mary Elizabeth. "Italian Immigrants and the Catholic Church in the Archdiocese of New York, 1880–1950." Ph.D. dissertation. Columbia University, 1967.

Gilheany, Juliana. "Subjects of History: English, Scottish and Welsh Immigrants in New York City, 1820–1860." Ph.D. dissertation. New York University, 1989.

Ryan, Stephen M. "An Historical Look at the Parish of St. Joseph, Greenwich Village." Seminar paper. St. Francis College, Brooklyn, N.Y., 1984.

Secondary Sources

Andreassi, Anthony D. "'The Cunning Leader of a Dangerous Clique?': The Burtsell Affair and Archbishop Michael Augustine Corrigan." *Catholic Historical Review* 86 (1999): 620–39.

Arlotta, Jack M. "Before Harlem: Black Catholics in the Archdiocese of New York and The Church of St. Benedict the Moor." *Dunwoodie Review* 16 (1992–1993): 69–108.

Aubert, Roger. "Les Nouvelles Frontières de l'Historiographie Ecclésiastique." *Revue d'Histoire Ecclésiastique* 95, no. 3 (2000): 757–81.

Barrett, William. "New Designs on Our Bohemia." *New York Times Magazine,* August 20, 1950, 20, 38–39.

———. "The Village Gone Bourgeois." *New York Times Magazine,* April 4, 1954, 19–20, 22.

Beard, Rick, and Leslie Cohen Berlowitz, eds. *Greenwich Village: Culture and Counterculture.* New York: Museum of the City of New York, 1993.

Bennett, William H. "Francis Cooper: New York's First Catholic Legislator." *Historical Records and Studies* 12 (1918): 29–38.

Blackmar, Elizabeth. *Manhattan for Rent, 1785–1850.* Ithaca, N.Y.: Cornell University Press, 1989.

Boroff, David. "An Appeal to Save the Village." *New York Times Magazine,* May 7, 1961, 32–33, 74, 77–78.

Brown, Mary Elizabeth. *Churches, Communities and Children: Italian Immigrants in the Archdiocese of New York, 1880–1945.* New York: Center for Migration Studies, 1995.

———. *From Italian Villages to Greenwich Village: Our Lady of Pompei.* New York: Center for Migration Studies, 1992.

———. *The Scalabrinians in North America, 1887–1934.* New York: Center for Migration Studies, 1996.

Browne, Henry J. *St. Ann's on East Twelfth Street, New York City, 1851–1952.* New York: Church of St. Ann, 1952.

Byrne, John F., C.Ss.R. *The Redemptorist Centenaries.* Philadelphia: The Dolphin Press, 1932.

Carey, Patrick. *People, Priests and Prelates: Ecclesiastical Democracy and the Tensions of Trusteeism.* Notre Dame, Ind.: University of Notre Dame Press, 1987.

Carthy, Mary Peter. *Old St. Patrick's: New York's First Cathedral.* New York: U.S. Catholic Historical Society, 1947.

Cohalan, Florence D. *A Popular History of the Archdiocese of New York.* New York: U.S. Catholic Historical Society, 1983.

Coles, Robert. *Dorothy Day: A Radical Devotion.* Reading, Mass.: Addison-Wesley Publishing Co., 1987.

Complete Works of the Most Reverend John Hughes. 2 vols. New York: Lawrence Kehoe, 1866.

Condon, Kevin, C.M. *The Missionary College of All Hallows, 1842–1891.* Dublin: All Hallows College, 1986.

Corrigan, Michael A. "Record of Clergy Laboring in the Archdiocese of New York from Early Missionary Times to 1885." *Historical Records and Studies* 2, no. 1 (1900): 31–81.

Curran, Francis X., S.J. "Archbishop Hughes and the Jesuits: An Anatomy of Their Quarrels." In *Fordham: The Early Years,* edited by Thomas C. Hennessy, S.J., 177–221. N.p.: Something More Publications, 1998.

Curran, Robert Emmett. "Prelude to 'Americanism': The New York Accademia and Clerical Radicalism in the Late Nineteenth Century." *Church History* 47 (1978): 48–65.

Davis, Cyprian, O.S.B. *The History of Black Catholics in the United States.* New York: Crossroad, 1990.

Day, Dorothy. *The Long Loneliness: The Autobiography of Dorothy Day.* New York: Harper and Brothers, 1952.

DeForest, Robert W., and Lawrence Veiller. *The Tenement House Problem.* 2 vols. New York: Macmillan, 1903.

Delaney, Edmund. *New York's Greenwich Village.* Barre, Mass.: Barre Publishers, 1968.

The Diary of George Templeton Strong, 1820–1875. Edited by Allan Nevins and Milton Halsey Thomas. 4 vols. New York: Macmillan, 1952.

DiGiovanni, Stephen M. *Archbishop Corrigan and the Italian Immigrants.* Huntington, Ind.: Our Sunday Visitor Press, 1994.

Dolan, Jay P. *The American Catholic Parish.* 2 vols. New York: Paulist Press, 1987.

———. *The Immigrant Church: New York's Irish and German Catholics, 1815–1865.* Baltimore: The Johns Hopkins University Press, 1975.

———. "New Dimensions in American Catholics History." In *New Dimensions in American Religious History,* edited by Jay P. Dolan and James P. Winds. Grand Rapids, Mich.: Eerdmans, 1993

Dubois, Jean. "Mission de New-York." *Annales de l'Association de la Propagation de la Foi* 22 (October 1830): 447–63.

Egan, Maurice Francis. "A Slight Appreciation of James A. McMaster." *Historical Records and Studies* 15 (1921): 7–18.

Ernst, Robert. *Immigrant Life in New York City, 1825–1863*. Reprint. Syracuse, N.Y.: Syracuse University Press, 1994.

Farley, John Cardinal. *The Life of John Cardinal McCloskey.* New York: Longmans, Green and Company, 1918.

Fishbein, Leslie. *Rebels in Bohemia: The Radicals of the Masses.* Chapel Hill: University Of North Carolina Press, 1982.

Fowler, Dorothy Ganfield. *A City Church: The First Presbyterian Church in the City of New York, 1716–1976* . New York: The First Presbyterian Church in the City of New York, 1981.

Gelb, Arthur and Barbara. *O'Neill.* New York: Harper and Row, 1962.

Gilje, Paul J. *The Road to Mobocracy: Popular Disorder in New York City, 1763–1834*. Chapel Hill: University of North Carolina Press, 1987.

Gleason, Philip. "Thanks to the Irish." *America,* May 14, 1966, 696–98.

"Gli Emigranti Italiani a Nuova York." *La Civiltà Cattolica* 55 (April 4, 1904): 172–79.

Gonnet, D. *La liberté religieuse à Vatican II: La contribution de John Courtney Murray.* Paris: Les Editions du Cerf, 1994.

Green, Jesse. "Where the Boys Went." *New York Times Magazine,* October 19, 1997, 66–70.

Green, Martin. *New York 1913: The Armory Show and the Paterson Strike Pageant.* New York: Collier Books, 1988.

Guilday, Peter. "Lay Trusteeism in New York." *Historical Records and Studies* 18 (1928): 7–73.

Hassard, John. *Life of the Most Reverend John Hughes.* New York: D. Appleton and Company, 1866.

Hersfeld, Al. "Counter Revolution in the Village." *New York Times Magazine,* April 23, 1944, 16, 35–36.

Janvier, Thomas A. "Greenwich Village." *Harper's New Monthly Magazine* 87 (1893): 339–57.

The John Carroll Papers. Edited by Thomas O'Brien Hanley, S.J. 3 vols. Notre Dame, Ind.: University of Notre Dame Press, 1976.

The Journal of the Fair to Aid in the Completion of the New St. Francis Xavier Church. New York: St. Francis Xavier Church, 1880.

Kaiser, Charles. *The Gay Metropolis.* New York: Harcourt Brace and Company, 1997.

Kwitchen, Mary Augustine. *James Alphonsus McMaster: A Study in American Thought.* Washington: The Catholic University of America Press, 1949.

The Letters and Diaries of John Henry Newman. Edited by C. S. Dessain, Edward F. Kelly, S.J., Thomas Gornall, S.J., and Ian Ker. 24 vols. London: Thomas Nelson; Oxford: Clarendon, 1961–1977.

Letters of John Pintard to His Daughter, Elise Noel Davidson, 1816–1833. 4 vols. New York: New York Historical Society, 1937–1941.

Lockwood, Charles. *Manhattan Moves Uptown.* Boston: Houghton Mifflin Company, 1976.

Longworth's American Almanac, New-York Register and City Directory. New York: Thomas Longworth, 1833–1837.

Lynch, Bernard J. "The Italians in New York." *The Catholic World* 47 (1888): 67–73.

Lynch, Thomas A. "'Above All Things the Truth': John P. Monaghan and the Church in New York." *Dunwoodie Review* 16 (1992–1993): 109–65.

MacGregor, Morris. *A Parish for the Federal City: St. Patrick's in Washington, 1794–1994.* Washington: The Catholic University of America Press, 1994.

———. *The Emergence of a Black Catholic Community: St. Augustine's in Washington.* Washington: The Catholic University of America Press, 1999.

McCadden, Joseph and Helen. *Father Varela: Torchbearer from Cuba.* New York: U.S. Catholic Historical Society, 1969.

McCaffrey, Lawrence J. *The Irish Diaspora in America.* Bloomington: Indiana University Press, 1976.

McClellan, George B., Jr. *The Gentleman and the Tiger.* Edited by Harold C. Syrett. Philadelphia: J. P. Lippincott Company, 1956.

McFarland, Gerald W. *Inside Greenwich Village: A New York City Neighborhood, 1898–1918.* Amherst: University of Massachusetts Press, 2001.

McNally, Michael J. *Catholic Parish Life on Florida's West Coast, 1860–1968.* Privately printed, 1996.

Meehan, Thomas F. "Evangelizing the Italians." *The Messenger* 39 (1903): 16–32.

———. "Some Schools in Old New York." *Historical Records and Studies* 2 (1901): 432–53.

"A Memoir of Archbishop Hughes, 1838–1858." Edited by Henry J. Browne. *Historical Records and Studies* 39–40 (1952): 129–90.

Mildred, M. "James A. McMaster, Pioneer Journalist." *Records of the American Catholic Historical Society of Philadelphia* 46 (1935): 1–21.

Miller, William D. *Dorothy Day: A Biography.* New York: Harper and Row, 1982.

Minihan, Mary Canisius. "James A. McMaster, A Pioneer Catholic Journalist." *Records of the American Catholic Historical Society of Philadelphia* 47 (1936): 87–131.

Morris, Jan. *Manhattan* '45. Reprint. Baltimore: The Johns Hopkins University Press, 1998.

Moses, Robert. "New York *Has* a Future." *New York Times Magazine,* January 30, 1955, 22–23, 71.

Murphy, Francis X., C.Ss.R. *The Centennial History of St. Alphonsus Parish.* New York: St. Alphonsus Church, 1947.

Minutes of the Common Council of the City of New York. New York: Common Council of the City of New York, 1784–1831.

New York Association for Improving the Condition of the Poor. *Annual Reports,* 1854–1859.

———. *First Report of a Committee on the Sanitary Condition of the Laboring Classes in the City of New York with Remedial Suggestions.* New York: John F. Trow, 1853.

New York City Guide. Reprint. New York: Random House, 1956.

New York State Senate. *Report of the Select Committee on the Report of Trinity Church Made in 1855.* Albany: Van Benthuysen, 1857.

Nolan, Charles E. *St. Mary's of Natchez: The History of a Southern Catholic Congregation.* 2 vols. Natchez, Miss.: St. Mary's Church, 1992.

Orsi, Robert A. *The Madonna of 115th Street: Faith and Community in Italian Harlem.* New Haven, Conn.: Yale University Press, 1985.

Pelotte, Donald. *John Courtney Murray: Theologian in Conflict.* New York: Paulist Press, 1976.

"Plan of St. Joseph's Church." *Records of the American Catholic Historical Society of Philadelphia* 21 (1910): 107–8.

Preston, Thomas. "American Catholicity." *American Catholic Quarterly Review* 16 (1891): 396–408.

Pierson, George William. *Tocqueville and Beaumont in America.* New York: Oxford University Press, 1938.

Purcell, Richard. "Patrick Keely, Builder of Churches." *Records of the American Catholic Historical Society of Philadelphia* 54 (1943): 208–27.

Report of the Council of Hygiene of the Citizens' Association of New York upon the Sanitary Condition of the City. New York: D. Appleton and Company, 1865.

Report of the New York State Legislative Assembly Tenement House Committee. Albany: James R. Lyon, 1895.

Rosenwaike, Ira. *Population History of the City of New York.* Syracuse, N.Y.: Syracuse University Press, 1972.

Ryan, Leo R. *Old St. Peter's: The Mother Church of Catholic New York.* New York: U.S. Catholic Historical Society, 1935.

Shaw, Richard. *Dagger John: The Unquiet Life and Times of Archbishop John Hughes of New York.* New York: Paulist Press, 1977.

Shea, John Gilmary. *The Catholic Churches of New York.* New York: Lawrence C. Goulding and Company, 1878.

Shelley, Thomas J. *Dunwoodie: The History of St. Joseph's Seminary.* Westminster, Md.: Christian Classics, 1992.

———. "Fordham Before the Jesuits: Bishop John Hughes and St. John's College, 1838–1846." In *Fordham: The Early Years,* edited by Thomas C. Hennessey, S.J., 53–76. N.p: Something More Publications, 1998.

———. "Irish-Americans and the Archdiocese of New York." *American Catholic Studies* 112 (2001): 1–22.

———. "'What the Hell Is an Encyclical?': Governor Alfred E. Smith, Charles C. Marshall, Esq., and Father Francis P. Duffy." *U.S. Catholic Historian* 15 (1997): 87–107.

Simkhovitch, Mary Kingsbury. *Neighborhood: My Story of Greenwich House.* New York: Norton, 1938.

Smith, John Talbot. *The Catholic Church in New York.* 2 vols. New York and Boston: Hall & Locke Company, 1905.

Spalding, Thomas W. *The Premier See: A History of the Archdiocese of Baltimore.* Baltimore: The Johns Hopkins University Press, 1989.

St. Anthony of Padua Church, New York City. South Hackensack, N.J.: Custombook, 1967.

St. Joseph's Parish Bulletin, 1971–1987.

St. Joseph's Parish Newsletter, 1987–2003.

Still, Bayrd. *Mirror for Gotham.* Westport, Conn.: Greenwood Press, 1980.

Stokes, Phelps. *The Iconography of Manhattan Island, 1498–1909.* 6 vols. New York: Robert Dodd, 1926.

Tomasi, Silvano. *Piety and Power: The Role of Italian Parishes in the New York Metropolitan Area.* New York: Center for Migration Studies, 1975.

Tourscher, Francis E., O.S.A. *The Hogan Schism and Trustee Troubles in St. Mary's Church, Philadelphia, 1820–1829.* Philadelphia: The Peter Reilly Company, 1930.

The Trial of John Moore and Others for Assault and Battery, New York City, 1824. American State Trials, 13:189–204. Edited by John D. Lawson. St. Louis: Thomas Law Book Company, 1921.

Tricario, Donald. *The Italians of Greenwich Village: The Social Structure and Transformation of an Ethnic Community.* New York: Center for Migration Studies, 1984.

Tuttle, H. P. Croswell. *History of St. Luke's Church in the City of New York.* New York: Appeal Printing Company, 1927.

The United States Catholic Almanac or Laity's Directory for the Year 1834. Baltimore: John Myers, 1834.

United States Documents in the Propaganda Fide Archives. 11 vols. Washington: Academy of American Franciscan History, 1966–1987.

Vecoli, Rudolph J. "Prelates and Peasants: Italian Immigrants and the Catholic Church." *Journal of Social History* 2 (1969): 217–68.

Walsh, Mary de Lourdes. *The Sisters of Charity of New York.* 3 vols. New York: Fordham University Press, 1960.

Walsh, Walter J. "Religion, Ethnicity and History." In *The New York Irish,* edited by Ronald H. Bayor and Timothy J. Meagher, 48–69. Baltimore: The Johns Hopkins University Press, 1996.

Ware, Caroline. *Greenwich Village, 1920–1930.* Reprint. Berkeley: University of California Press, 1994.

Washington Square Association Yearbook, 1908–1931.

White, E. B. *Here Is New York.* Reprint. New York: The Little Book Room, 1999.

Index

Greenwich Village Catholics: St. Joseph's Church and the Evolution of an Urban Faith Community, 1829–2002 was designed and composed in Minion by Kachergis Book Design, Pittsboro, North Carolina, and printed on 60-pound Sebago 2000 Eggshell and bound by The Maple-Vail Book Manufacturing Group of York, Pennsylvania.